THE INITIATIVE

THE INITIATIVE

Citizen Law-Making

Joseph F. Zimmerman

Westport, Connecticut
London

Library of Congress Cataloging-in-Publication Data

Zimmerman, Joseph Francis, 1928–
    The initiative : citizen law-making / Joseph F. Zimmerman.
      p.   cm.
    Includes bibliographical references and index.
    ISBN 0–275–96729–8 (alk. paper)
    1. Referendum—United States. I. Title.
    KF4881.Z55   1999
    328.273—dc21   99–34428

British Library Cataloguing in Publication Data is available.

Library of Congress Catalog Card Number: 99–34428
ISBN: 0–275–96729–8

First published in 1999

Praeger Publishers, 88 Post Road West, Westport, CT 06881
An imprint of Greenwood Publishing Group, Inc.
www.praeger.com

Printed in the United States of America

The paper used in this book complies with the
Permanent Paper Standard issued by the National
Information Standards Organization (Z39.48–1984).

10 9 8 7 6 5 4 3 2 1

For Kieran

Contents

Preface

In the 1890s, voter dissatisfaction with the representativeness of many state legislatures and city councils, which could be attributed primarily to public exposure of corruption in the law-making process, led to amendment of state constitutions and city charters or ratification of new ones to provide for three correctives — the initiative, the protest or citizen referendum, and the recall activated by voter petitions. The first two correctives were incorporated into the South Dakota state constitution by a constitutional amendment in 1898, and all three correctives were included in the new charter for the City and County of San Francisco ratified by voters in the same year.

The initiative allows voters by petitions to place proposed constitutional amendments or statutes on the state ballot and proposed charters, charter amendments, and ordinances on the local ballot. The protest referendum authorizes the electorate, by petition, to suspend implementation of a newly enacted statute or ordinance and to vote in a referendum on the question of repealing the statute or ordinance. The recall is a petition process for placement of the question of the immediate removal from office of an elected officer on the referendum ballot. These three participatory devices were unconventional when adopted but have become important reserved powers of voters in the state and local governments, where the devices are authorized, and can be exercised whenever elected officers fail to be responsive to the will of the people.

The direct initiative, an affirmative-forcing mechanism, challenges the fundamental theory of representative law-making by allowing voter law-making whenever a majority of those participating in a referendum decide to supersede the representative law-making body relative to establishing a specific public policy embodied in the proposition. The filing of a large number of petition signatures in favor of a proposition could persuade the legislative body to enact the proposition or a similar bill into law, thereby obviating the need for a referendum.

Not surprisingly, defenders of representative law-making have advanced numerous arguments against the initiative since it first was proposed. Historically, law-making in the United States, except in New England towns, was predicated upon the leadership-feedback theory under which elected officers propose new governmental policies, receive feedback from individuals and organizations, and may revise their original proposals to reflect these views before enacting a statute or ordinance.

This process, in theory, assumes that when elected officers propose a new policy they genuinely are interested in obtaining the views of the citizenry and will consider such views carefully when drafting or revising bills for enactment. The failure of many legislative bodies in the United States to live up to democratic ideals led to the public's loss of confidence in these bodies. The solution, according to populist and progressive reformers, involved voters taking into their own hands the responsibility for determining public policies on important issues in the event a legislative body failed to establish a policy favored by a majority of the voters.

The initiative is authorized by the constitution in twenty-three states, by statute in Utah for state use, by local government charter, and by state constitutional or statutory provisions in numerous local governments. Because each state, by its constitution or statutes, can determine the features of the initiative, there has been a great variation in the degree of difficulty and frequency of use of this popular device. The practical political workings of the device also vary and result in criticisms that differ between individual initiative states and local governments.

This book describes the origin and spread of the initiative, its legal foundation, the role of the judiciary in interpreting constitutional and statutory initiative provisions, and initiative proposition campaigns. The arguments of the proponents and opponents of this popular law-making device are evaluated, and conclusions are drawn about its desirability and effectiveness. A model is presented to guide state and local governments that are considering adoption of the initiative or revision of current constitutional or statutory provisions.

Acknowledgments

Although it is not possible to acknowledge individually the many state and local government officers, individuals, and organizations that supplied information in response to my many requests, a special debt of gratitude must be expressed to my research assistants — Christopher C. Sarver, Troy E. Smith, Adegboyega A. Somide, and Jordan Wishy — who collected a large amount of data and materials, and to Addie Napolitano for excellence in preparing the manuscript.

1

Unassembled Law-Making

The initiative, a petition process that allows voters to place one or more propositions on the referendum ballot, continues to this day to be a controversial mechanism and raises fundamental questions about the nature of representative government and the role of voters in the United States. The value of an active citizenry in promoting the health of the polity was recognized in ancient times. Aristotle, for example, placed greater faith in the collective wisdom of citizens than in the sagacity of any individual.[1] Nevertheless, political theorists and elected officers have different views about the proper role of citizen participation in the law-making process.

Advocates of direct democracy favor the traditional New England town meeting in which assembled voters enact all bylaws after discussing each article in the warrant, the fixed agenda, issued by the selectmen who are the town's plural executive.[2] Such law-making is traceable in origin to the Athenian *ecclesia* of the fifth century B.C. At the other extreme, advocates of representative law-making favor periodic election of legislators who lead public opinion by advancing proposals and soliciting feedback on them from the citizenry. The premise of this leadership-feedback theory is based on the belief that elected officers will consider seriously the views of the people on legislative proposals and will follow the wishes of the majority.

In the latter part of the nineteenth century, many populist proponents of the initiative were convinced that state legislatures were only pseudo-representative institutions, which did the bidding of special interests, such as major railroads and trusts, and refused to enact bills into law favored by the majority of the citizens. One of the populists' cardinal solutions was the initiative supplemented by the protest referendum, which allows voters by petition to call a referendum to repeal statutes enacted by the legislature, and the recall, which allows voters by petition to call a special election for the purpose of determining whether a named officer should be removed from office.[3] The initiative is a logical extension of the mandatory referendum — for the adoption of proposed constitutions, constitutional amendments, and pledging the full faith and credit of the state as support for bond issues — that had become well established by the latter half of the nineteenth century.

The populists were successful in amending the South Dakota Constitution on November 8, 1898, by adding the initiative and protest or petition referendum activated by petitions signed by 5 percent of the registered voters of the state. The amendment provides:

The legislative power shall be vested in a legislature which shall consist of a Senate and House of Representatives. Except that the people expressly reserve to themselves the right to propose measures, which measures the legislature shall enact and submit to a vote of the electors of the state, and also the right to require that any laws which the legislature may have enacted shall be submitted to a vote of the electors of the state before going into effect (except such laws as may be necessary for the immediate preservation of the public peace, health, or safety, support of state government and the existing public institutions).[4]

This provision explicitly stipulates that a member of the state legislature cannot be denied the right to propose a bill and exempts initiated measures from the gubernatorial veto.

San Francisco freeholders in the same year adopted a new city-county charter, providing among other things, for the initiative and the protest referendum.[5]

ORIGIN AND SPREAD OF THE INITIATIVE

The origin of the legislative initiative generally has been attributed to Swiss cantons in the nineteenth century and an 1898 South Dakota constitutional amendment. Nevertheless, voters in Massachusetts towns were empowered by the General Court (provincial legislature) on December 22, 1715, to require the selectmen (plural executive) to include in the warrant (calling a town meeting) any article accompanied by a petition signed by ten or more voters.[6] Currently, voters in all New England towns with open town meetings possess this power of initiative.

A second eighteenth-century example of an authorization for voter employment of the initiative is found in the Georgia Constitution of 1777, framed and adopted by a convention but not submitted to the electorate for ratification. The amendment article of this fundamental document provided for the calling of a constitutional convention to revise the organic law only upon receipt of "petitions from a majority of the counties and the petitions from each county . . . signed by a majority of voters in each county."[7]

Several Swiss cantons, following the revolutionary movement of 1830, drafted constitutions authorizing the employment of the constitutional initiative. In 1848 the new federal constitution required all cantons to adopt the device, which also could be used to place proposed national constitutional amendments on the ballot.[8] The statutory initiative first was authorized by the Vaud cantonal constitution of 1845 and subsequently was authorized by the cantonal constitutions in Aargau in 1852, Baselland in 1863, and Solothrun, Thurgau, and Zurich in 1869. In Switzerland, the initiative is referred to as the "Imperative Petition" of the voters.

In the United States, the California State Legislature in 1883 enacted "An Act to Provide for the Organization, Incorporation, and Government of Municipal Corporations" to implement the home rule provision of the 1879 state constitution. This act authorized incorporation of a city by petitions, signed by 100 registered voters within the limits of the proposed city and filed with the county board of supervisors. Voters subsequently approved a charter incorporating the new city and providing for its governmental structure and power.[9]

The drafters of the early state constitutions, who feared a strong governor and placed great trust in legislative bodies, limited suffrage, despite the emphasis on the equality of all men in the Declaration of Independence, and limited the role of the electorate primarily to the periodic selection of representatives.

To protect the public against capture of the government by a faction and to ensure that governmental policies were in accord with the desires of the majority of the citizens, the drafters of state constitutions divided political power among three branches of government and instituted a system of checks and balances. This governance system, according to the populists, had broken down, and the farmers and industrial workers were at the mercy of an economic oligarchy.

The initiative, as developed outside of the New England towns, generally is rooted in the agrarian discontent that followed the Civil War. This was a period when railroads often had a monopoly on bulk transportation. The agitation for governmental control of railroad monopolies and reform of state legislatures started with the granger movement and its associated greenbackism in the Midwest in the 1870s, and continued with the emergence of the populist movement. George McKenna explained "the farmers and their champions turned back to the vast literature of rural romanticism, the eulogies of decentralized government, the methods of Andrew Jackson and Thomas Jefferson — turned to them not for solace but for strength, which they then mixed with their own evangelical Protestantism to create a powerful fighting faith."[10] Populist leaders were aware of the use of the constitutional and statutory initiative in Switzerland.

Populists contended that institutional arrangements stressed the wrong values. They charged that too much emphasis was placed upon centralization of political power in the state legislature, whereas too little attention was paid to responsiveness as a criterion of democratic government. They were convinced that the supercentralization of power resulted in enactment of policies that favored special economic interests and alienated many citizens. In effect, populists were preaching a type of political fundamentalism and calling for institutional and procedural changes that putatively would maximize citizen participation and neutralize the nefarious influence of the invisible government; that is, the economic special interests. They argued that only by embodying the initiative, the protest referendum, and the recall in the state constitution would citizen government be restored. In other words, political realities, as reflected in legislative abuses of the public trust, would necessitate a new procedural system, which would permit a redistribution of political power and would revitalize legislative decision-making and invigorate citizen participation.

The populists believed that grassroots citizenry had the capacity to make proper decisions, often superior to those made by legislatures, and it is an undemocratic system that deprives voters of the opportunity to make important policy decisions. The mechanisms advocated by the populists also would maximize *vox populi* by giving citizens a greater stake in, and enhance the legitimacy of, the governmental system. Although the populists placed great faith in the direct initiative and its obligatory referendum, they did not advocate the replacement of a representative democracy with a plebiscitarian democracy.

The National People's Party (Populist), an amalgam of the Farmers' Alliance and a number of urban labor organizations, recommended at its first national convention on July 4, 1892, the adoption of the initiative and the protest (petition) referendum as correctives for the problems of state legislatures.[11] In the same year, the American Federation of Labor officially recommended the adoption of the initiative and the referendum. The National People's Party gained control of the South Dakota Legislature as a result of the 1896 elections, and in 1897 it proposed a direct legislation constitutional amendment that was ratified by the voters in 1898. San Francisco freeholders in the same year adopted a new city-county charter providing, among other things, for the initiative and the petition referendum.[12] South Dakota voters, however, were not the first ones to utilize the initiative. Oregon, which adopted the device in 1902, holds that honor; voters on June 6, 1904, approved a direct primary proposition and a county local option liquor proposition. In Oregon, the initiative was promoted actively by labor unions, Henry George's single-taxers, and the Grange, a farmers' organization.[13] South Dakota voters first employed the initiative in November 1908.

The Progressive movement developed at the turn of the century as the populist movement declined, and the two movements to an extent blended into one reform movement. Whereas the populist movement was agrarian based, the progressive movement had two bases — agrarian and urban. Richard Hofstadter explained: "Progressivism differed from populism in the fact that the middle classes of the cities not only joined the trend toward protest but took over its leadership."[14] The progressives generally were led by Yankee protestants who placed great emphasis upon the responsibilities of citizenship to ensure the public good was promoted.

The direct legislation drive gained important support from the Progressive movement during the first two decades of the twentieth century. In California, progressives were upset greatly by what they perceived to be control of the state legislature by corporations, and concluded that the initiative and petition referendum could break monopoly control and machine politics.[15] Robert M. LaFollette, a leading progressive in Wisconsin, wrote:

For years the American people have been engaged in a terrific struggle with the allied forces of organized wealth and political corruption. . . . The people must have in reserve new weapons for every emergency, if they are to regain and preserve control of their governments.

Through the initiative, referendum, and recall the people in any emergency can absolutely control.

The initiative and referendum make it possible for them to demand a direct vote and repeal bad laws which have been enacted, or to enact by direct vote good measures which their representatives refuse to consider.[16]

Public enthusiasm in favor of law-making by unassembled citizens was strong in the period 1898 to 1918 as nineteen states adopted the initiative as part of their respective state constitutions. All were west of the Mississippi River except Maine, Massachusetts, and Ohio. No state subsequently adopted the initiative until 1959 when Alaska entered the Union with a constitutional provision for the initiative. Wyoming adopted the initiative by constitutional amendment in 1968, Illinois voters in 1970 ratified a proposed constitution providing for the initiative relative to the legislative article only of the constitution, and Florida adopted the constitutional initiative in 1972. The Illinois Supreme Court ruled in 1976 that only voter-approved, initiated constitutional amendments proposing structural and procedural changes in the legislative article of the constitution are valid.[17] Mississippi readopted the initiative in 1992 after its 1916 adoption was invalidated by the state supreme court in 1922.[18] The *Utah Code* (consolidated statutes) first authorized the initiative in 1900.

The initiative, protest referendum, and the recall also were promoted by the municipal reform movement. These three participatory mechanisms were incorporated in the commission form of municipal government commencing in Des Moines in 1907 and subsequently in council-manager charters. Richard S. Childs, originator of the council-manager plan of municipal government and cofounder with Woodrow Wilson of the National Short Ballot Organization, was convinced in 1916 that elected officers were irresponsible and that "our representative system is mis-representative."[19]

THE INITIATIVE

The initiative today is authorized by state constitutional or statutory provisions that vary in terms of authorized types of initiatives, restrictions on use, petition signature requirements, ballot title preparation, system of verifying signatures, voter information pamphlets, approval requirements, and legislative amendment or repeal. Whether the petition requirements are easy or difficult to meet often determines the frequency with which the initiative will be employed.

The constitutions of twenty-three states and the *Utah Code* contain provisions authorizing state voters to use one or more types of initiatives (see Chapter 2). Constitutional provisions for direct legislation in some states — Idaho and South Dakota are examples — are brief, and implementation of the provisions is the responsibility of the state legislature. In contrast, the Colorado and Ohio constitutions contain detailed procedural provisions. In nine states, the constitutional provisions for the initiative and protest referendum are self-executing, that is, no implementing legislation is required.

In eighteen states, the initiative can be employed in the process of amending the state constitution. The Florida and Mississippi constitutions permit use of the initiative to amend only the constitution, and the Illinois constitution restricts use of the device to amendment of the legislative article of the constitution. The initiative in twenty-two states can be utilized to enact ordinary statutes. The veto power of the governor does not extend to voter-approved initiated measures. As authorized by the state constitution, state statute, or local government charter, the initiative can be employed in most states to adopt and amend local government charters and ordinances.

The initiative can be direct, indirect, or advisory. Under the former, the entire legislative process is circumvented when propositions are placed directly on the referendum ballot, if the requisite number and distribution of valid signatures are collected and certified. This initiative is employed in sixteen states to amend the constitution and in seven states to enact statutes. On the substate level, the direct initiative commonly is employed to place local government charters or charter amendments on the referendum ballot. Although the New York City Charter authorizes the use of the initiative to propose charter amendments, the initiative seldom has been employed.[20]

The indirect statutory initiative, employed in nine states, involves a more cumbersome process. A proposition is referred to the legislative body when the required number of certified signatures is filed. Failure of the legislative body to approve the proposition within a specified number of days, varying from forty days in Michigan to adjournment of the Maine state legislature, leads to the proposition appearing automatically on the referendum ballot. In three states, additional certified signatures must be collected to place the proposition on the ballot as follows: one-half of 1 percent and 10 percent of the votes cast for governor in the last general election in Massachusetts and Utah, respectively, and 3 percent of the registered voters in Ohio.

Only the Massachusetts and Mississippi constitutions authorize the indirect initiative for constitutional amendments. To appear on the Massachusetts referendum ballot, the initiative proposal must be approved by each of two successive joint sessions of a successively elected General Court (state legislature) or receive the affirmative vote of 25 percent of all members in each of two successive joint sessions.[21] The state legislature in five states — Maine, Massachusetts, Michigan, Nevada, and Washington — is authorized to place a substitute proposition on the referendum ballot whenever an initiative proposition appears on the ballot.[22] Regarding proposed statutes, Alaska, Maine, Massachusetts, Michigan, and Wyoming provide only for the indirect initiative. Nevada, Ohio, Utah, and Washington authorize use of both the indirect and the direct initiative.

The initiative also can be employed by voters in numerous, general-purpose, local governments to place propositions on the referendum ballot. Eight state constitutions and statutes in six additional states authorize such use. Furthermore, home rule constitutional provisions in several other states allow voters to adopt charters or charter amendments providing for this participatory device (see Chapter 2).

The advisory initiative allows voters to circulate petitions to place non-binding questions on the ballot at an election and is a mechanism citizens and groups can employ to pressure legislative bodies to take a certain course of action. If petition circulators are successful in collecting the required number of verified signatures for a referendum, a large favorable vote on the question exerts great pressure on the legislative body to accede to the desires of the electorate.

Until the late 1970s, the advisory initiative was employed relatively infrequently and generally attracted only local notice. The growth of the environmental and nuclear freeze movements, along with movements opposing United States involvement in Central America, resulted in media attention being focused upon advisory referenda as national and regional groups employed the initiative to place questions on the election ballots. In 1983, for example, voters approved Proposition 9, which directed the mayor and the board of supervisors of the city and county of San Francisco to notify President Ronald Reagan and Congress that the voters favor the repeal of the provisions of the federal Voting Rights Act that require the city and county to provide ballots, voter pamphlets, and other materials on voting in Chinese and Spanish as well as English.[23]

VIEWS OF ADVOCATES AND CRITICS

The initiative was controversial in 1898 when adopted by South Dakota and San Francisco, but currently has wide acceptance in many general-purpose, local governments and a number of states. The device is a populist extension of the constitutional referendum first authorized by the Massachusetts State Constitution of 1780, which also directed the General Court to issue precepts to selectmen of towns and plantations that directed them to hold town and plantation meetings of voters in 1795 to decide whether a convention should be called to revise the constitution.[24]

New Hampshire followed Massachusetts' lead in submitting its proposed constitution to the voters in 1783, and Maine adopted the same practice when it entered the Union as a state in 1820. Subsequently, other states adopted the principle that changes proposed by constitutional conventions or state legislatures do not become effective unless adopted by a majority of voters casting ballots on the question of ratification.[25] By 1860, the principle was well established in most northern states. The constitutional referendum spread to all states except Delaware, whose constitution can be amended by a two-thirds vote of the members elected to each house of the state legislature in two consecutive sessions separated by an election.[26]

As noted, there are two profoundly different views of law-making by citizens. Although the populists and progressives hailed the initiative as an effective device to make legislative bodies more responsive to the will of the popular majority, elected officers and a number of political observers condemned the initiative on the ground it effectively would destroy representative law-making and replace it with whimsical and emotional law-making. Several observers viewed the initiative as reactionary because it appears to be a return to the ancient Greek and New England town meetings of assembled voters. The arguments of the proponents and opponents are evaluated in Chapter 5.

Advocates

The populists and other advocates of the initiative advanced proposals that followed in the Jeffersonian and Jacksonian traditions. Jefferson opposed a strong national government and placed his faith in the common citizens who must be educated. He stressed: "In every government on earth is some trace of human weakness, some germ of corruption and degeneracy, which cunning will discover, wickedness insensibly open, cultivate, and improve. Every government degenerates when trusted to the rulers of the people alone. The people themselves therefore are its only safe depositories. And to render even them safe, their minds must be improved to a certain extent."[27]

Andrew Jackson similarly distrusted government officers and recommended their frequent election, often annually, as a guard against unethical behavior. He stated:

There are perhaps few men who can for any great length of time enjoy office and power, without being more or less under the influence of feelings unfavorable to the faithful discharge of their public duties. Their integrity may be proof against improper considerations immediately addressed to themselves; but they are apt to acquire a habit of looking with indifference upon the public interests, and of tolerating conduct from which an unpracticed man would revolt. Office is considered as a species of property, and Government rather as a means of promoting individual interests than as an instrument created solely for the service of the People. Corruption in some and in others a perversion of correct feelings and principles divert Government from its legitimate ends, and make it an engine for the support of the few at the expense of the many.[28]

Richard Hofstadter attributed the "agrarian myth" to the Revolutionary War farmer soldiers and to Jefferson's faith in the yeoman farmer, and maintained that the myth "encourages farmers to believe they were not themselves an organic part of the whole order of business enterprise and speculation that flourished in the city, partaking of its character and sharing in its risks, but rather the innocent pastoral victims of a conspiracy hatched in the distance."[29]

The conspiracy theory influenced populist thinking and their efforts to improve the economic condition of farmers and establish governments controlled by the citizenry rather than the special economic interests. Albert M. Kales wrote in 1914 that "unpopular government is, and indeed always has been a government of the few, by the few, and for the few, at the expenses and against the wish of the many."[30] There was general agreement among populists that legislative dominance of the citizenry must be ended.

Dr. John R. Haynes — a prominent promoter of the initiative, protest referendum, and recall in the City of Los Angeles, reflected upon the initiative in a 1917 speech in Washington, D.C., that was published by the Government Printing Office. He stated the initiative and the protest referendum, "by bringing the people's servants under a more strict responsibility and a more direct control, has greatly improved the work of representative assemblies."[31] Haynes provided evidence, based upon California experience, that voters did distinguish carefully between the initiated measures that appeared on the referendum ballot and made sound decisions. He added: "From an educational standpoint the initiative and referendum have been worth their cost a thousandfold. They have acted as a sort of great popular university to stimulate the intellectual faculties of the people. They have made the individual less selfish, more thoughtful of the welfare of others; they have given him a new feeling of social solidarity."[32]

Delos F. Wilcox explained "representative assemblies have become so unwieldy as deliberative bodies that they have been driven to harness themselves with iron rules and submit themselves to guidance by tyrants whose powers Pisistratus himself would have envied."[33] He was convinced voters were less likely to take ruinous action than a legislative body because the issue would have been framed and discussed in the newspapers and at meetings for weeks prior to referendum day.[34]

He advanced four major arguments in favor of the initiative. First, the device "would utilize the individuals in politics" by tapping their wisdom and employing their energies to solve governmental problems directly.[35] Second, bills would be drafted by individuals who wanted the bills to succeed in achieving their goals, and the bills would be submitted unamended to the voters.[36] He specifically noted that hostile legislators typically amend measures sponsored by reformers to ensure that they will be defeated or will not achieve their goals.

Third, Wilcox argued that the initiative enables the sovereign people to exercise their right to make laws without the need for approval by the legislature or other intermediaries. He elaborated that the initiative would free citizens "from the domination of our own representatives and it would be possible by direct action to solve" major problems.[37]

Wilcox's fourth argument stresses that the initiative "would provide an orderly means for the restriction or the extension of the suffrage in accordance with the will of the majority and free from the interference of elected persons whose representative function makes it particularly inappropriate for them to tamper with the suffrage."[38] This argument, of course, was a potent one during the period when women generally were denied the right to vote and questions were raised about the desirability of lowering the voting age below twenty-one.

William B. Munro commented on the ineffectiveness of constitutional restrictions placed upon the discretion of state legislatures in the nineteenth century and concluded that the restrictions in general resulted in less competent individuals being elected to serve in these bodies.[39] He identified two major arguments in favor of the initiative and referendum. The first argument is based upon the contention that citizens are not represented properly by elected legislators. Munro wrote that in the decade prior to the constitutional adoption of direct legislation in California "it would be a gross perversion of obvious facts to allege that the voters of the state got what they wanted in the way of legislation."[40] Munro also explained the educational value of the initiative which promotes "a spirit of legislative enterprise . . . among the voters" who are able to develop proposed legislation with a guaranty that the proposal will receive careful consideration by the voters if the requisite number of petition signatures is obtained.[41] The civic education of the voters also is promoted by the distribution at public expense of informational pamphlets containing the proposed statute and pro and con arguments.

Theodore Roosevelt, a leading progressive, was an advocate of the New England open town meeting, the initiative, and the referendum. He referred to the latter two as merely the next stage of the former and added: "Personally I should like to see the initiative and referendum, with proper safeguards, adopted generally in the states of the Union, and personally I am sorry that the New England town meeting has not spread throughout the Union."[42] Roosevelt was a pragmatist and favored the adoption of every participatory device that is theoretically good, provided experience supports the theory.[43]

A second prominent progressive, Woodrow Wilson, contended the legislative initiative and the referendum would restore representative government by abolishing secret decision-making under the control of economic interest groups.[44] He emphasized these participatory devices would ensure that legislators would be "bound in duty and in mere policy to . . . represent the sovereign people whom they profess to serve and not the private interests which creep into their counsels by way of machine orders and committee conferences."[45]

Richard S. Childs in 1916 reflected the popular suspicion of the quality of representative government and noted "it often fails to register the will of the people and in fact may brazenly and successfully defy the people on a given issue."[46] He highlighted the fact that the Oregon electorate overwhelmingly approved propositions that the state legislature had scorned. Referring specifically to municipal governments, he wrote the people's "nominal agents and servants in the representative system will frequently maintain a successful indifference or resistance election after election."[47] Childs, however, did not call for the abandonment of representative government, but advocated a number of reform measures, including the initiative, protest referendum, recall, and short ballot.

The populist theme of the need to break the stranglehold of the plutocrats on governments was echoed by Robert M. LaFollette, a leading progressive, who explained:

For years the American people have been engaged in a terrific struggle with the allied forces of organized wealth and political corruption. . . . The people must have in reserve new weapons for every emergency, if they are to regain and preserve control of their governments.

Through the initiative, referendum, and recall the people in any emergency can absolutely control.

The initiative and referendum make it possible for them to demand a direct vote and repeal bad laws which have been enacted, or to enact by direct vote good measures which their representatives refuse to consider.[48]

LaFollette was convinced that only a united people using the instruments of direct democracy could regain popular control of governments.

John D. Hicks identified two key populist propositions: The need to "restrain the selfish tendencies of those who profited at the expense of the poor and needy" and to replace a plutocracy by a democracy.[49] According to Hicks, populists accepted as reality the ability of voters to draft, enact, and implement statutes "to redeem themselves from the various sorts of oppression that were being visited upon them."[50]

The most common themes of the populists and progressives were empowerment of the people and the educative value of the initiative and associated referendum. Lewis J. Johnson provided a third theme; that is, direct legislation offers "an attractive field of usefulness for such of her citizens as do not care to give up their whole time to public life."[51] Johnson, of course, was referring to the fact the initiative allows voters on occasion to become legislators without serving as elected lawmakers on a full or part-time basis. Because the potential use of the initiative encourages legislators to enact bills desired by the majority of their respective constituents, the affirmative-forcing mechanism would not have to be employed by the voters.

A most interesting justification of the initiative was made by U.S. Senator Mark O. Hatfield of Oregon, who in 1979 argued "the initiative is an actualization of the citizens' first amendment right to petition the Government for redress of grievances."[52] Of course, this statement could not have been made by the populists or the progressives because the first amendment to the U.S. Constitution, which specifically was designed to limit the powers of Congress, had not yet been incorporated into the fourteenth amendment by the U.S. Supreme Court. Hatfield's statement is related more directly to the indirect initiative than to the direct initiative.

Critics

The political theory of the direct initiative and obligatory protest referendum challenges the fundamental assumptions of the theory of representative government and suggests elected officers are little more than delegates to legislative assemblies with detailed instructions on how to vote on bills. Not surprisingly, the emergence of the direct democracy movement sparked a spirited response and attack by defenders of the institutional status quo. A. Lawrence Lowell in an 1895 article, for example, argued the initiative "has not been a success in its native country, and there is no reason to suppose it would work any better elsewhere."[53] The more extreme opponents of direct democracy clearly were fearful these participatory instruments would lead to a most undemocratic result: an ocholocracy.

One of the most vitriolic attacks on direct democracy was published in 1912. James Boyle, a former Consul of the United States at Liverpool, England, complained that direct legislation was "impracticable, revolutionary, and reactionary, and that it would be followed by a train of evils greater than those of which they complain."[54] In his view, any evil in the system of representative government is attributable to the failure of the voters to assume fully their civic responsibilities. He justified his description of the participatory democracy as revolutionary on the ground proponents are opposed to the current representative system and as reactionary because they want to retrogress to town meeting government, which he asserted is unsuited to the conditions of today.[55]

Boyle particularly resented the inability of the voters or the legislature to amend propositions placed on the referendum ballot by only 8 percent of the registered voters that are approved and observed that the initiative is inferior to town meeting government in which the majority can make the decisions.[56]

The dulling of the sense of responsibility of legislators was another major argument advanced by Boyle who elaborated: "The people can initiate laws; the people can pass laws; therefore let the people be responsible; — and the argument is sound. But who will "Referendum" or "Recall" the people? Yet the people sometimes make mistakes, — though it is almost rank treason in these days of cheap fawning demagogy to say so — God's truth though it be!"[57]

Boyle was convinced that initiative propositions never would draw a majority of the registered voters to the ballot box and hence would result in minority rule. Although he admitted that a high percentage of voters were turning out to make decisions on initiated propositions in Oregon, he dismissed the turnout on the grounds that the initiative was a novelty, public interest was generated by the women's suffrage campaign, and several leaders of the national movement for the initiative and referendum were residents of Oregon.[58] The national and state platforms of the Socialist Party called for the adoption of the initiative and protest referendum. Building upon this fact and the general aversion to socialism in the United States, Boyle labeled direct legislation "the Gate-Way to Socialism."[59] Recalling the colonists' cry of no taxation without representation, Boyle alleged the initiative and the referendum "would place the tremendous

'Ladies and gentlemen, you're looking at the place where
California's laws are formulated; next to it is the state Legislature.'

Source: Denis Renault, Editorial Cartoon, October 29, 1996, *The Sacramento Bee*. Reprinted with
permission of *The Sacramento Bee*.

power of taxation — the highest power any State can exercise, next only to that of imprisonment or inflicting the death penalty — in the hands of selfish groups and classes of organized minorities."[60] Boyle was not done with his litany of direct legislation defects. He asserted such legislation would be crude legislation in need of amendment and would have to be accepted or rejected *en toto* without amendment.[61] After citing the negative views of other critics of direct legislation and concluding that "the Swiss people are weary of their many elections under the initiative and referendum," Boyle ended his tirade with the statement that the direct legislation system "is not only a failure as an effective and satisfactory instrument of Democratic government, but that it is full of vicious possibilities."[62]

Walter E. Weyl noted in 1912 that the initiative and protest referendum tended to limit the discretionary authority of legislators and maintained that the devices turned solons "into mere delegates; into mere mechanical forecasters and repeaters of popular deliverances; into parrot-like, political phonographs."[63] This theme occurs frequently in the writings of persons opposed to direct legislation.

Two years later, Albert M. Kales concluded that voters were burdened by a long ballot prior to the adoption of the initiative that added to the length of the ballot, which possibly contained other propositions on the same subjects as the initiative propositions.[64] In addition, he believed "the power of the extra-legal government to advise and direct the politically ignorant voter how to vote will be just as effective in the normal election to carry or defeat an act of an initiative or referendum as it is to place men loyal to it in the offices of the legal government."[65] In essence, government will continue to be dominated by special interest groups, regardless of whether the initiative is available to the voters.

Reviewing Oregon's early experience with the initiative and the referendum, James D. Barnett wrote that it often was difficult for voters to determine who were the genuine authors of initiative propositions, and special interests on a number of occasions were behind the propositions.[66] This theme also appears in the writings of other opponents.

In 1915, Herbert Croly explained that the initiative grants a most important power — the ability to place a proposition without amendment on the ballot — to a small group of voters who "might frequently be able to wear down or circumvent the opposition of a less able and tenacious majority."[67]

The most eminent early opponent of the initiative was former President William H. Taft, who questioned in 1913 whether the voters possessed the ability to act upon numerous initiative propositions on a single referendum ballot and whether the failure of representative government was due to the inability of the electorate to choose representatives intelligently. He used strong words to describe the negative impact of direct legislation on legislative bodies.

The effect of the initiative and referendum upon the legislative branch of government, even if it be retained, is necessarily to minimize its power, to take away its courage and independence of action, to destroy its sense of responsibility and to hold it up as unworthy of confidence. Nothing would more certainly destroy the character of a law-making body. No one with just pride and proper self-respect would aspire to a position in which the sole standard of action must be the questions what the majority of the electorate, or rather a minority likely to vote, will do with measures the details of which there is neither time nor proper means to make the public understand. The necessary result of the compulsory referendum and following initiative is to nullify and defeat the very advantages of the representative system which made it an improvement upon direct government.[68]

Taft also objected to direct legislation because it removed the distinction between fundamental law, a constitution, and ordinary statutes since both receive the identical sanction of the voters.[69] In his view, this was the strongest objection to the use of the initiative and the referendum.

To many, direct legislation ran counter to the guaranty clause of the U.S. Constitution that provides "the United States shall guarantee to every State in this Union a Republican form of Government."[70] A republic is a representative form of government, and opponents of the initiative strongly believed direct legislation was facially unconstitutional. This question is examined in Chapter 3.

The controversy over the desirability of the initiative has not died out with the passage of time. Professor Eugene C. Lee of the University of California, Berkeley, noted the paradox that this participatory device no longer is direct democracy in California.

In 1990, representative government is threatened, not by a private monopoly, but by the initiative process itself. . . . It is a force that has produced occasional benefits but at an extraordinary cost — an erosion of responsibility in the executive and legislative branches of state government, a simultaneous overload in the judiciary, and an overamended state constitution alongside a body of inflexible "quasi-constitutional" law. At a time when the ultimate in statecraft is required to achieve even a minimum of coordinated public policies, the initiative offers the politics of simplification.[71]

Lee acknowledged that approved initiative propositions in a number of instances have been beneficial to the public, but doubted whether these benefits outweigh the shortcomings of direct democracy. Although he recommended several actions to improve the existing process, he placed special emphasis upon an option not available to California voters — the indirect initiative.[72]

Professor Preble Stolz of the University of California, Berkeley, School of Law directed his criticism of the initiative to its effect upon the courts. Stressing that the California Supreme Court can consider a maximum of approximately 140 cases a year, he noted initiative cases occupy the time of the courts that could be devoted to other important issues.[73] He added: "The best way to fix the initiative process is to get rid of it. The Supreme Court could help by applying the single-subject rule more rigorously to initiatives than it has to statutes. Since legislative statutes are the product of extensive hearings and negotiations, the wording represents a compromise. That process is absent from initiatives, which are written by partisans and put before the voters on an all-or-nothing basis. Initiatives invite log rolling the single-subject rule was intended to prevent."[74]

The widespread negative view of elected officers to the initiative is reflected in a 1997 E-mail message to the author from the executive director of a state association of counties — "Thank goodness we do not have initiative."

THE INITIATIVE AND DEMOCRATIC LAW-MAKING

The term democracy is derived from two Greek words, which translate into English as power of the people. Hence, it appears direct law-making by citizens, whether in a New England open town meeting or by means of the initiative and its compulsory referendum, is the most democratic method for enacting statutes.

The views of the critics cited above suggest that initiated constitutional amendments and statutes might be the result of well-financed interest group action and might not necessarily represent the views of the majority of voters because the amendments and statutes might have been approved by a minority of the registered voters or by a majority of voters who might not have been well-informed or were confused by the wording of the referendum questions. Critics also argue that statutes passed through the legislative process are improved, in contrast to initiated measures, which are placed on the ballot without the benefit of review and needed amendments.

The relatively widespread authorization for employment of the initiative, particularly by local government voters, and numerous uses of the device for nearly one century provide a large body of evidence that can be utilized to evaluate the desirability of this participatory mechanism. The thesis examined in this book is the belief of early proponents that voter employment of the initiative results in the enactment of *pro bono publico* constitutional amendments and statutes. Specifically, I examine whether special interests have captured control of the initiative process as they have captured control of legislative decision-making on certain subjects. I also examine whether the initiative has helped to reinvigorate representative law-making by acting as a Sword of Damocles and persuading legislators to enact all statutes desired by the majority of their constituents.

Chapter 2 focuses upon the legal foundations for the initiative, including state constitutional and statutory provisions and local government charters, restrictions on its use, pre-election review of initiated propositions, conferences with sponsors, ballot titles, paid and unpaid petition circulators, petition signature requirements, approval requirements, legislative amendment or repeal of initiated statutes, and types of initiatives.

The initiative immediately raised a number of legal issues, including whether it violated the guarantee clause of the U.S. Constitution. Chapter 3 examines the major court decisions relating to the guarantee issue, number of propositions allowed on a single election ballot, solicitation of petition signatures on private property, use of paid circulators, constitutional single subject requirement, privacy of petitioners' signatures, validity of signatures, campaign finance, federal preemption, civil rights, state preemption, excluded subjects, legislative reapportionment, and legislative organization and rules.

Chapter 4 is devoted to major initiative campaigns, including the tax revolt propositions in California and Massachusetts. The successful use of the initiative to limit the property tax in these and other states had major repercussions for state and local governments and interest groups desiring increased governmental expenditures.

The arguments of the proponents and opponents of the initiative are evaluated in Chapter 5, and conclusions are drawn as to their validity.

The final chapter builds upon the findings and conclusions of Chapters 2 through 5 to develop a model, constitutional or local government, charter initiative provision to guide citizens interested in adopting the initiative or modifying an existing provision. This chapter also suggests supplementary actions that should be initiated to ensure that state and local governments are accountable and responsible to the voters.

NOTES

1.　Benjamin Jowett, trans., *Aristotle's Politics* (New York: Carlton House, n.d.), pp. 145–56.

2.　For details, see Joseph F. Zimmerman, *The New England Town Meeting: Democracy in Action* (Westport, CT: Praeger Publishers, 1999).

3.　Joseph F. Zimmerman, *The Recall: Tribunal of the People* (Westport, CT: Praeger Publishers, 1997).

4.　*Constitution of South Dakota*, art. III, § 1.

5.　*Charter for the City and County of San Francisco*, art. 2, chap. 1, § 20–22 (1898).

6.　*The Acts and Resolves of the Province of the Massachusetts Bay* (Boston: Wright and Potter, 1874), vol. 2, p. 30.

7.　*Constitution of Georgia*, art. LXIII (1777).

8.　William E. Rappard, "The Initiative, Referendum, and Recall in Switzerland," *The Annals of the American Academy of Political and Social Science*, September 1912, pp. 131–32. Pages 119–21 of this article contain an extensive bibliography. See also Kris W. Kobach, *The Referendum: Direct Democracy in Switzerland* (Aldershot, England: Dartmouth Publishing Company, 1993), pp. 25–30.

9.　*Constitution of California*, art. XI (1879) and *California Laws of 1883*, chap. 49.

10.　George McKenna, ed., *American Populism* (New York: G.P. Putnam's Sons, 1974), pp. 85–86.

11.　Rappard, "The Initiative, Referendum, and Recall in Switzerland," p. 124.

12.　*Charter for the City and County of San Francisco*, art. 2, chap. 1, §§ 20–22 (1898).

13.　Lloyd Sponholtz, "The Initiative and Referendum: Direct Democracy in Perspective, 1898–1920," *American Studies*, Fall 1973, p. 46.

14.　Richard Hofstadter, *The Age of Reform* (New York: Alfred A. Knopf, 1955), p. 130.

15.　George E. Mowry, *The California Progressives* (Berkeley: University of California Press, 1951), p. 289. See also William Deverell and Tom Sitton, *California Progressivism Revisited* (Berkeley: University of California Press, 1994).

16.　Ellen Torelle, comp. *The Political Philosophy of Robert M. LaFollette* (Madison, WI: The Robert M. LaFollette Company, 1920), pp. 173–74.

17.　*Coalition for Political Honesty v. State Board of Elections*, 65 Ill.2d 453, 359 N.E.2d 138 (1976).

18.　*Power v. Robertson*, 93 So. 769 (Miss. 1922).

19.　Richard S. Childs, *The Short Ballot: A Movement to Simplify Politics* (New York: The National Short Ballot Organization, 1916), p. 4.

20.　*Charter of the City of New York*, § 42.

21. *Constitution of Massachusetts*, articles of amendment, art. 48, § 5.

22. *Constitution of Maine*, art. 4, part III, § 18; *Constitution of Massachusetts*, articles of amendment, art. 48, the initiative, part III, § 2; *Constitution of Michigan*, art. 2, § 9; *Nevada Revised Statutes*, § 295.025-3; *Constitution of Washington*, art. 2, § 1(a).

23. Judith Cummings, "San Francisco's Absentees Decide Smoking and Building Measures," *The New York Times*, November 10, 1983, p. D26.

24. *Constitution of the Commonwealth of Massachusetts*, art. X.

25. Joseph F. Zimmerman, *State and Local Government*, 3rd ed. (New York: Barnes & Noble Books, 1978), pp. 40–42.

26. *Constitution of Delaware*, art. XVI, § 1.

27. Paul L. Ford, ed., *The Writings of Thomas Jefferson* (New York: G.P. Putnam's Sons, 1894), vol. 4, p. 64.

28. Henry S. Commager, ed., *The Era of Reform: 1830–1860* (New York: Van Nostrand Reinhold, 1960), p. 71.

29. Richard Hofstadter, *The Age of Reform: From Bryan to F.D.R.* (New York: Alfred A. Knopf, 1955), p. 55.

30. Albert M. Kales, *Unpopular Government in the United States* (Chicago, IL: University of Chicago Press, 1914), p. 7.

31. John R. Haynes, *Direct Government in California* (Washington, DC: Government Printing Office, 1917), p. 8.

32. *Ibid.*, p. 10.

33. Delos F. Wilcox, *Government by All the People* (New York: The Macmillan Company, 1912), pp. 7–8.

34. *Ibid.*, pp. 104 and 111.

35. *Ibid.*, pp. 112–14.

36. *Ibid.*, pp. 115–19.

37. *Ibid.*, p. 119.

38. *Ibid.*, p. 126.

39. William B. Munro, ed., *The Initiative, Referendum, and Recall* (New York: D. Appleton and Company, 1912), p. 19.

40. *Ibid.*, p. 21.

41. *Ibid.*

42. Theodore Roosevelt, "Nationalism and Popular Rule" in *Ibid.*, p. 63.

43. *Ibid.*, p. 65.

44. Woodrow Wilson, "The Issue of Reform" in Munro, ed., *The Initiative, Referendum, and Recall*, p. 87.

45. *Ibid.*, p. 88.

46. Childs, *The Short Ballot*, p. 3.

47. *Ibid.*, p. 4.

48. Ellen Torelle, comp. *The Political Philosophy of Robert M. LaFollette* (Madison, WI: The Robert M. LaFollette Company, 1920), pp. 173–74.

49. John D. Hicks, *The Populist Revolt: A History of the Farmers' Alliance and the People's Party* (Minneapolis: The University of Minnesota Press, 1931),

p. 406.

50. *Ibid.*, p. 413.

51. Lewis J. Johnson, "Direct Legislation as an Ally of Representative Government" in Munro, ed., *The Initiative, Referendum, and Recall*, p. 151.

52. Mark O. Hatfield, "Voter Initiative Amendment," *Congressional Record*, February 5, 1979, p. S 1062.

53. A. Lawrence Lowell, "The Referendum and Initiative: Their Relation to the Interests of Labor in Switzerland and in America," *International Journal of Ethics*, vol. 6, 1895, p. 62.

54. James Boyle, *The Initiative and Referendum: Its Folly, Fallacies, and Failure*, 3rd ed. (Columbia, OH: A.H. Smythe, 1912), p. 8.

55. *Ibid.*, p. 19.

56. *Ibid.*, p. 21.

57. *Ibid.*, p. 25.

58. *Ibid.*, p. 35.

59. *Ibid.*, p. 42.

60. *Ibid.*, p. 46.

61. *Ibid.*, pp. 47–48.

62. *Ibid.*, pp. 81 and 108.

63. Walter E. Weyl, *The New Democracy: An Essay on Certain Political and Economic Tendencies* (New York: The Macmillan Company, 1912), p. 307.

64. Albert M. Kales, *Unpopular Government in the United States* (Chicago: University of Chicago Press, 1914), pp. 119–20.

65. *Ibid.*, p. 121.

66. James D. Barnett, *The Operation of the Initiative, Referendum, and Recall in Oregon* (New York: The Macmillan Company, 1915), pp. 13 and 21.

67. Herbert Croly, *Progressive Democracy* (New York: The Macmillan Company, 1915), p. 306.

68. William H. Taft, *Popular Government* (New Haven: Yale University Press, 1913), pp. 63–64.

69. *Ibid.*, p. 64.

70. *United States Constitution*, art. IV. § 4.

71. Eugene C. Lee, "Hiram Johnson's Great Reform Is an Idea Whose Time Has Passed," *Public Affairs Report*, July 1990, p. 1.

72. *Ibid.*, pp. 2–3.

73. Preble Stolz, "Initiatives Sap Courts and Threaten Reform," *Public Affairs Report*, July 1990, p. 10.

74. *Ibid.*

2

The Legal Foundation

The initiative can be authorized directly or indirectly by the state constitution and similarly by statute. Currently, the constitutions of twenty-three
states and the *Utah Code* authorize state voters to employ the initiative to
place proposed constitutional amendments or statutes on the referendum
ballot (Table 2.1). The constitution of eight states and statutes in an additional nine states authorize voters in all or specified types of municipal
subdivisions to place propositions on the ballot by means of the initiative.
Data on initiative provisions for general purpose, local governments with
a population exceeding 2,500 — classified by population size, geograph-
ic region, and central city, suburban, and independent municipalities —
are shown in Table 2.2.

An indirect authorization is a constitutional or statutory provision
granting home rule to all or certain types of general purpose, local governments by empowering their voters to draft new charters that include
provisions for the initiative, and other general purpose governments to
amend their charters to include this participatory device.[1] The municipal
reformers who promoted home rule and the commission and council-manager forms of government generally were advocates of the initiative, referendum, and recall; not surprisingly, commission and council-manager
charters often contain provisions for these popular control devices.[2] In
Alabama, a non-home rule state, only cities with the commission form of
government are authorized by the state legislature to employ the initiative.

TABLE 2.1
Constitutional and Statutory State Initiative Provisions, 1999

State	Constitutional Provision	Statutory Provision
Alabama	None	Code of Alabama, tit. 11, art. 2, § 11-44-105 (commission form of government
Alaska	art. 11, §§ 1-7	Alaska Statutes, tit. 15, §§ 15.45.010-15.45.245
Arizona	art. 4, Part 1, §§ 1-2; art. 21, § 1; art. 22, § 14	Arizona Revised Statutes, tit. 19, §§ 19-102 to 19-144
Arkansas	7th & 65th amendments	None
California	art. 2, §§ 8, 10-12; art. 4, § 1; art. 16, § 11	California Civil Procedure Code, § 2015; Election Code, §§ 100-02, 104, 106, 336, 9001-002, 9004, 9007, 9014, 9020-022, 9030-035, 9060-090, 18370, 18600-8603, 18610-8614, 18620-8622, 18630-8631, 18640, 18650, 18660-8661, 18670; Government Code, §§ 6253, 84101, 84200, 84202
Colorado	art. 5, § 1	Colorado Revised Statutes, tit. 31, art. 40, §§ 1-40-101 to 1-40-133; 1-41-101 to 1-41-103; §§ 31-11-101 to 31-11-117
Connecticut	None	None
Delaware	None	None
Florida	art. 11, §§ 3, 5(a)	Florida Statutes, tit. 9, §§ 15.21, 16.061, 100.371, 101.161, 106.03
Georgia	art. 9, § 2 (I-II) (cities and counties)	None
Hawaii	None	None
Idaho	art. 3, § 1	Idaho Code, tit. 18, § 18-2318; tit. 34, §§ 34-1801 to 34-1823
Illinois	art. 14, § 3	Illinois Annotated Statutes, chap. 5, § 28-1 (municipalities)
Indiana	None	None
Iowa	None	None
Kansas	None	Kansas Statutes Annotated, § 3013 (cities)
Kentucky	None	None
Louisiana	None	None
Maine	art. 4, Part 3, §§ 18-22	Maine Revised Statutes, tit. 21-A, chap. 11, §§ 901-06
Maryland	None	None
Massachusetts	48th, 74th, and 81st amendments	Massachusetts General Laws, chap. 43, §§ 9-10, 38, 42, 129-30; chap. 44, § 8A; chap. 53, §§ 7, 18, 21, 22A; chap. 54, §§ 42A, 42C, 48, 52-54, 58A, 61-65; chap. 55B, §§ 5, 8; chap. 56, § 11; chap. 138, § 11A

State	Constitutional Provision	Statutory Provision
Michigan	art. 2, § 9; art. 12, § 2	Michigan Compiled Laws, Election Law, chap. 22, § 168.471
Minnesota	None	Minnesota Statutes, § 205.10(1) (cities)
Mississippi	art. 15, § 273 (3-13)	Mississippi Code, §§ 23-17-1-61, 23-25-1 to 23-15-951, 97-13-1 to 97-13-39
Missouri	art. 3, §§ 49-53; art. 12, § 2(b)	Missouri Annotated Statutes, §§ 116.010-340
Montana	art. 3, § 4; art. 4, § 7; art. 14, §§ 2, 9	Montana Code, §§ 13-27-101 to 13-27-504, § 78.573, § 78.575
Nebraska	art. 3, § 2; art. 3, § 4	Revised Statutes of Nebraska, §§ 14-210 to 14-211, 18-2501 to 18-2537, 32-1401 to 32-1417, 32-628 to 32-632
Nevada	art. 19, §§ 2-6	Nevada Revised Statutes, §§ 195.015, 195.056(2), 195.07 (county), 218.276, 218.493, 293.12793-.12795, 293.250, 294A.150, 295.195 (municipal)
New Hampshire	None	None
New Jersey	None	None
New Mexico	None	None
New York	None	None
North Carolina	None	None
North Dakota	art. 3, §§ 1-9	North Dakota Century Code, §§ 16.1-01-09, 16.1-01-10, 16.1-01-11, 16.1-06-09, 40-120-03 to 40-12-13
Ohio	art. 2, §§ 1, 1a, 1b, 1g; art. 16, § 1	Ohio Revised Code, §§ 705.91, 731.28, 3501-05, 3501.38, 3519.01-.22
Oklahoma	art. 5, §§ 1-8; art. 18, §§ 4(a-6); art. 24, § 3	Oklahoma Statutes, tit. 11, §§ 15-101, 15-102, 15-104; tit. 34, §§ 22-25
Oregon	art. 4, § 1	Oregon Revised Statutes, §§ 250.005-.355, 251.005-.435, 260.555, 260.558, 260.560
Pennsylvania	None	None
Rhode Island	Articles of amendment, art. 28, § 6 (city & town charters)	None
South Carolina	None	None
South Dakota	art. 3, § 1; art. 23, § 1	South Dakota Codified Laws, §§ 2-1-1 to 2-1-14, 7-18A-8 to 7-18-14, 9-20-1 to 9-20-19
Tennessee	None	None
Texas	None	None
Utah	None	Utah Code, §§ 20A-7-101 to 20A-7-512
Washington	art. 1, § 1(a, c, e)	Revised Code of Washington, §§ 29.79.010 to 29.79.500
West Virginia	None	None
Wisconsin	None	Wisconsin Statutes, § 9.20 (cities and villages)
Wyoming	art. 3, § 52	Wyoming Statutes, §§ 15-6-203, 15-9-106, 22-23-1002 to 22-23-1007, 22-24-101 to 22-24-125, 22-24-201, 22-25-101 to 22-25-102, 22-25-106

The state legislature in many states has enacted one or more statutes authorizing voters in named municipalities to employ the initiative, referendum, recall, or two of the three, or all three.

TABLE 2.2
General Purpose Local Governments: Initiative Provisions, 1998

	Initiative		
Classification	Number Reporting (A)	Number	Percent of (A)
Total, all cities	3,018	1,752	58.1
Population group			
Over 1,000,000	2	1	50.0
500,000–1,000,000	7	7	100.0
250,000–499,999	23	19	82.6
100,000–249,999	64	49	76.6
50,000–99,999	165	133	80.6
25,000–49,999	357	239	66.9
10,000–24,999	749	468	62.5
5,000–9,999	746	401	53.8
2,500–4,999	702	333	47.4
Under 2,500	203	102	50.2
Geographic division			
New England	395	274	69.4
Mid-Atlantic	301	109	36.2
East North Central	636	359	56.4
West North Central	334	176	52.7
South Atlantic	346	127	36.7
East South Central	87	22	25.3
West South Central	344	224	65.1
Mountain	197	146	74.1
Pacific Coast	378	315	83.3
Metro status			
Central	242	182	75.2
Suburban	1,676	959	57.2
Independent	1,100	611	55.5

Source: Tari Renner and Victor S. DeSantis, "Municipal Form of Government: Issues and Trends," *The Municipal Year Book 1998* (Washington, DC: International City/County Management Association, 1998), p. 41. Reprinted with permission of the Association.

The authorizing provision can be brief as in South Dakota, whose constitution simply provides that "However, the people expressly reserve to themselves the right to propose measures, which shall be submitted to a vote of the electors of the state. . . . No more than five percent of the qualified electors of the state shall be required to invoke either the initiative or the referendum."[3] In contrast, the Colorado constitutional provisions occupy two pages of fine print detailing the procedure for its use.[4] The constitutional authorization in twenty-two states is supplemented by statutes spelling out procedures in greater detail or authorizing all or certain general purpose, local governments to employ the initiative.

The constitutional initiative provision might be self-executing or might require implementing legislation before voters can use the participatory device. Nine states — Alaska, Arizona, Arkansas, Colorado, Michigan, Nevada, North Dakota, Ohio, and Wyoming — have self-executing provisions. The Alaska constitution stipulates "the provisions of this constitution shall be construed to be self-executing whenever possible."[5] The Arizona constitution declares that the initiative is "in all respects, self-executing."[6] Although the Michigan and Wyoming constitutions have a self-executing initiative provision, the supreme court in each state has taken a narrow view of the provision as explained in Chapter 3. The California Constitution specifically stipulates that the state legislature shall provide the manner in which the initiative will be operated.[7]

Sixteen of the eighteen states authorizing the use of the initiative to place proposed constitutional amendments on the referendum ballot allow only the direct initiative, which bypasses completely the state legislature (Table 2.3). Massachusetts and Mississippi authorize only the indirect initiative to place proposed constitutional amendments on the ballot (see Chapter 1). The constitutions in Florida and Mississippi permit proposals only of constitutional amendments by the direct initiative. The Illinois initiative can be used only to place on the ballot proposed constitutional amendments relating to the state legislature.

Voters are empowered by nineteen state constitutions to place proposed state statutes on the referendum ballot by means of initiative petitions. In addition, Utah statutes sanction use of the participatory device to add proposed statutes to the ballot. Although the Arkansas and Illinois constitutions authorize use of the statutory initiative, the state legislatures have not enacted enabling statutes.

TABLE 2.3
Statewide Initiative and Referendum

	Changes to constitution			Changes to statutes			
	Initiative		Referendum	Initiative		Referendum	
State or other jurisdiction	Direct (a)	Indirect (a)	Legislative (b)	Direct (c)	Indirect (c)	Legislative	Citizen petition (d)
Alabama	...	...	...	...	...	...	...
Alaska	...	...	★	...	★	...	★
Arizona	★	...	★	★	...	★	★
Arkansas	★	...	★	★	...	★	★
California	★	...	★	★	...	★	★
Colorado	★	...	★	★	...	...	...
Connecticut	...	...	★	...	...	...	...
Delaware*	...	...	★	...	...	★	...
Florida	★	...	★	...	...	...	...
Georgia	...	...	★	...	...	...	...
Hawaii	...	...	★	...	...	...	...
Idaho	...	...	★	★	...	★	★
Illinois	★	...	★	★	...	★	...
Indiana	...	...	★	...	...	...	...
Iowa	...	...	★	...	...	...	...
Kansas	...	...	★	...	...	...	...
Kentucky	...	...	★	...	...	★	★
Louisiana*	...	...	★	...	...	...	...
Maine	...	...	★	...	★	★	★
Maryland	...	...	★	...	...	★	★
Massachusetts	...	★	★	...	★	★	★
Michigan	★	...	★	...	★	★	★
Minnesota	...	...	★	...	...	...	...
Mississippi	...	★	★	...	...	...	...
Missouri	★	...	★	★	...	★	★
Montana	★	...	★	★	...	★	★
Nebraska	★	...	★	★	...	★	★
Nevada	★	...	★	★	★	★	★
New Hampshire	...	...	★	...	...	...	...
New Jersey	...	...	★	...	...	...	...
New Mexico	...	...	★	...	...	★	★
New York	...	...	★	...	...	...	...
North Carolina	...	...	★	...	...	...	...
North Dakota	★	...	★	★	...	★	★
Ohio	★	...	★	★	★	★	★
Oklahoma	★	...	★	★	...	★	★
Oregon	★	...	★	★	...	★	★
Pennsylvania	...	...	★	...	...	...	...
Rhode Island	...	...	★	...	...	...	...
South Carolina	...	...	★	...	...	...	...
South Dakota	★	...	★	★	...	★	★
Tennessee	...	...	★	...	...	...	...
Texas	...	...	★	...	...	...	...
Utah	...	...	★	★	★	★	★
Vermont	...	...	★	...	...	...	...
Virginia	...	...	★	...	...	...	...
Washington	...	...	★	★	★	★	★
West Virginia*	...	...	★	...	...	...	...
Wisconsin	...	...	★	...	...	...	...
Wyoming	...	...	★	...	★	...	★
U.S. Virgin Islands	...	★	...	★	...	★	★

Sources: State election administration offices, state constitutions and statutes, except where noted by * where data are from *The Book of the States, 1996-97.*

Note: This table summarizes state provisions for initiatives and referenda. *Initiatives* may propose constitutional amendments or develop state legislation and may be formed either directly or indirectly. The *direct initiative* allows a proposed measure to be placed on the ballot after a specific number of signatures have been secured on a citizen petition. The *indirect initiative* must be submitted to the legislature for a decision after the required number of signatures has been secured on a petition and prior to placing the proposed measure on the ballot.

Referendum refers to the process whereby a state law or constitutional amendment passed by the legislature may be referred to the voters before it goes into effect. Three forms of referenda exist: (1) citizen petition, whereby the people may petition for a referendum on legislation which has been considered by the legislature: (2) submission by the legislature (designated in table as "Legislative"), whereby the legislature may voluntarily submit laws to the voters for their approval; and (3) constitutional requirement, whereby the state constitution may require that certain questions be submitted to the voters.

Key:

★ — State Provision.

... — No state provision.

(a) See Table 1.3, "Constitutional Amendment Procedure: By Initiative," for more detail.

(b) See Table 1.2, "Constitutional Amendment Procedure: By the Legislature," for more detail.

(c) See Tables 5.16 through 5.19 on *State Initiatives*, for more detail.

(d) See Tables 5.20 through 5.23 on *State Referenda*, for more detail.

Source: *The Book of the States 1998–1999* (Lexington, KY: The Council of State Governments, 1998), p. 210. © 1999 The Council of State Governments. Reprinted with permission from *The Book of the States.*

RESTRICTIONS ON USE

The initiative is subject to the same prohibitions as the state legislature with respect to enactment of statutes. Furthermore, thirteen state constitutions — Alaska, California, Illinois, Massachusetts, Mississippi, Missouri, Montana, Nebraska, Nevada, North Dakota, Ohio, South Dakota, and Wyoming — exempt certain subjects from the initiative or place restrictions on its exercise. Appropriations, the judiciary, emergency measures, and support of the government typically are not subject to the initiative.

The longest list of exempted matters is contained in the Massachusetts Constitution:

No measure that relates to religion, religious practices or religious institutions; or to the appointment, qualification, tenure, removal, recall or compensation of judges; or to the reversal of a judicial decision; or to the powers, creation or abolition of courts; or the operation of which is restricted to a particular town, city, or other political division or to particular districts or localities of the commonwealth; or that makes a specific appropriation of money from the treasury of the commonwealth, shall be proposed by an initiative petition; but if a law approved by the people is not repealed, the general court shall raise by taxation or otherwise and shall appropriate such money as may be necessary to carry such law into effect.

Neither the eighteenth amendment of the constitution, as approved and ratified to take effect on the first day of October in the year nineteen hundred and eighteen, nor this provision for its protection, shall be the subject of an initiative amendment.

No proposition inconsistent with any one of the following rights of the individual, as at present declared in the declaration of rights, shall be the subject of an initiative or referendum petition. The right to receive compensation for private property appropriated to public use; the right of access to and protection in courts of justice; the right of trial by jury; protection from unreasonable search, unreasonable bail, and the law martial; freedom of the press, freedom of speech, freedom of elections, and the right of peaceable assembly.

No part of the constitution specifically excluding any matter from the operation of the popular initiative and referendum shall be the subject of an initiative petition; nor shall this section be the subject of such a petition.

The limitations on the legislative power of the general court in the constitution shall extend to the legislative power of the people as exercised hereunder.[8]

The Nevada constitution forbids the use of the initiative to appropriate funds unless an initiated measure provides for the levying of a tax to supply the finds.[9] The Maine Constitution stipulates that an initiated measure authorizing expenditures exceeding the amount appropriated becomes invalid forty-five days after the state legislature convenes.[10]

Fifteen state constitutions, including the ones in California and Missouri, restrict an initiative to a single subject. This restriction has led to challenges that many initiated propositions violate the constitutional requirement, a subject examined in detail in Chapter 3.

The Illinois statutes limit the number of propositions on the referendum ballot of a political subdivision to three, and the *Mississippi Code* allows only the first five certified propositions to appear on the referendum ballot.[11] By way of contrast, the Arkansas Constitution specifically stipulates "no limitations shall be placed upon the number of constitutional amendments, laws, or other measures which may be proposed and submitted to the people by either initiative or referendum petition."[12]

The constitutions of Nebraska and Wyoming do not allow a defeated initiative proposition to be placed upon the ballot a second time for a period of three years and five years, respectively.[13] A Mississippi statute stipulates that, if a constitutional amendment proposed by the initiative is rejected by the electorate, no identical or substantially similar proposed amendment shall be placed upon the referendum ballot for a minimum of two years.[14] If neither of two competing propositions in Oklahoma is approved by the majority of those voting in the referendum, the proposition receiving the most votes automatically will appear by itself on the next referendum ballot provided the proposition received at least one-third of the votes cast in favor of the two propositions.[15]

JUDICIAL INTERPRETATION

No state constitution addresses the question of whether courts should interpret the initiative provisions liberally, but a South Dakota statute directs that all initiative petitions shall be liberally construed.[16] In the absence of a constitutional provision, courts have been called upon to determine whether the authorization for the electorate to utilize the initiative should be interpreted broadly. To date, the highest courts in twelve states have issued opinions that the constitutional authorization provisions are to be liberally construed. These decisions are examined in Chapter 3.

To fully understand the initiative provisions of constitutional, statutory, and local government charters one must examine the decisions of U.S. and state courts and the opinions of state attorneys general. Opponents of the initiative petition can file a suit in a state court, which challenges the validity of filed petition signature sheets on the grounds that the constitutional or statutory provisions have not been complied with fully, the single subject rule has been violated, and other grounds. In addition, an aggrieved person or the U.S. Department of Justice can file suit against an initiated measure, alleging it violates the contract clause, commerce clause, or other clause of the U.S. Constitution or a preemption statute. Decisions of trial courts can be appealed to appellate courts, including the U.S. Supreme Court if a federal question is involved, and the latter can affirm or overturn the trial court decisions. Key court decisions and opinions of state attorneys general are reviewed in Chapter 3.

PETITION REQUIREMENTS

With the exception of Alaska, states that authorize the use of the initiative require that a proposed petition be filed first with the attorney general, the lieutenant governor (Alaska and Utah), or the secretary of state (commonwealth) who checks that it conforms with constitutional and statutory requirements (Figure 2.1). In Alaska, sponsors file the preliminary petition with the lieutenant governor, who also receives all signed petitions submitted by the filing deadline date. Three states require a deposit — $100 in Alaska, $200 in California, and $500 in Wyoming — when an application for the initiative is filed. The deposit is refunded if the proposition qualifies for the ballot.

In most initiative states, only one voter needs to sign the preliminary filing application, although a few states require additional signatures — a total of 10 signatures on an application for a constitutional or statutory initiative in Massachusetts, 25 signatures on either type of initiative in North Dakota and Oregon, 5 signatures on a statutory application in Utah, and 100 signatures on a statutory application in Wyoming.

In Arizona, a person filing a preliminary application for a proposed constitutional amendment or statute is required to set "forth his name or, in an organization, its name and the names of its officers, address, his intention to circulate and file a petition, a description of no more than one hundred words of the principal provisions of the proposed law, constitutional amendment, or measure and the text of the" proposal "in no less than eight point type" and apply "for issuance of an official serial number."[17]

The Oregon election laws require a prospective petition to contain a sponsorship statement signed by twenty-five voters, a complete copy of the measure to be initiated, designation of the names and addresses of three chief petitioners, and "a statement declaring whether one or more persons will be paid money or other valuable considerations for obtaining signatures on the initiative . . . petition" and a statement of the organization of a political committee and appointment of a treasurer and directors.[18]

FIGURE 2.1

<table>
<tr>
<td>SEL 310
REV. 9/97
ORS 250.045</td>
<td colspan="2" align="center">PROSPECTIVE PETITION FOR STATE
☐ INITIATIVE   REFERENDUM ☐
MEASURE</td>
<td>STATUTORY ☐
CONSTITUTIONAL ☐</td>
</tr>
</table>

TO THE SECRETARY OF STATE:

We, the undersigned, request the Attorney General prepare a ballot title for the attached proposed measure to be submitted to the people of Oregon for their approval or rejection at the election to be held on _____ , 19 _____ .

DESIGNATING CHIEF PETITIONER(S)

Every petition shall designate not more than three persons as chief petitioners, setting forth the name, residence address and title (if officer of sponsoring organization) of each.

1. NAME (PRINT) _____ SIGNATURE _____
   RESIDENCE ADDRESS _____
   MAILING ADDRESS (IF DIFFERENT) _____
   CITY, STATE, ZIP CODE _____ DAY TELEPHONE _____
   SPONSORING ORGANIZATION (IF ANY) _____

2. NAME (PRINT) _____ SIGNATURE _____
   RESIDENCE ADDRESS _____
   MAILING ADDRESS (IF DIFFERENT) _____
   CITY, STATE, ZIP CODE _____ DAY TELEPHONE _____
   SPONSORING ORGANIZATION (IF ANY) _____

3. NAME (PRINT) _____ SIGNATURE _____
   RESIDENCE ADDRESS _____
   MAILING ADDRESS (IF DIFFERENT) _____
   CITY, STATE, ZIP CODE _____ DAY TELEPHONE _____
   SPONSORING ORGANIZATION (IF ANY) _____

INSTRUCTIONS

FOR CIRCULATORS	FOR SIGNERS
Only registered voters of the state of Oregon may sign a petition.	Only registered voters of the state of Oregon may sign a petition.
All signers on any one signature sheet must be registered voters of the same county.	Sign your full name, as you did when you registered to vote, and fill in the date on which you signed the petition, your residence address and your precinct in the spaces provided.
It is advisable to use a pen or indelible pencil for signing petitions.	
Do not use ditto marks.	A woman should sign her own name, not her husband's or her husband's initials (for example: not "Mrs. John A. Jones" or "Mrs. J. A. Jones").
A petition circulator must be a registered voter of the state.	
Only one circulator may collect signatures on any one sheet of a petition.	Be sure to print your name clearly in the space provided.
	It is unlawful to sign any person's name other than your own. Do not sign another person's name under any circumstances.
It is unlawful for a petition circulator to knowingly make any false statement to any person who signs it or requests information about it.	It is advisable to use a pen or indelible pencil for signing petitions.
	Do not use ditto marks.
It is unlawful to circulate or file a petition knowing it to contain a false signature.	It is unlawful to sign a petition more than once.
	It is unlawful for a person to knowingly sign a petition when the person is not qualified to sign it.

Source: Office of the California Secretary of State.

Statutes often spell out in detail the duties of the public officer who receives an initiative application. The Utah lieutenant governor, for example, is directed to "reject the application and not issue circulation sheets if: (a) the law proposed by the initiative is patently unconstitutional; (b) the law proposed by the initiative is nonsensical; or (c) the proposed law could not become law if passed."[19]

Conference with Sponsors

A major objection to the initiative over the years, despite statutory instructions to write in clear and simple language, has been faulty draftsmanship that makes a proposition difficult for voters to understand or causes serious implementation problems if it is approved by the voters.

To avoid draftsmanship problems, Colorado, Idaho, Washington, and Wyoming statutes provide for conferences with initiative petition filers at which state officers explain wording problems, if any, and offer suggestions to overcome the problems. In Colorado, the directors of the legislative council and office of legislative legal services, within two weeks of the filing of a petition must provide comments to the sponsors who "may amend the petition in response to some or all of the comments."[20] If a major amendment is made to a petition other than in response to the comments received, the amended petition must be resubmitted for comments.

An Idaho initiative petitioner files a proposition with the secretary of state who is instructed by statute to transmit it for review to the attorney general who may confer with the sponsors and within twenty days must "recommend to the petitioner such revision or alteration of the measure as may be deemed necessary and appropriate."[21] The comments are advisory only and can be rejected totally or partially by the petitioner. In other words, the petitioner can freeze the wording of the referendum question at the time of filing the petition.

The Washington secretary of state upon receiving an initiative petition must transmit a copy to the code reviser who is authorized to confer with the petitioner and within seven working days must "review the proposal for matters of form and style, and such matters of substantive import as may be agreeable to the petitioner, and shall recommend to the petitioner such revision or alteration of the measure as may be deemed necessary and appropriate."[22] The recommendations, however, are advisory only. Similarly, the Wyoming secretary of state is directed to discuss format or content of the proposition with the sponsoring committee.[23]

Ballot Title and Summary

In most initiative states, the attorney general (lieutenant governor in Alaska) is directed to prepare a ballot title and a summary of the proposition that will be printed at the top of each petition signature sheet. The *Washington Revised Code Annotated* specifically stipulates the attorney general must formulate and transmit to the secretary of state a concise statement of the proposition that "shall be the ballot title . . . unless changed on appeal."[24] The code also stipulates that: "When practicable, the question posed by the ballot title shall be written in such a way that an affirmative answer to such question and an affirmative vote on the measure would result in a change in then current law, and a negative answer to the question and a negative vote on the measure would result in no change to then current law."[25] In Alaska, the lieutenant governor simply is directed by the state constitution to prepare a title and summary for placement on the referendum ballot.[26] The ballot title and summary can be challenged in court as explained in Chapter 3.

Estimate of Cost

The Mississippi Constitution and statutes in eight additional states require that a cost estimate be prepared for each initiative petition. In Mississippi, the sponsor must "identify the amount and source of revenue to implement the initiative" and the chief legislative budget officer prepares a summary fiscal analysis of each initiative and each legislative alternative for inclusion on the referendum ballot.[27]

Similarly, the Missouri secretary of state is required by statute to submit any petition received to the state auditor who, within twenty days of receipt of a petition, must "prepare a fiscal note and a fiscal note summary for the proposed measure" that contains an estimate of the cost or savings that would result to the state or a local government if the proposition is approved.[28] The note summary is limited to a maximum of fifty words and cannot be argumentative in nature. The *Arizona Revised Statutes* direct the legislative council to analyze each proposed initiative and prepare a report for inclusion in the voter information pamphlet.[29]

In Montana, the budget director has six days after receiving an initiative petition from the attorney general to draft a cost estimate for submittal to the attorney general, who prepares a fiscal statement limited to a maximum of fifty words.[30] The Ohio secretary of state, upon receiving a verified copy of a proposed constitutional amendment or state statute providing for the levy of a tax necessitating the expenditure of funds by the state or local government, must request the state tax commissioner to prepare "an estimate of any annual expenditure of public funds proposed and the annual yield of any proposed taxes."[31] The secretary of state also is mandated to include the estimates in the informational pamphlet distributed to voters prior to the referendum.

In Oregon, the cost estimates are prepared jointly by the secretary of state, state treasurer, director of the department of administrative services, and director of the department of revenue.[32] The estimate must identify the recurring annual amount or the total amount in the event there are no recurring costs, and the amount must be included in the voter information pamphlet. The Oregon lieutenant governor prints a voter information pamphlet containing, among other subjects, an estimate of the fiscal impact of an initiative petition and the Wyoming secretary of state similarly prepares a cost estimate and explanation of the fiscal impact that is disclosed to the sponsors who then could attempt to persuade the secretary of state to revise the estimates.[33]

Printing of Petitions

Five states require the sponsors to print copies of petitions to be circulated for signatures of voters. The *Mississippi Code* stipulates: "The person proposing an initiative measure shall print blank petitions upon single sheets of paper of good writing quality not less than eight and one-half inches in width and not less than fourteen inches in length. Each sheet shall have a full, true, and correct copy of the proposed measure referred to therein printed on the reverse side of the petition or attached thereto."[34] The *Idaho Code* provides for printing of petitions by sponsors after they receive approval from the secretary of state. Nebraska statutes direct the secretary of state to provide five camera-ready copies of the petition to sponsors for printing. The Utah law stipulates that the lieutenant governor shall provide sponsors with one copy of the initiative petition and one copy of the signature sheet. The Washington statute simply directs the sponsor to print blank petitions.[35]

Signature Requirements and Deadline

All state constitutions that authorize the initiative require a specified minimum number of signatures of registered voters on petitions to validate a proposition for placement on the referendum ballot (Table 2.4). Each circulator must sign an affidavit or jurat on each petition sheet attesting the signatures contained thereon are those of eligible registered voters (see Figure 2.2). Circulators typically are required to be qualified voters, and hence each circulator can sign the petition. Political committees circulating initiative petitions are subject to state corrupt practices

TABLE 2.4
Statewide Initiatives: Circulating the Petition

State or other jurisdiction	Basis for signatures (see key below)		Maximum time period allowed for petition circulation (a)	Can signatures be removed from petition (b)	Completed petition filed with	Days prior to election	
	Const. amdt.	Statute				Const. amdt.	Statute
Alabama		10% TV from 2/3 ED		Y	(c)		
Alaska	15% VG	10% VG	1 yr.	Y	SS	4 mos.	4 mos.
Arizona	10% VG	8% VG	2 yr.	N	SS	4 mos.	4 mos.
Arkansas	10% VG	5% VG	6 mos.	Y	SS (d)	131 days	131 days
California	8% VG	5% VSS	150 days	N	SS	3 mos.	3 mos.
Colorado	5% VSS	5% VSS	6 mos.		SS		
Connecticut							
Delaware*							
Florida	8% VEP, 8% from 1/2 CD		4 yr.	Y	SS	91 days	
Georgia				Y			4 mos.
Hawaii			(e)				
Idaho	8% VG	6% EV	2 yr.	Y		6 mos.	
Illinois							
Indiana							
Iowa							
Kansas							
Kentucky			1 yr.	Y	SS		(f)
Louisiana*	10% VG	10% VG		N	SS	(f)	
Maine					SS		
Maryland						(i)	(i)
Massachusetts	3% VG, no more than 25% from 1 county	3% VG, no more than 25% from 1 county (g)	(h)	Y	SS (d)	90 days prior to LS	
Michigan	10% VG	8% VG		N	SS	4 mos.	
Minnesota							
Mississippi	12% VG	12% VG	1 yr.	N	SS		4 mos.
Missouri	8% VG, 8% each from 2/3 CD	5% VG, 5% each from 2/3 CD	2 yrs.	Y	SS		
Montana	10% VG, 10% each from 2/5 SLD	5% VG, 5% each from 1/3 SLD	1 yr.	Y	SS	(j)	(j)
Nebraska	10% EV, 5% each from 2/5 counties	7% EV, 5% each from 2/5 counties	(k)		.	90 days	30 days prior to LS
Nevada	10% TV, 10% each from 3/4 counties	10% TV, 10% each from 3/4 counties					
New Hampshire							
New Jersey							
New Mexico			1 yr.				
New York				N	SS		
North Carolina	4% resident population	2% resident population			SS	90 days	90 days
North Dakota	10% VG, 1.5% each from 1/2 counties	3% VG, 1.5% each from 1/2 counties (l)		N	SS	90 days	90 days
Ohio		8% VH	90 days	N (m)			
Oklahoma	15% VH	6% VG			SS	4 mos.	4 mos.
Oregon	8% VG				SS		
Pennsylvania							
Rhode Island							
South Carolina							

See footnotes at end of table.

Source: *The Book of the States 1998–1999* (Lexington, KY: The Council of State Governments, 1998), pp. 212–13. © 1999 The Council of State Governments. Reprinted with permission from *The Book of the States.*

South Dakota	10% VG	...	1 yr.	...	SS	...	1 yr.	...	182 days
Tennessee	...	...	...	...	...	...
Texas	...	...	...	...	...	...
Utah	10% VG, 10% each from 1/2 counties	...	2 election cycles	Y	LG	...	June 1
Vermont	...	...	...	...	...	...
Virginia	...	...	...	...	...	...
Washington	8% VG	...	(i)	Y	SS	...	(n)
West Virginia*	...	...	...	...	...	...
Wisconsin	...	...	...	...	...	...
Wyoming	15% TV, from 2/3 counties	...	18 mos.	Y	SS	...	120 days
U.S. Virgin Islands	10 % ED	...	180 days	...	SBE	...	90 days

Source: State election administration offices, except where noted by * where data are from *The Book of the States, 1996-97.*

Key:

... — Not applicable.
VG — Total votes cast for the position of governor in the last election.
EV — Eligible voters.
VH — Total votes cast for the office receiving the highest number of votes in last general election.
TV — Total voters in last election.
VSS — Total votes cast for all candidates for the office of secretary of state at the previous general election.
VEP — Total votes cast in the state as a whole on the last presidential election.
ED — Election district.
CD — Congressional district.
SBE - State Board of Elections.
SLD - State legislative district.
LG — Lieutenant Governor
SS — Secretary of State
LS — Legislative session
Y — Yes
N — No

(a) The petition circulation period begins when petition forms have been approved and provided to sponsors. Sponsors are those individuals granted permission to circulate a petition, and are therefore responsible for the validity of each signature on a given petition.
(b) Should an individual wish to remove his/her name from a petition, a request to do so must be submitted in writing to the state officer with whom the petition is filed.
(c) Director of elections.
(d) Petitions first must be submitted to county circuit clerks for signature certification.
(e) 6% of qualified voters at most recent general election including 6% each from 22 counties. Pending initiative would change requirements. 18 months from receipt of ballot title or April 30 of year of election on initiative, whichever occurs earlier.
(f) To be placed on November ballot, petitions must be submitted to SS by 5:00 p.m. on 50th day after convening of Legislature in 1st regular session, or by 5:00 p.m. on 25th day in 2nd regular session.
(g) First Wednesday in December.
(h) In Michigan, signatures dated more than 180 days prior to the filing date are ruled invalid.
(i) Constitutional amendment--not less than 120 days prior to the next general election; statute--approximately 160 days prior to the next general election.
(j) Third Friday of the fourth month prior to election (3 months).
(k) Constitutional amendment--276 days; Amend or create a statute--291 days.
(l) Direct--6 months; Indirect--10 months.
(m) Not after petition has been filed.
(n) Direct--4 months; Indirect--2 weeks prior to legislative session.

acts, and must register and file financial reports with a specified state officer.

The number of required signatures is based on a percentage of the votes cast at the most recent general election or a percentage of the votes cast for governor (secretary of state in Colorado). Signature requirements for constitutional amendment initiatives vary from 3 percent of the vote for governor in Massachusetts (with no more than one-quarter from one county) to 15 percent of the votes cast for governor in Arizona. Oklahoma also has a 15 percent requirement, but it is based upon the total votes cast for the state office receiving the largest number of votes in the previous general election.

The Massachusetts Constitution only authorizes the indirect constitutional initiative. Therefore, petitions must be submitted to the General Court (state legislature), which must place the initiated proposition on the referendum ballot only if at least one-fourth of the members in two consecutive sessions approve the petition. When placed on the ballot, the proposed amendment is ratified if approved by a majority of the votes cast on the proposal and if the majority includes 30 percent of the total number of ballots cast in the election.[36]

Signature requirements for statutory initiatives range from 3 percent of the votes cast for governor in the preceding general election in Massachusetts (with no more than 25 percent of the signatures from one county) to 15 percent of the electorate participating in the last general election and residing in at least two-thirds of the counties in Wyoming. Although North Dakota has a 2 percent petition requirement, the base is the state's population in the latest federal census that produces a higher signature requirement than the Massachusetts requirement.

Massachusetts voters are restricted to employing the indirect statutory initiative. If the required number of signatures is certified, the petition is submitted to the General Court, which by the first Wednesday in May must vote on the question of enacting the initiative petition into law.[37] If the General Court rejects the petition or fails to act on it, sponsors of the proposal are authorized to collect additional signatures by the first Wednesday in July equal to 0.5 percent of the total votes cast for governor in the previous general election. If these additional signatures are filed and certified, the secretary of the commonwealth must place the initiative proposition on the next state election ballot. To be approved, a petition must receive the sanction of a majority of those voting on the proposition, provided the majority includes at least 30 percent of the ballots cast at the election.

FIGURE 2.2
Declaration of a Petition Circulator

[A one inch blank space must be left at the top of each page of the petition.]

The Attorney General of California has prepared the following Title and Summary of the chief purposes and points of the proposed measure.

[*INSERT* ATTORNEY GENERAL TITLE AND SUMMARY]

NOTICE TO THE PUBLIC

THIS PETITION MAY BE CIRCULATED BY A PAID SIGNATURE GATHERER OR A VOLUNTEER. YOU HAVE THE RIGHT TO ASK.

This column for official use only

1.			
	PRINT YOUR NAME	RESIDENCE ADDRESS ONLY	
	YOUR SIGNATURE AS REGISTERED TO VOTE	CITY	ZIP
2.			
	PRINT YOUR NAME	RESIDENCE ADDRESS ONLY	
	YOUR SIGNATURE AS REGISTERED TO VOTE	CITY	ZIP
3.			
	PRINT YOUR NAME	RESIDENCE ADDRESS ONLY	
	YOUR SIGNATURE AS REGISTERED TO VOTE	CITY	ZIP
4.			
	PRINT YOUR NAME	RESIDENCE ADDRESS ONLY	
	YOUR SIGNATURE AS REGISTERED TO VOTE	CITY	ZIP
5.			
	PRINT YOUR NAME	RESIDENCE ADDRESS ONLY	
	YOUR SIGNATURE AS REGISTERED TO VOTE	CITY	ZIP

DECLARATION OF CIRCULATOR
(to be completed after above signatures have been obtained)

I, _____, am registered to vote in the County (or City and County) of _____.
   (Print name)

My residence address is _____.
                                            (Address, city, state, zip)

I circulated this section of the petition and witnessed each of the appended signatures being written. Each signature on this petition is, to the best of my information and belief, the genuine signature of the person whose name it purports to be. All signatures on this document were obtained between the dates of _____ and _____.
                                                            (Month, day, year)   *(Month, day, year)*

I declare under penalty of perjury under the laws of the State of California that the foregoing is true and correct.

Executed on _____, 19___ at _____
              (Month and day)   *(Place of signing)*

_____
                                        (Complete signature of circulator)

[Dates of circulation, printed name and residence address must be in circulator's own hand.]

[NOTE: It is recommended that a space approximately 1/2 inch wide be left along the left margin opposite the signatures, as shown for the clerks' use in verifying signatures.]

Source: Office of the California Secretary of State.

Seven states have constitutional provisions with respect to the distribution of signatures on petitions for constitutional amendments ranging from 1.5 percent of the votes cast for governor in each of one-half of the counties in Ohio to 10 percent of the registered voters in each of 40 percent of the legislative districts in Montana. The purpose of the distributional requirement is to ensure that there is general support in various sections of the state for an initiative proposition. The petition signature threshold or distribution requirements affect significantly the relative ease or difficulty of employing the initiative to place a proposition on the referendum ballot.

Twenty-one states have established a maximum time limit for the collection of initiative petitions. These limits range from ninety days in Oklahoma to four years in Florida, and differ in certain states in accordance with whether the proposition is a constitutional or statutory one, or a direct or indirect one. In Nevada, the time limit is 276 days for a constitutional amendment proposition and 291 days for a statutory one. Washington allows six months for a direct initiative petition and ten months for an indirect one, suggesting the state is encouraging the use of the indirect initiative.

Similarly, twenty-one states have established a deadline date — number of days or months before the election — for filing state initiative petitions with the certifying officer. For constitutional initiative petitions, Nevada, North Dakota, and Ohio selected ninety days, Colorado three months, and Florida ninety-one days. South Dakota established the earliest deadline — one year before the election where the proposition will be voted upon. For statutory propositions, six states established a deadline day of four months before the election, but the South Dakota deadline is the first Tuesday in May before the election.

Paid Petition Circulators

Prior to 1976, eight states — California, Colorado, Idaho, Massachusetts, Ohio, Oregon, South Dakota, and Washington — by statute restricted or prohibited organizers of initiative petition campaigns to pay petition circulators.

In 1976, the California Supreme Court voided a provision of a 1974 statute limiting payments for petition signatures to twenty-five cents per signature as infringing "impermissibly upon rights of free speech and association guaranteed by the First Amendment to the United States Constitution."[38] The court noted that decisions of courts in other states upholding broad regulation of paid circulators of petitions, cited by the state, were rendered before the U.S. Supreme Court's decision in *Buckley v. Valeo*, striking down several congressional provisions limiting campaign expenditures.[39]

A U.S. District Court judge in 1982 invalidated Oregon's ban on paid petition circulators as violating the right of free speech guaranteed by the First Amendment to the U.S. Constitution by restricting "the discussion of issues that normally accompanies the circulation of petitions . . . and . . . the size of the audience that can be reached."[40]

Today, Arkansas has a constitutional amendment and six states have statutes relating to paid petition circulators. The Arkansas amendment stipulates: "No law shall be passed to prohibit any person or persons from giving or receiving compensation for circulating petitions, nor to prohibit the circulation of petitions, nor in any manner interfering with the freedom of the people in procuring petitions, but laws shall be enacted prohibiting and penalizing perjury, forgery, and all other felonies or other fraudulent practices in securing of signatures or filing of petitions."[41]

Colorado statutes require initiative petition proponents to file a monthly circulator disclosure report containing:

(a) The names of the proponents;
(b) The name and the residential and business addresses of each of the paid circulators;
(c) The name of the proposed ballot measure for which petitions are being circulated by paid circulators; and
(d) The amount of money paid and owed to each paid circulator for petition circulation during the month in question.[42]

A 1997 Idaho law makes it unlawful for any person to solicit initiative petition signatures by contracting to hire a person to obtain signatures unless the following is printed on the petition in bold red type: "THIS INITIATIVE PETITION IS BEING CIRCULATED BY A PAID SIGNATURE GATHERER. THE SIGNATURE GATHERER IS EMPLOYED BY OR HAS BEEN CONTRACTED WITH . . . , THE MAIN OFFICE OR HEADQUARTERS OF WHICH IS LOCATED AT (city and state)."[43] Statutes in Maine, North Dakota, and Wyoming forbid petition circulators to be paid based upon the number of signatures collected.[44] These statutes specifically note they do not prevent a circulator from being paid to collect signatures. Oregon's election laws require the chief petitioners to include with the prospective petition a notation whether any person will be paid money or other consideration to obtain petition signatures and notify the secretary of state if they discover that a person is being paid after indicating on the prospective petition that no person will be paid.[45]

The Washington State Legislature included the following finding in a 1993 statute:

The legislature finds that paying a worker, whose task it is to secure the signatures of voters on initiative or referendum petitions, on the basis of the number of signatures the worker secures on the petitions, encourages the introduction of fraud in the signature gathering process. Such a form of payment may act as an incentive for the worker to encourage a person to sign a petition for a ballot measure even if the person has already signed a petition for the measure. Such payments also threaten the integrity of the initiative and referendum process by providing an incentive for misrepresenting the nature or effect of a ballot measure in securing petition signatures for the measure.[46]

In effect, this provision suggests that proponents of an initiative petition have a moral obligation not to employ paid circulators.

Withdrawal of Signatures

Alaska, Idaho, Montana, Nebraska, Utah, and Wyoming have statutes authorizing withdrawal of signatures from initiative petitions. *Alaska Statutes* stipulate that "(a) person who has signed the initiative petition may withdraw the person's name only by giving written notice to the lieutenant governor before the date the petition is filed."[47] An Idaho voter can cross out, deface, or obliterate his or her signature on an initiative petition until it is presented to the county clerk for verification, and subsequently can have his or her name removed by presenting to the county clerk a signed statement expressing the desire that his or her name be removed from the petition.[48] The Washington Supreme Court in 1924 opined that once the secretary of state accepts an initiative petition for filing the secretary cannot permit the withdrawal of signatures in view of the absence of explicit statutory instructions relative to withdrawal of signatures.[49]

Petition Verification

Petitions are submitted for verification to one of the following officers: secretary of state, lieutenant governor, county clerk or recorder, or register of voters. The certifying officer has a stipulated number of days — ranging from ten in Arkansas to sixty in Alaska and Wyoming — to complete the signature verification process for state initiatives (Table 2.5). The

TABLE 2.5
State Initiatives: Preparing the Initiative to be Placed on the Ballot

State or other jurisdiction	Signatures verified by: (a)	Within how many days after filing	Number of days to amend/appeal a petition that is: Incomplete (b)	Not Accepted (c)	Penalty for falsifying petition (denotes fine, jail term)	Petition certified by: (d)
Alabama						
Alaska	Director of elections	60 days			Class B misdemeanor	LG
Arizona	County recorder	10 days		30 days	Class 1 misdemeanor	SS
Arkansas	SS	30 days	30 days	15 days	$50-$100, 1-5 yrs.	SS
California	Clerk or registrar of voters	30 days		15 days		SS
Colorado	SS	30 days	15 days			SS
Connecticut					(e)	
Delaware*						
Florida	Supervisor of elections					SS
Georgia						
Hawaii						
Idaho	County clerk	60 days		10 days		SS
Illinois	SBE and election authority	14 days			$5,000, 2 yrs.	SBE
Indiana						
Iowa						
Kansas						
Kentucky						
Louisiana*						
Maine	Registrar of voters, SS					
Maryland					§§	
Massachusetts	Local board of registrar	2 weeks	4 weeks (f)		$1,000, 1 yr.	SS
Michigan	City & township clerks					BSC
Minnesota						
Mississippi	Circuit clerk	2 weeks			$1,000, 1 yr.	SS
Missouri	SS, local election authority				$1,000, 1 yr. Class A misdemeanor	SS
Montana	County clerk and recorder	4 weeks			$500, 6 mos.	SS
Nebraska	County clerk or election commissioner	40 days			Class IV felony	SS
Nevada	County clerk or registrar	20-50 days		10 days	$10,000, 1-10 yrs.	SS
New Hampshire						
New Jersey						
New Mexico						
New York						
North Carolina			20 days			
North Dakota	SS		10 days			SS
Ohio	County board of elections	35 days			$1,000, 6 mos.	SS
Oklahoma						
Oregon	SS, county elections official	15 days	(g)		$1,000, 1 yr. Class C felony (possible)	SS
Pennsylvania						
Rhode Island						
South Carolina						

See footnotes at end of table.

Table 2.5, continued

State or other jurisdiction	Signatures verified by: (a)	Within how many days after filing	Number of days to amend/appeal a petition that is:		Penalty for falsifying petition (denotes fine, jail term)	Petition certified by: (d)
			Incomplete (b)	Not Accepted (c)		
South Dakota	SS	...	...	...	...	SS
Tennessee	...	...	...	...	...	...
Texas	...	...	...	...	...	...
Utah	County clerk	...	...	...	$500, 2 yrs.	LG
Vermont	...	...	...	...	...	...
Virginia	...	...	...	...	...	SS
Washington	SS	(h)	...	10 days (i)	Class C felony	SS
West Virginia*	...	...	...	...	...	...
Wisconsin	...	...	...	...	...	...
Wyoming	SS	60 days	30 days	30 days	$1,000, 1 yr.	SS
U.S. Virgin Islands	Supervisor of elections	60 days	30 days	30 days	...	SBE

Sources: State election administration offices, except where noted by * where data are from *The Book of the States,* 1996-97.

Key:

... — Not applicable.
SS — Secretary of State.
LG — Lieutenant Governor.
BSC — Board of State Canvassers.
SBE — State Board of Elections.

(a) The validity of the signatures, as well as the correct number of required signatures must be verified before the initiative is allowed on the ballot.

(b) If an insufficient number of signatures is submitted, sponsors may amend the original petition by filing additional signatures within a given number of days after filing. If the necessary number of signatures has not been submitted by this date, the petition is declared void.

(c) In some cases, the state officer will not accept a valid petition. In such a case, sponsors may appeal this decision to the Supreme Court, where the sufficiency of the petition will be determined. If the petition is determined to be sufficient, the initiative is required to be placed on the ballot.

(d) A petition is certified for the ballot when the required number of signatures has been submitted by the filing deadline, and are determined to be valid.

(e) No more than $500, one year in county jail, or both.

(f) Applies to statutory initiatives.

(g) If an initiative petition is submitted not less than 165 days before the election and if the secretary of state determines there are insufficient signatures, but the deadline for filing the signatures has not passed, the petitioners may submit additional signatures.

(h) Direct—no specific limit; Indirect—45 days.

(i) In Washington, a petition that is not accepted may be appealed within 10 days.

Source: The Book of the States 1996–1997 (Lexington, KY: The Council of State Governments, 1996), pp. 214–15. © 1999 The Council of State Governments. Reprinted with permission from *The Book of the States.*

Oregon Revised Statutes mandate that "the Secretary of State by rule shall designate a statistical sampling technique to verify whether a petition contains the required number of signatures of electors" and seek professional advice in determining the sampling technique.[50] Similarly, the Missouri, Nevada, and Washington secretaries of state are authorized to employ statistical sampling in the verification process.[51]

If the certifying officer determines that insufficient verified signatures were filed, the petition circulators typically are allowed to seek additional signatures, provided the deadline for filing signatures has not passed. The Arizona Supreme Court in 1947 ruled that any citizen can question the legal sufficiency of an initiative petition before it appears on the referendum ballot and in 1972 opined that courts lack jurisdiction to enjoin an initiative petition referendum on grounds of alleged illegality or unconstitutionality of the proposed action.[52]

Opponents of initiative petitions often challenge the validity of filed signatures. If either the proponents or opponents are dissatisfied with the verification ruling, it can be appealed to the courts. As explained in Chapter 3, charges of fraudulent signatures on petitions are common, and questions have been raised in court proceedings as to whether one fraudulent signature or jurat on a petition sheet invalidates all signatures on the sheet. Similarly, certified petitions have been challenged on procedural grounds or the petitions allegedly violate the single subject rule or the U.S. Constitution.

If the state legislature is opposed to a certified initiative petition on policy grounds or poor draftsmanship, the legislature typically is authorized to place an alternative proposition on the referendum ballot. The Massachusetts Constitution stipulates: "The General Court may, by resolution passed by yea and nay vote, either by the two houses separate, or in the case of a constitutional amendment by a majority of those voting thereon in joint session in each of two years as hereinafter provided, submit to the people a substitute for any measure introduced by initiative petition, such substitute to be designated on the ballot as the legislative substitute for such an initiative measure and to be grouped with it as an alternative therefor."[53]

Voter Information Pamphlets

The secretary of state (the nonpartisan research staff of the Colorado General Assembly and the Utah lieutenant governor) is directed by statute to prepare and post to each registered voter an official pamphlet describing or containing the full text of each initiated or referred proposition that

will appear on the forthcoming ballot and the arguments pro and con relative to each proposal. The California legislative analyst is required to
prepare a fiscal note on each proposition (see Figure 2.3).

FIGURE 2.3
California Proposition 213 of 1996

Analysis by the Legislative Analyst

PROPOSAL

This measure would limit the ability of certain people to sue to recover losses suffered in accidents.

Limits on Uninsured Motorists and Drunk Drivers

Under existing law, someone who has suffered an injury in a car accident may sue the person, business, or government at fault for the injury in order to recover related losses. These losses can include both *economic* losses (such as lost wages, medical expenses, and property damage) and *noneconomic* losses (such as pain and suffering).

This measure would prohibit the recovery of *noneconomic* losses in certain car accidents. Specifically, an uninsured driver or a driver subsequently convicted of driving under the influence of alcohol or drugs ("drunk drivers") at the time of an accident could not sue someone at fault for the accident for noneconomic losses. (These drivers could still sue for economic losses.) If, however, an uninsured motorist is injured by a drunk driver in an accident, the uninsured motorist could still sue to recover noneconomic losses from the drunk driver.

Limits on Convicted Felons

Currently, in certain cases a person who is injured while breaking the law may sue on the basis of another person's negligence to recover any losses resulting from the injury. For example, a person convicted of a robbery who was injured because he or she slipped and fell while fleeing the scene of the crime can sue to recover losses resulting from the injury.

This measure prohibits a person convicted of a felony from suing to recover any losses suffered while committing the crime or fleeing from the crime scene *if* these losses resulted from another person's negligence. Convicted felons, however, would still be able to sue to recover losses for some injuries suffered while committing or fleeing a crime—for instance those resulting from the use of "excessive force" during an arrest.

FISCAL EFFECT

Restricting the ability of people to sue for injury losses in the above situations would reduce the number of lawsuits handled by the courts. This would reduce annual court-related costs to state and local governments by an unknown but probably minor amount. These restrictions would also result in fewer lawsuits filed against state and local governments. Thus, there would be an unknown savings to state and local governments as a result of avoiding these lawsuits.

In addition, the restrictions placed on uninsured motorists and drunk drivers could result in somewhat lower costs, or "premiums," for auto insurance. Under current law, insurance companies doing business in California pay a tax of 2.35 percent of "gross premiums." This tax is called the gross premiums tax and its revenues are deposited in the state's General Fund. Any reduction in insurance premiums would also reduce gross premiums tax revenue to the state. We estimate that any revenue loss would probably be less than $5 million annually.

Source: *California Ballot Pamphlet, November 5, 1996* (Sacramento, CA: Office of the Secretary of
   State, 1996), p. 49.

The 1994 official Massachusetts pamphlet contained the above information plus information on how to vote, how to apply for an absentee ballot, services of the office of the secretary of state, and a checklist that
voters were urged to tear out and take to the polls. The Ohio secretary of
state is required to include in the voter information pamphlets "an estimate of any annual expenditure of public funds proposed and the annual
yield of any proposed taxes" prepared by the state tax commissioner.[54]

The *Oregon Revised Statutes* authorize any person to publish pro or con
arguments in the voters' pamphlet provided they "fit within a 19.9 square
inch space limitation, approximately 325 words" at a cost "of $300 per

argument" or filing of a "Petition for Measure Argument Signatures Sheets" containing the verified signatures of 1,000 registered voters.[55]

The voter information pamphlet prepared for the Multnomah County, Oregon, general election of November 3, 1998, holds the record for length. Volume 1 contains 154 pages relating to 14 statewide questions and 248 arguments for and against the measures. Volume 2 contains 192 pages, including 76 pages of state information and the 116-page Mult-nomah County information pamphlet.[56] San Francisco voters in the November 3, 1998, election received a 152-page county pamphlet and a 128-page state voter information guide.

General or Special Election

Constitutional and statutory provisions typically specify whether an initiative petition will appear on the general or special election ballot. The Alaska Constitution, for example, directs initiative petitions to be placed on the first statewide election ballot "no more than 120 days after adjourn-ment of the legislative session following the filing."[57] Similarly, the *Utah Code* specifies such petitions will appear at the regular general election.[58]

The Maine Constitution stipulates "the Legislature may order a special election on any measure that is subject to a vote of the people" and the Missouri Constitution provides that referred statutory measures shall appear on the general state election ballot "except when the General Assembly shall order a special election."[59] Missouri constitutional amend-ments proposed by the initiative appear on the general state election unless the governor calls a special election "prior thereto."[60] The North Dakota Supreme Court ruled in 1983 that a primary, general, or special election is a statewide election provided all electors are authorized to vote in the election.[61]

APPROVAL REQUIREMENTS

The constitutions of thirteen states provide that a constitutional amend-ment proposed by the initiative becomes effective if ratified by a majori-ty of those voting on the proposition. Four other state constitutions have additional ratification requirements. In Illinois, an amendment proposed by the initiative becomes effective if approved by either a majority of those voting in the election or 60 percent of those voting on the proposal.[62] The Massachusetts ratification requirement is an affirmative majority vote provided it includes 30 percent of the ballots cast at the election.[63] The Nebraska Constitution contains a provision similar to the Massachusetts one, except that the affirmative majority must include a minimum of 35 percent of the votes cast at the election.[64] The ratification requirement in Nevada is the affirmative majority vote on the proposed constitutional amendment in two consecutive general elections.[65]

Relative to the statutory initiative, propositions are approved by a simple affirmative majority vote, except in Massachusetts where the affirmative majority also must include at least 30 percent of the ballots cast at the election. If two or more conflicting propositions concurrently receive the required affirmative majority in eight of the fourteen states with constitutional or statutory provisions addressing such conflicts, the proposition receiving the largest vote is approved.[66]

Sections of an approved initiative proposition that received the smaller number of votes are invalid in five states only if they conflict directly with sections of a second approved initiative that received a larger number of votes.[67] The California Supreme Court had followed this principle of harmonizing provisions of two approved propositions on the same subject until it issued an opinion in 1990 interpreting the key section of the state constitution as not requiring a section-by-section reconciliation in all cases.[68] The court, in a case involving two campaign finance propositions, invalidated the one that received the fewest votes.[69]

Should voters reject conflicting propositions in Maine and Oklahoma, the proposition receiving the most votes will appear on the next general election ballot provided this initiative received one-third or more of the total votes cast on the conflicting propositions.[70]

The Maine Supreme Court in 1996 opined that the state legislature cannot enact a statute whose effectiveness is contingent on an initiated bill being rejected by the voters on the ground that such a measure is a competing measure that would have to be placed on the referendum ballot with the initiated measure.[71]

Opponents of an initiative petition certified as receiving the required votes of approval have from two days in Michigan to sixty days in Arkansas to contest the result (Table 2.6). Approved initiatives are not subject to a veto by the governor.[72] However, the state legislature in fifteen states can amend approved statutory initiatives, subject to restrictions in certain states as explained in a subsequent section.

Constitutions and statutes contain provisions relating to the effective date of an initiated constitutional amendment or statute approved by the electorate. The Arizona Constitution stipulates that a measure "shall become law when approved by a majority of the votes cast thereon and upon proclamation of the governor, and not otherwise."[73] The California Constitution, on the other hand, declares that an initiated statute

TABLE 2.6
State Initiatives: Voting on the Initiative

State or other jurisdiction	Ballot (a)		Election where initiative voted on	Effective date of approved initiative (b)		Days to contest election results (c)	Can an approved initiative be:			Can a defeated initiative be refiled?
	Title by:	Summary by:		Const. amdt.	Statute		Amended?	Vetoed?	Repealed?	
Alabama	...	...	...	...	...	...	...	...	...	...
Alaska	LG,AG	LG,AG	(d)	...	90 days (e)	10	Y	N	after 2 yrs.	Y
Arizona	...	...	GE	IM (f)	IM (f)	5	Y (g)	N (f)	Y (g)	Y
Arkansas	AG	AG	GE	30 days	30 days	20	Y	N	N	...
California	AG	AG	GE,PR or SP	1 day	IM	5	Y (h)	N	Y	Y
Colorado	SS,AG,LSS	SS,AG,LSS	(i)	30 days	30 days	...	Y	N	Y	Y
Connecticut	...	...	...	...	...	...	...	...	...	...
Delaware*	...	...	...	...	...	...	..	..	..	...
Florida	P,AG	P,AG	GE	(j)	...	10	Y	N	N	Y
Georgia	...	...	...	...	...	...	...	...	...	...
Hawaii	...	...	...	...	...	...	..	...	...	...
Idaho	AG	AG	GE	...	30 days	20	Y	N	Y	Y
Illinois	(k)	(k)	GE	20 days	...	15	...	...	...	...
Indiana	...	...	...	...	...	...	...	...	...	...
Iowa	...	...	...	...	...	...	...	...	...	...
Kansas	...	...	...	...	...	...	...	...	...	...
Kentucky	...	...	...	...	...	...	...	...	...	...
Louisiana*	...	...	...	...	...	...	...	...	...	...
Maine	...	...	REG or SP	...	30 days (f)	...	Y	N	Y	...
Maryland	...	...	...	...	...	...	...	...	...	...
Massachusetts	AG	AG	GE	30 days	30 days	10	Y	Y	Y	after 2 biennial elections
Michigan	BSC	BSC	GE	45 days	10 days	2 (l)	Y	N	Y	Y
Minnesota	...	...	...	...	...	...	...	...	...	...
Mississippi	AG	AG	GE	30 days	...	...	Y	N	Y	after 2 yrs.
Missouri	SS,AG	LC	GE or SP	30 days	IM	30	Y (m)	N	Y (m)	Y
Montana	...	AG	GE	July 1	Oct. 1	...	...	N	...	...
Nebraska	AG	AG	GE 4 mos. after filing	10 days	10 days	40	...	N	...	Y
Nevada	SS,AG	SS,AG	GE	10 days (n)	10 days (n)	14 (o)	N	N	N	...
New Hampshire	...	...	...	...	...	...	...	...	...	...
New Jersey	...	...	...	...	...	...	...	...	...	...
New Mexico	...	...	...	...	...	...	...	...	...	...
New York	...	...	...	...	...	...	...	...	...	...
North Carolina	...	...	...	...	...	...	...	...	...	...
North Dakota	AG,SS	AG,SS	PR,SP or GE	30 days	30 days	14	w/i 7 yrs. (p)	N	w/i 7 yrs. (p)	Y
Ohio	SS	Ohio Ballot Board	(q)	30 days	30 days	15	...	N	...	Y
Oklahoma	P,AG	P,AG	REG or SP	IM	IM	...	...	N	Y	after 3 yrs.
Oregon	AG	AG	GE even yrs.	30 days	30 days	40	Y	N	Y	Y
Pennsylvania	...	...	...	...	...	...	...	...	...	...
Rhode Island	...	...	...	...	...	...	...	...	...	...
South Carolina	...	...	...	...	...	...	...	...	...	...
South Dakota	AG	AG	GE	1 day	1 day	10	Y	N	Y	Y
Tennessee	...	...	...	...	...	...	...	...	...	...
Texas	...	...	...	...	...	...	...	...	...	...
Utah	LC	LC	GE	...	5 days (r)	40	Y	N	Y	Y
Vermont	...	...	...	...	...	...	...	...	...	...
Virginia	...	...	...	...	...	...	...	...	...	...
Washington	AG	AG	GE	...	IM	3	after 2 yrs.	...	after 2 yrs.	Y
West Virginia*	...	...	...	...	...	...	...	...	...	...
Wisconsin	...	...	...	...	...	...	...	...	...	...
Wyoming	SS	SS,AG	GE 120 days after LS	...	90 days	...	Y	N	after 2 yrs.	after 5 yrs.
U.S. Virgin Islands	SBE	SBE	LC	IM	IM	30	Y	N	N	Y

See footnotes at end of table.

Table 2.6, continued

Source: *The Book of the States 1998–1999* (Lexington, KY: The Council of State Governments, 1998), pp. 216–17. © 1999 The Council of State Governments. Reprinted with permission from *The Book of the States.*

"approved by a majority vote thereon takes effect the day after the election unless the measure provides otherwise."[74] The Florida Constitution specifies that a constitutional initiative becomes effective "on the first Tuesday after the first Monday in January following the election, or on such other date as may be specified in the amendment or revision."[75]

The *Mississippi Code* specifies that an approved initiative becomes effective thirty days after the official declaration of the vote by the secretary of state unless a different date is provided in the measure.[76] A statutory initiative in Montana is implemented on October 1 following its approval, unless the petition establishes a different effective date.[77]

AMENDMENT AND REPEAL

Although the purpose of an initiative might be thwarted if the state legislature is free to amend an initiated measure at will, such a provision is contained in the constitutions of thirteen states.[78] The *Utah Code* permits the state legislature to amend an approved initiative measure in a subsequent legislative session.[79]

The Arizona Constitution specifically stipulates that an initiated measure cannot be amended by the state legislature if the proposition was approved by a majority of the registered voters.[80] The Arkansas Constitution permits an amendment or repeal of an approved state or city initiative proposition only by an affirmative vote of two-thirds of all members elected to the concerned body.[81] The North Dakota Constitution forbids the Legislative Assembly to amend an initiated statute for a period of seven years unless such amendment is approved by a two-thirds vote of the members elected to each house.[82] The Michigan Constitution contains a similar provision requiring a three-fourths affirmative vote of all members elected to each house to amend an initiated measure but does not specify a time period.[83]

The California Constitution allows amendment of such a statute only with the permission of the voters, unless the proposition permits an amendment without their consent.[84] The electorate, if it so chooses, can attach conditions to its authorization of a legislative amendment.[85] The Washington Constitution permits the state legislature to amend an initiated measure two years after its approval by a two-thirds vote of the members elected to each house and adds "no amendatory law adopted in accordance with this provision shall be subject to referendum. But such enactment may be amended or repealed at any general regular or special election by direct vote of the people thereon."[86]

Seven state constitutions contain a provision on the repeal of an initiated statute. Alaska and Wyoming do not permit a repeal for two years, Arizona prohibits a repeal statute, and California authorizes a repeal only if the repealer is approved by the voters or the initiated measure allows a repeal without the approval of the electorate.[87]

Such a measure can be repealed in Arkansas by a two-thirds vote of the members elected to each house of the state legislature, in Michigan by a three-fourths vote of each house unless the measure provides otherwise, and in North Dakota by a two-thirds vote of the members elected to each house after the measure has been in effect for seven years.[88] The Colorado Supreme Court ruled in 1913 that an act repealing an initiated measure was constitutional, and the General Assembly has the authority to enact any measure.[89] A similar decision was rendered by the Idaho Supreme Court in 1943.[90]

No state constitution prohibits sponsors of a defeated proposition from placing an identical proposition on the referendum ballot in the future, although five states require the elapse of a period of time varying from two years in Mississippi to five years in Wyoming. It is not unusual for rejected measures to reappear on the ballot, but they typically have been amended to make them more attractive to the voters.

The amount of funds spent by proponents or opponents of an initiative proposition can vary from a few hundred dollars in a small local government campaign, if the advocacy work is performed by volunteers, to millions of dollars in a California statewide initiative campaign. The spending of large amounts of money by corporations and other special interests to promote or defeat a proposition raises concerns about whether the process has been corrupted and no longer is a citizen corrective, a subject examined in more detail in Chapter 5.[91]

All state legislatures and Congress have enacted corrupt practices acts regulating campaign finance. Although these statutes often contain loopholes that allow the spending of large sums, the statutes have placed some restrictions on excessive contributions and spending to promote or defeat an initiative proposition by individuals and corporations. As explained in Chapter 3, the U.S. Supreme Court in 1978 extended to corporations the protection of the free speech and association guarantee of the First Amendment to the U.S. Constitution, thereby allowing these incorporeal entities to spend as much as they desire to promote their views on whether an initiative proposition should be approved or rejected.[92]

SUMMARY

The ease or difficulty of using the initiative to place propositions on the referendum ballot is determined by the constitution makers or state legislators. The most liberal constitutional initiative provision, however, might be of no use to the electorate if the provision is not self-executing, and the state legislature refuses to enact the necessary implementing statute.

Several states rightly do not permit the initiative to enact measures relating to appropriations, emergencies, and the judiciary. Similarly, a provision requiring the sponsors of a proposition to confer with knowledgeable state officers about the wording of the proposal is highly desirable because the ballot language might be improved if the required number of signatures are collected.

Voters must be provided with a copy of the complete text of a proposition and arguments for and against it if they are to make intelligent decisions on referendum day. Consequently, it is incumbent upon the responsible state officer to be diligent in preparing and distributing to each registered voter an information pamphlet in advance of the referendum.

The constitutional and statutory provisions authorizing voters to employ the initiative have been subject to numerous court challenges over the decades. Chapter 3 examines the initiative in court.

NOTES

1. See, for example, *Constitution of the State of New York*, art. 9, § 2.

2. Joseph F. Zimmerman, *The Recall: Tribunal of the People* (Westport, CT: Praeger Publishers, 1997). See also Richard S. Childs, *The First 50 Years of the Council-Manager Plan of Municipal Government* (New York: National Municipal League, 1965).

3. *Constitution of South Dakota*, art. 3, § 1.

4. *Constitution of Colorado*, art. 5, § 1.

5. *Constitution of Alaska*, art. XII, § 9.

6. *Constitution of Arizona*, art. 4, § 1(15).

7. *Constitution of California*, art. 1, § 10(e).

8. *Constitution of the Commonwealth of Massachusetts*, article 48 of the articles of amendment, the initiative, II, § 2.

9. *Constitution of Nevada*, art. 19, § 6.

10. *Constitution of Maine*, art. 4, part 3, § 19.

11. *Illinois Annotated Statutes*, chap. 5, § 28-1 and *Mississippi Code*, § 23-17-39.

12. *Constitution of Arkansas*, amendment 7.

13. Constitution of Nebraska, art. 3, § 2 and Constitution of Wyoming, art. 2, § 52(d).

14. *Mississippi Code*, § 23-27-43.

15. *Oklahoma Statutes*, tit. 34, § 21.

16. *South Dakota Codified Laws*, § 2-1-11.

17. *Arizona Revised Statutes*, § 19-111.

18. *Oregon Revised Statutes*, §§ 250.045 and 260.118.

19. *Utah Code*, § 20A-7-202(1).

20. *Colorado Revised Statutes*, § 1-40-105 (1-2).

21. *Idaho Code*, §§ 34-2804 and 34-1808.

22. *Washington Revised Code Annotated*, § 29.79.015.

23. *Wyoming Statutes*, § 22-24-105.

24. *Washington Revised Code Annotated*, § 19.70.040.

25. *Ibid*.

26. *Constitution of Alaska*, art. XI, § 4.

27. *Constitution of Mississippi*, art. 15, §§ 273(4) and 273(6).

28. *Missouri Code Annotated*, § 116.175(1).

29. *Arizona Revised Statutes*, § 19-124.

30. *Montana Code*, § 13-27-312.

31. *Ohio Revised Code*, § 3519.04.

32. *Oregon Revised Statutes*, § 250.125.

33. *Wyoming Statutes*, § 22-24-105(c).

34. *Mississippi Code*, § 13017-17(1).

35. *Idaho Code*, § 34-1805; *Revised Statutes of Nebraska*, § 32-1405(3); Utah Code, § 20A-7-204(2); and *Revised Code of Washington*, § 29.79.080.

36. *Constitution of Massachusetts*, articles of amendment, art. 48, the initiative, IV, §§ 3 and 5, and art. 81, § 1.

37. *Ibid.*, art. 81, § 2.

38. *Hardie v. Eu*, 18 Cal.3d 971, 556 P.2d 301 (1976).

39. *Buckley v. Valeo*, 424 U.S. 1 at 143 (1976).

40. *The Libertarian Party of Oregon v. Paulus*, civil case number 81-521-FR, U.S. District Court, District of Oregon (1982).

41. *Constitution of Arkansas*, amendment no. 7.

42. *Colorado Revised Statutes*, § 1-40-121.

43. *Idaho Code*, tit. 34, § 1814(1).

44. *Maine Revised Statutes*, tit. 21-A, § 904-A; *North Dakota Century Code*, § 16.1-01-12(11); and *Wyoming Statutes*, § 22-24-125(a).

45. *Oregon Revised Statutes*, § 250.045.

46. *Revised Code of Washington*, § 29-79.500.

47. *Alaska Statutes*, § 15.45.120.

48. *Idaho Code*, § 34-1803B(1).

49. *People v. Hinkle*, 130 Wash. 419, 227 P.861 (1924).

50. *Oregon Revised Statutes*, § 250.105(4-5).

51. *Missouri Annotated Statutes*, § 116.120(1), *Constitution of Nevada*, art. 19, § 3(2), and *Revised Code of Washington*, § 29.79.200.

52. *Renck v. Superior Court of Maricopa County*, 66 Ariz. 320, 187 P.2d 656 (1947) and *Queen Creek Land & Cattle Corporation v. Yavapai County Board of Supervisors*, 108 Ariz. 449, 501 P.2d 391 (1972).

53. *Constitution of Massachusetts*, articles of amendment, art. 48, the initiative, III, § 2.

54. *Ohio Revised Code*, § 3519.04.

55. *Oregon Revised Statutes*, § 251.255.

56. "Oregon, California Ballot Pamphlets May Deliver Information Overload," *Election Administration Reports*, November 23, 1998, p. 5.

57. *Constitution of Alaska*, art. IX, § 4.

58. *Utah Code*, § 201-7-206.

59. *Constitution of Missouri*, art. 3, § 52(b).

60. *Ibid.*, art. 12, § 2(b).

61. *Haugland v. Meier*, 339 N.W.2d 100 (N.D. 1983).

62. *Constitution of Illinois*, art. XIV, § 3.

63. *Constitution of Massachusetts*, articles of amendment, art. 48, the initiative, V, § 1.

64. *Constitution of Nebraska*, art. 3, § 4.

65. *Constitution of Nevada*, art. 19, § 2(4).

66. See, for example, *Constitution of Missouri*, art. 3, § 51.

67. For examples, consult *Constitution of Arizona*, art. IV, pt. 1, § 12 and *Idaho Code*, § 34-1811.

68. *Taxpayers to Limit Campaign Spending v. Fair Political Practices Commission*, 799 P.2d 1220 at 1235 (Cal. 1990).

69. *Ibid.* at 1236-237.

70. *Constitution of Maine*, art. IV, part 3, § 18 and *Oklahoma Statutes Annotated*, tit. 34, § 21.

71. *Opinion of the Justices*, 680 A.2d 444 (Me. 1996).

72. See, for example, *Constitution of Massachusetts*, articles of amendment, art. 48, general provisions, V.

73. *Constitution of Arizona*, art. IV, § 1(5).

74. *Constitution of California*, art. 2, § 10(a).

75. *Constitution of Florida*, art. XI, § 5(c).

76. *Mississippi Code*, § 23-17-41.

77. *Montana Code*, § 13-27-105(1).

78. For example, see *Constitution of Alaska*, art. XI, § 6, and *Constitution of Wyoming*, art. 3, § 52(f).

79. *Utah Code*, § 20A-7-311(2)(b).

80. *Constitution of Arizona*, art. IV, § 1(6).

81. *Constitution of Arkansas*, amendment no. 7.

82. *Constitution of North Dakota*, art. 3, § 8.

83. *Constitution of Michigan*, art. 2, § 9.

84. *Constitution of California*, art. 2, § 10(c). See *Americans for Nonsmokers' Rights v. State*, 59 Cal.Rpt.2d 416, 51 Cal.App.4th 724 (App. 3 Dist. 1996).

85. *Amwest Surety Insurance Company v. Wilson*, 48 Cal.Rpt.2d 12, 11 Cal.4th 1243, 906 P.2d 1112 (1995).

86. *Constitution of Washington*, art. II, § 1(c).

87. *Constitution of Alaska*, art. XI, § 6; *Constitution of Wyoming*, art. 3, § 52(f); *Constitution of Arizona*, art. IV, § 1(6); and *Constitution of California*, art. 2, § 10(c).

88. *Constitution of Arkansas*, amendment number 7; *Constitution of Michigan*, art. 2, § 9; and *Constitution of North Dakota*, art. 3, § 8.

89. *In re Senate Resolution No. 5*, 54 Colo. 262, 130 P.333 (1913).

90. *Luker v. Curtis*, 64 Idaho 703, 136 P.2d 978 (1943).

91. See, for example, David R. Lagasse, "Undue Influence: Corporate Political Speech Power, and the Initiative Process," *Brooklyn Law Review*, Winter 1995, pp. 1347–397.

92. *First National Bank of Boston et al. v. Bellotti*, 435 U.S. 765 (1978).

3

The Initiative in Court

The initiative was challenged almost immediately after its adoption as violating the U.S. Constitution, which guarantees each state a republican form of government.[1] Opponents argued in court that a republican form of government is a representative form of government and there is no constitutional provision authorizing states to allow their respective voters to propose statutes by initiative petition and to adopt them by the referendum.

The Oregon Supreme Court in 1903 rejected these arguments by ruling direct legislation "does not abolish or destroy the republican form of government or substitute another in its place. The representative character of the government still remains. The people simply reserved to themselves a larger share of legislative power."[2] Nine years later, the U.S. Supreme Court upheld the constitutionality of direct legislation in Oregon by pointing out that Congress, in effect, had recognized a republican form of government in Oregon when the state's representatives and senators were seated in Congress.[3]

As noted in Chapter 2, the degree of difficulty encountered by voters in employing the initiative is associated with the requirements specified in the enabling constitutional, statutory, or charter provisions. Similarly, the ease of use has been affected by numerous court decisions interpreting specific sections of the enabling provision or alleged conflicts between the subject matter of the initiative and state and federal constitutional guarantees.

LEGAL ISSUES

Opponents and proponents of initiative measures typically seek judicial decisions to strengthen their respective positions and opponents of successful initiated measures often file suit seeking to invalidate them. In addition to challenging the initiative as a violation of the guarantee clause of the U.S. Constitution, suits involving this participatory device have been related to its scope, the requirement that petition circulators must be residents of the state, prohibition of paid signature collectors, solicitation of petition signatures on private property, privacy of petitioners' signatures, petition signature requirements, petition fraud, validity of petition signatures, constitutional single subject requirement, number of propositions allowed on any given referendum ballot, ballot question wording or summary, preemption of the subject matter by Congress or the state legislature, calling a limited constitutional convention, excluded subjects, legislative reapportionment, term limits, legislative organization and rules, balanced federal budget, campaign finance, financial disclosure, and required majority approval vote.

Legal challenges to initiative provisions are brought in state courts and U.S. courts. The U.S. Supreme Court in 1997 announced a flexible standard the Court would employ to determine the constitutionality of state statutes regulating the electoral process:

When deciding whether a state election law violates the First and Fourteenth Amendment associational rights, this Court must weight the character and magnitude of the burden the State's rule imposes on those rights against the interests the State contends justify that burden, and consider the extent to which the State's concerns make the burden necessary. Regulations imposing severe burdens must be narrowly tailored and advance a compelling state interest. Lesser burdens, however, trigger less exacting review, and a State's important regulatory interests will usually be enough to justify reasonable nondiscriminatory restrictions.[4]

Scope of the Initiative Power

As noted in Chapter 2, courts in twelve states have been called upon to determine whether the constitutional or statutory initiative provisions are to be interpreted liberally. All decisions were affirmative, including the following ones.

The Colorado Supreme Court in 1938 noted "it has generally been held by the courts of all jurisdictions that a constitutional provision for the initiative and referendum, and statutes enacted in connection therewith, should be liberally construed."[5] In 1942, the Arizona Supreme Court opined "every reasonable intendment is in favor of a liberal construction of those requirements and the effect of a failure to comply therewith, unless the Constitution expressly makes any departure therefrom fatal."[6]

More recently, the Michigan Court of Appeals in 1976 ruled that constitutional and statutory initiative provisions are to be construed liberally to effectuate their purposes and to facilitate rather than hamper the exercise by voters of their reserved rights.[7] The Washington Supreme Court in 1983 bluntly declared deliberate attempts by a legislature to circumvent the initiative will not be looked upon favorably.[8]

In 1995, the California Supreme Court emphasized that the initiative is not a right granted to the voters, but it is a power reserved by them and consequently constitutional; charter initiative provisions must be construed liberally in favor of the electorate's right to exercise the reserved power.[9] In 1996, the Colorado Supreme Court opined that the constitutional and statutory initiative provisions involved rights of great importance and hence must be interpreted liberally to facilitate voters' use of the participatory device, which should not be hampered by technical statutory provisions or a technical construction of such provisions.[10]

Resident Petitioner Circulators

A number of state legislatures enacted statutes limiting the circulation of initiative petitions to residents of a state or county, or to registered voters. The declared purpose of each such statute is to prevent fraud in signature collection.

The right to circulate a petition in Nebraska since 1919 had been limited to the home county of the circulator but did not apply to a circulator who registered with the Secretary of State and filed a $500 bond. A 1992 statute removed the exemption and made a violation of the restriction a class I misdemeanor.[11] The repealer was advocated on the ground it would protect the initiative process from fraud by outsiders. The Attorney General sought a temporary restraining order and a permanent injunction of implementation of the repealer in the Nebraska Supreme Court. The Court quickly issued a restraining order and subsequently issued a permanent injunction on the ground the act impeded the initiative and referendum processes by requiring advocates of an initiative to organize thirty-eight separate campaigns to collect petition signatures, thereby hindering initiative proponents lacking adequate funds in their efforts to collect signatures.[12]

In 1995, the Nebraska State Legislature enacted a statute stipulating that only a Nebraska voter could circulate petitions to collect signatures and that violations of this provision would result in criminal penalties.[13] This statutory provision was challenged by the co-chairman of the Nebraska Term Limits Committee that circulated petitions to place a term limit provision on the referendum ballot. The committee was unsuccessful in its efforts to hire petition circulators who complied with the statute and decided to ignore the thirty-day requirement.

The U.S. District Court in 1996 struck down the requirement as violating the First Amendment to the U.S. Constitution because the requirement reduced "the number of circulators who can be hired or recruited as volunteers to spread the message of the various petition-drive organizers" and diminished the prospects that petition promoters could collect the required number of signatures, thereby limiting their opportunity to make their proposition the subject of discussion by citizens of the state.[14] In 1997, the U.S. Court of Appeals for the Eighth Circuit upheld the lower court's decision by emphasizing the state "has an adequate arsenal of safeguards to protect against signature fraud" and the voter registration requirement "is not narrowly tailored to serve the State's compelling interest."[15]

An analogous suit was brought by the American Constitutional Law Foundation in the U.S. District Court challenging the constitutionality of a Colorado statute restricting petition circulators to registered electors at least eighteen years of age.[16] The court in 1996 ruled the petition process is not a right granted by the U.S. Constitution and hence the statute was not reviewable.[17] In 1997, the U.S. Court of Appeals for the Tenth Circuit reversed the lower court's decision by ruling that the statutory requirement imposed impermissible restraints on First amendment activity and added "it is irrelevant that the statutory restriction is based upon a constitutional provision enacted by petition. The voters may no more violate the United States Constitution by enacting a ballot issue than the general assembly may by enacting legislation."[18]

A similar decision was rendered in 1997 by the U.S. District Court for the Southern District of Mississippi. The Term Limits Leadership Council, Inc., challenged a provision of the *Mississippi Code Annotated* stipulating "only a person who is a qualified elector of this state may circulate a petition or obtain signatures on a petition."[19] The state argued non-resident petition circulators would abuse the initiative process because they are disinterested in the subject of an initiative petition and might offer misleading or false information to induce voters to sign petitions. The court rejected this argument and explained it "fails to perceive the logic in the reasoning by which the state concludes that persons who are disinterested in whether an initiative makes it to the ballot are more likely to offer false and misleading information to induce signatures than persons who are zealously interested in the success of an initiative petition drive."[20]

Petition and Handbill Circulators

As noted in Chapter 2, eight states had statutes prohibiting the payment of circulators of petitions in 1988 when the U.S. Supreme Court invalidated the Colorado provision. The origin of the court's decision can be attributed to several individuals and Coloradans for Free Enterprise, Inc., who launched an initiative campaign in the form of a proposed constitutional amendment that would remove motor carriers from the jurisdiction of the Colorado Public Utilities Commission. After meeting the various requirements for an initiative proposition, they brought a suit in the U.S. District Court seeking an injunction that would prevent the Colorado Attorney General and Secretary of State from enforcing a criminal statute that forbids the payment of petition circulators.[21]

The court in an unpublished opinion upheld the constitutionality of the statute on the ground it did not prevent the plaintiffs from advocating their initiative petition. A three-judge panel of the U.S. Court of Appeals for the Tenth Circuit in 1984 affirmed the District Court's decision.[22] The appellate court, however, in 1987 agreed to review the panel's decision *en banc* and reversed the District Court's and the three-judge appellate court's decisions.[23] The decision was appealed to the U.S. Supreme Court, which in *Grant v. Meyers* in 1988 upheld the decision of the Court of Appeals.[24]

The Supreme Court applied exacting scrutiny to the Colorado statute because it involves core political speech under the First Amendment to the U.S. Constitution. The court specifically found the statute restricts the number of persons conveying the appellees' views and their ability to obtain the required number of signatures to place their proposition on the referendum ballot.[25]

In a critical review of the decision, Daniel H. Lowenstein and Robert M. Stern commented:

It is true that the Colorado statute does, in form, define a felony, and that the possibility exists that a person could be prosecuted for violating it. These facts facilitate viewing the statute as one aimed at the conduct of private individuals, and therefore as falling within a conventional first amendment framework. The practical thrust of the statute is not, however, to regulate individual conduct but to regulate the state's conduct, namely, the circumstances in which the State will place propositions on the ballot.[26]

Lowenstein and Stern were convinced there was no need for an extra-ordinary state justification for the prohibition of paid petition circulators under the First Amendment and, referring to a 1973 decision, wrote "we believe the Supreme Court of Washington was correct in concluding that the possible association of paid petition circulators with improper prac-tices was sufficient to justify a ban on paid circulators as an exercise of the police power."[27] In 1995, the U.S. Supreme Court invalidated an Ohio statute prohibiting the circulation of anonymous campaign literature and made circulators of such materials subject to a fine.[28] The Court specifi-cally opined: "Under our constitution, anonymous pamphleteering is not a pernicious, fraudulent practice, but an honorable tradition of advocacy and of dissent. Anonymity is a shield from the tyranny of the majority. . . . It thus exemplifies the purpose behind the bill of rights, and of the First Amendment in particular: to protect unpopular individuals from retaliation — and their ideas from suppression at the hand of an intolerant society."[29]

The American Constitutional Law Foundation, Inc., brought an action in the U.S. District Court, which challenged Colorado statutes regulating the petition process, and the Court upheld certain statutes and struck down other ones.[30] In 1997, the U.S. Court of Appeals for the Tenth Circuit opined that Colorado statutes, which require initiative and referendum petition circulators to be registered voters and to wear personal identifi-cation badges, and that proponents of an initiative proposition must report the name and address of each paid circulator and the amount paid to the circulator, violated the First Amendment to the U.S. Constitution.[31]

The U.S. Supreme Court in 1999 upheld the decision of the Court of Appeals, although Chief Justice William H. Rehnquist wrote a strong dis-senting opinion rejecting the Court of Appeals contention that a paid cir-culator should not have to surrender his or her anonymity and explaining "even after today's decision the identity of the circulators as well as the total amount of money paid to circulators will be a matter of public record" since each circulator is required to submit an affidavit that includes the circulator's name and address.[32]

In 1997, the U.S. District Court for the Southern District of Mississip-pi invalidated a Mississippi statutory provision stipulating "it is unlawful for a person that pays or compensates another person for circulating a petition or for obtaining signatures on a petition to base the pay or com-pensation on the number of petitions circulated or the number of signa-tures obtained."[33] Noting that the *Meyer* decision made it clear that the burden was on the state to demonstrate paid petition circulators were more likely to commit fraud than volunteer petition circulators, the court stressed "the State's burden in the case at bar is to show that circulators

who are paid per signatures are more likely to commit fraud. . . . There is
. . . simply no proof to support such a finding."[34]

Signature Solicitation on Private Property

Can the owners of shopping centers prohibit initiative, protest referendum, and recall petition circulators from soliciting signatures in shopping
centers? The California Supreme Court in 1979 opined that the state constitution protects the reasonable exercise of speech and petitioning in a
privately owned shopping center.[35]

This decision was appealed to the U.S. Supreme Court by appellants
who argued their Fourteenth Amendment rights to exclude appellees from
use of appellants' private property cannot be restricted by a state constitutional provision or by judicial interpretation of a state's private property laws. The appellants based their case largely upon *Lloyd Corporation
v. Tanner*, a 1972 U.S. Supreme Court decision, holding property does not
"lose its private character merely because the public is generally invited
to use it for designated purposes" and "the essentially private character of a
store and its privately owned abutting property does not change by virtue
of being large or clustered with other stores in a modern shopping center."[36] This case dealt with a shopping center ban of handbill distribution.

The California Supreme Court's decision was upheld by the U.S.
Supreme Court, which in 1980 opined that its "reasoning in *Lloyd* . . . does
not . . . limit the authority of the state to exercise its police power or its
sovereign right to adopt in its own constitution individual liberties more
expansive than those conferred by the federal constitution."[37] In sum, the
court concluded that the appellant's federally recognized property rights
and First Amendment rights were not abridged by the decision of the California Supreme Court.

The following year, the Washington State Supreme Court addressed the
same issue and held "signature gathering in a shopping mall furthers the
exchange of ideas and the initiative process. . . . To bar this activity would
significantly undermine free speech and particularly the effectiveness of
the initiative process."[38]

In 1985, however, the Michigan Supreme Court opined that the state
constitution's declaration of rights provision guarantees free speech,
assembly, and petition, and the initiative with respect to legislation and
amending the constitution did not prohibit the owners of large shopping
malls from denying or restricting access to individuals seeking to exercise
the declared rights.[39]

A California shopping center had regulations on the exercise of speech permitting political petitioning, distribution of explanatory literature, and use of visual presentations. Groups desiring to distribute leaflets in the center were required to make a $50 cleaning deposit. The center's rules were challenged, and the California Court of Appeals in 1987 upheld the cleaning deposit, but struck down the center's unwritten rule as to whether an application for a permit to engage in petitioning would be accepted or rejected as violating the First Amendment to the U.S. Constitution because its standard — whether the activity would "adversely affect the shopping center environment, atmosphere, or image" — was constitutionally flawed because it conferred broad and unlimited discretion on the center's management to reject a request.[40]

In 1993, the Oregon Supreme Court upheld a shopping center's rule restricting petitioning to designated areas of the mall as reasonable, but the required twenty-four hours' advance notice, limitation of the number of individuals who could solicit signatures, and prohibiting petitioning at specific times were unreasonable.[41]

Privacy of Petition Signers

Should organizers of a petition campaign be precluded by state law from access to petitions in order to obtain the names and addresses of petition signers who could be enlisted in a future petition campaign? Would release of the names of petition signers violate their privacy rights? California voters in 1972 ratified a state constitutional amendment adding the right of privacy to its enumeration of inalienable rights in the constitutional bill of rights. The 1974 state legislature amended several sections of the elections code and inserted the following section: "No circulator of an initiative, referendum, or recall petition shall permit the list of signatures or the petition to be used for any purpose other than qualification of the initiative or referendum measure or recall question for the ballot. Violation of this section is a misdemeanor."[42]

The constitutionality of the section was challenged by proponents of an initiative petition providing for the mandatory establishment of smoking and non-smoking sections in enclosed public places, including employment and educational facilities, and health facilities and clinics. Proponents desired to use the names and addresses of signers to post (1) blank petition forms to them with the request they circulate and return signed petitions to the proponents, and (2) campaign events information to the signers. The California Attorney General issued an opinion that such use of petition signatures would violate the statute.[43]

Proponents of the use of initiative petition signatures contended the statute violated their First and Fourteenth Amendment rights guaranteed by the U.S. Constitution and rights guaranteed by the California Constitution. The California Court of Appeals placed emphasis on the fact freedoms of speech and association protected by the First and Fourteenth amendments are not absolutes and certain forms of speech are outside the scope of their provisions. The court noted:

We believe it a mistake to suppose that a person who signs an initiative or other petition may automatically be deemed to have enlisted in the cause of the proponent. Although many persons undoubtedly sign because they strongly believe in the measure, some may sign because they believe it appropriate to qualify the measure for the ballot so that the voters may decide. Still others may sign because of a yielding to the moral pressure of the moment. The legislature could properly conclude that, whatever his reason, a signer has the right to the privacy of his decision, secure in the knowledge that the fact of his signing will not be used for any purpose beyond the minimum necessary to forward the initiative process.[44]

The court, in upholding the constitutionality of the section, noted it is broad in scope. However, proponents of an initiative petition are not prevented from contacting signers of an earlier petition, provided the former do not obtain their names and addresses from the signed petitions. The U.S. Supreme Court in 1982 dismissed an appeal by the proponents for want of a federal question.[45]

Petition Signature Requirements

To ensure there is statewide interest in an initiative proposition, the state constitution or statute authorizing the initiative typically includes a county signature distribution requirement, or establishes a limit on the number of signatures from any one county that can be counted toward meeting the signature requirement. The Massachusetts Constitution contains a provision limiting the number of certified signatures from any one county to one-fourth of the required number of certified signatures.[46]

The Massachusetts Public Interest Research Group (PIRG) decided to collect petition signatures for an indirect initiative proposition that would establish a Telephone Consumer's Action Group. The attorney general determined the petition was in proper form, and the subject matter was not excluded from the initiative. PIRG collected 87,500 petition signatures and 61,176 signatures were certified by the Secretary of the Commonwealth. However, application of the county distribution requirement reduced the number of signatures to 54,528, which was less than the number required for transmittal of the petition to the General Court (state legislature).

PIRG filed an action for declaratory relief and alleged the requirement violated the right to equal protection of the law and contended the Massachusetts Supreme Judicial Court, which has original jurisdiction over all cases arising in equity, should apply a strict scrutiny standard of review.[47] The court in 1978 rejected the plaintiffs' contention that the right to vote encompassed the right to have an initiative petition signature counted and ruled the county distribution requirement was valid.[48]

The court decided to apply a rational basis standard for its review of the restriction placed on the collection of initiative petitions. The court concluded there was no fundamental right to have an initiative proposition placed on the ballot because neither representation nor an election was involved.[49] In the court's opinion an initiative petition is simply a method for establishing a threshold of demonstrated minimum support before a proposition is submitted to the voters. Specifically, the court found the county distribution rule served the valid state purpose of preventing the appearance of localized issues on the statewide ballot.[50]

The 1980 Illinois constitutional initiative proposition reducing the size of the House of Representatives from 177 to 120 members and abolishing cumulative voting was challenged on the grounds of insufficient petition signatures and violation of the constitutional prohibition of two separate and unrelated questions.

The Illinois State Board of Elections, by a five to three vote, invalidated all signatures on a petition page of persons who were not from the same election jurisdiction as the other persons who had signed the page. The Illinois Supreme Court in 1980 reversed the board's decision, invalidated the statutory requirement that all signatures on a petition sheet must be those of registered voters of the same election jurisdiction, and held the initiative proposition consisted of related questions and did not violate the constitutional prohibition of multiple questions in a single proposition as the two questions were related.[51]

The Arizona Supreme Court in 1983 struck down an initiative proposition requiring voter approval for freeway and parkway construction in Tucson on the ground the bulk of the petitions were notarized improperly.[52]

Sponsors of a Nebraska constitutional initiative petition brought an action in the U.S. District Court seeking to have invalidated a provision of a state constitution requiring sponsors to obtain certified signatures equal to 10 percent of the number of Nebraska registered voters on the day the petitions are submitted to the Secretary of State for verification. The plaintiffs maintained their First Amendment constitutional rights of free speech and procedural due process were violated because they were unable to determine the number of signatures required to place an initiative proposition on the referendum ballot until after the deadline for filing petitions.

The issue in this case involved the Nebraska Supreme Court's construction of sections of the state constitution relative to the determination of the number of signatures to place a proposition on the ballot. Until 1988, the number of required signatures was based on the number of votes cast in the previous gubernatorial election. Voters in 1988, however, amended sections 2 and 3 of article III of the constitution to change the wording in the initiative section of the constitution from "electors" to "registered voters" but did not change the wording of section 4 of article III. Consequently, section 1 refers to 10 percent of the registered voters, and section 4 stipulates that the required number of signatures is based on the number of votes cast in the previous gubernatorial election. The Nebraska Supreme Court unanimously held in 1994 that the required number of signatures is equal to 10 percent of the number of registered voters on the day petitions are submitted to the secretary of state.[53] The court concluded that the conflict between the two sections of the constitution could not be reconciled and the most recent amendment is controlling.

The U.S. District Court rejected the plaintiffs' arguments and opined "the plaintiffs have no federal constitutional right to define the state constitutional right of the initiative contrary to the written will of the people of Nebraska as expressed in the document defining their own government and interpreted by their own high court."[54] This decision was upheld by the U.S. Court of Appeals in 1997.[55]

Petition Fraud

A major potential problem with the use of the initiative, the protest referendum, and recall is fraudulent petition signatures. The costs, in terms of time and money, of collecting signatures tempt unscrupulous petition circulators to forge signatures on petitions. The secretary of state or state ballot law commission is charged with the responsibility of examining and certifying signatures on state initiative petitions, and local government clerks or board of registrars of voters typically are charged with a similar responsibility relative to employment of the initiative in local governments.

The complexity of determining the validity of petitions signatures is illustrated by a 1963 Massachusetts controversy over protest referendum petitions seeking to invalidate a state statute increasing the salary of members of the General Court.[56] The petitioners made a timely filing of 88,159 signatures from 12 counties; a total of 32,637 signatures were required. The state ballot law commission held public hearings regarding challenges to the validity of signatures, and all commission members agreed there were instances of fraud and perjury relative to the petitions. The majority of the commission members ruled that only 29,299 signatures were valid, and the minority argued 39,040 signatures were valid. The difference involved the legal issue of whether a false jurat on a petition sheet invalidates the entire sheet and whether a forged signature on a sheet invalidates the entire sheet because the forgery affects the jurat of the circulator. The Supreme Judicial Court in 1964 rejected the contention that a provision in state law applicable to jurats on nomination papers applied to protest referendum petitions and ordered the printing of ballots containing the referendum question and an explanatory pamphlet for voters.[57]

Another example of petition fraud involved six Missouri individuals indicted in 1972 on the basis of testimony by nine teenagers who had been promised $5 for each signing of names from street directories on initiative petition forms to place a proposed $7.3 million transportation bond issue on the statewide referendum ballot.[58]

Single Subject Requirement

As explained in Chapter 2, fifteen of the twenty-four states authorizing the use of the initiative by state voters have a constitutional provision restricting a proposition to one subject. Although one might assume it should be easy to determine whether a proposition complied with this requirement, such has not been the case, particularly in California.

Reacting to a series of initiatives in the 1930s and 1940s known as "ham and eggs" ones involving pension plans, the California Constitution was amended to restrict an initiative proposition to a single subject, a requirement similar to the constitutional single subject requirement for bills enacted by a state legislature. As part of a process of constitutional revision, the single subject initiative provision was reworded in 1966 to read: "An initiative measure embracing more than one subject may not be submitted to the electors or have any effect."[59]

The requirement has been justified on two principal grounds. The first is to prevent voter confusion that might occur if a multi-subject proposition appeared on the referendum ballot. Daniel H. Lowenstein concluded in 1983 that the rule fails to achieve its first purpose because the rule will prevent a number of simple propositions, such as changing the date of the primary election and increasing the sentence for rape, from appearing on the ballot and allowing exceptionally complex ones, such as school finance revision, to appear on the referendum ballot.[60] The second justification for the single subject rule is to prevent logrolling involving several interest groups building a coalition and each group including a provision in the proposition or sponsors adding a popular rider to a proposition to increase its prospects of gaining voter approval.

The rule first was examined in 1949 by the California Supreme Court in *Perry v. Jordan* and was construed in the same manner as the single subject rule is applied to acts of the state legislature; that is, the rule "is not to receive a narrow or technical construction in all cases, but is to be construed liberally to uphold proper legislation, all parts of which are reasonably germane."[61] California voters in June 1982 approved initiative Proposition 8, entitled the "Victims Bill of Rights." Its validity was challenged on the ground that the proposition violated the state constitutional provision restricting an initiative proposition to a single subject. The California Supreme Court, by a four to three vote, upheld the validity of the proposition even though it dealt with several subjects, including school safety, elimination of plea bargaining, restrictions of the insanity defense, and provisions for longer prison terms for recidivists.[62] The majority wrote:

We are reinforced in our conclusion that Proposition 8 embraces a single subject by observing that the measure appears to reflect public dissatisfaction with the several prior judicial decisions in the area of criminal law. In our democratic society, in the absence of some compelling, overriding constitutional imperative, we should not prohibit the sovereign people from either expressing or implementing their own will on matters of such direct and immediate importance as their own perceived safety.[63]

The California Court of Appeals in 1988 issued two decisions interpreting the single subject initiative rule. In *California Trial Lawyers Association v. Eu*, the court examined an initiative proposition creating a no-fault insurance system and containing provisions with regard to insurance companies' rates and practices. The court held that the initiative petition violated the rule because the proposition protected the right of interest groups to make campaign contributions to state elected officers and exempted them from disqualification in acting on official matters affecting contributors.[64] The court noted that the proponents of the petition did not attempt to explain how the exemption of state officers from rules disqualifying them from acting on matters related to the interests of campaign contributors "would operate to advance the initiative's announced purpose of controlling spiraling insurance costs."[65]

In the second case, the court ruled on a request for issuance of a writ of mandate directing the secretary of state to refrain from placing an insurance initiative (allowing banks to engage in the insurance business) on the referendum ballot on the ground the proposition violates the single subject rule. The court quoted its decision in *California Trial Lawyers Association* that "initiatives encompassing a wide range of diverse measures will withstand challenge so long as their provisions are 'either functionally related' to one another 'or . . . reasonably germane' to one another or the objects of the enactment's" [citing *Harbor v. Deukmejian*, 43 Cal.3d 1078 at 1100, 240 Cal.Rptr. 569 (1987)].[66]

The court rejected the request and noted that the section repealing the prohibition of banks engaging in the insurance business was related directly to consumer protection announced in the initiative's title. Petitioners maintained the section on attorneys' fees violated the single subject requirement because the section applies to all attorneys' fees. The court responded that a "narrow rule would probably be over inclusive since some overbreath is inevitable in virtually all legislation that is not under inclusive. In other words, the drafters do not have to score a bull's eye, they need only be on target."[67]

In 1990, the California Supreme Court upheld Proposition 115, approved by the voters in 1990, even though it contained a wide range of topics relating to preliminary hearings, duties and rights of prosecutors, discovery, *voir dire*, joinder, hearsay, independence of state constitutional rights, the felony-murder rule, sentencing of juveniles, special circumstances, and the crime of torture. The court struck down part of the proposition as a revision, rather than an amendment, of the state constitution, but opined that "although the provisions of Proposition 115 seem somewhat disparate, . . . they reflect a consistent theme or purpose to nullify particular decisions of our court affecting various aspects of the criminal justice system."[68]

Number of Ballot Questions

The Mississippi Constitution limits the number of initiative propositions on the ballot to five and the Massachusetts General Laws restricts the number of advisory initiative questions on the ballot to three.[69] The Illinois State Legislature limits to three the number of referendum questions that can appear on an election ballot on the ground that voter confusion would be produced if a large number of propositions were included in the ballot and many would not receive thoughtful consideration.[70] A group of DuPage County voters petitioned for an advisory referendum on a nuclear arms freeze, but four binding referenda questions already had qualified for the ballot. Qualifying questions not specifying a date for a referendum in excess of three are placed on the next local election ballot.

Judge William T. Hart of the U.S. District Court for the Northern District of Illinois in 1982 upheld the Illinois law concerning the number of ballot questions but invalidated the requirement that petitions for advisory referenda need the signatures of 25 percent of the registered voters.[71] The nuclear freeze group collected only one-eighth of the required signatures, and the judge ruled "we can not suppose the legislature intended that professional canvassers be employed in order to allow citizens to exercise their statutory right to place on the ballot advisory public questions."[72]

Ballot Language

Ballot language restricts voters to a yes or no choice. If several questions are on the referendum ballot, proponents of one proposal might discover that their campaign urging the electorate to vote yes inadvertently might encourage the electorate also to vote yes on a second proposition that the group opposes.

On the November 4, 1972, ballot in Yonkers, New York, there were two propositions one.[73] The League of Women Voters favored one proposition one, a state environmental bond issue, and opposed a second proposition one, a city charter amendment that would provide for a strong mayor as a replacement for the city manager. Because the environmental bond issue was the first state proposition on the ballot, the proposition was labeled number one. Similarly, the city charter amendment was the first local proposition and also was labeled number one. Citizens for Continued City Manager Government discovered the wording problem after distributing 50,000 flyers urging the defeat of proposition one.

In 1981, the Ohio Supreme Court directed the Ohio Ballot Board, a five-member bipartisan body charged with drafting the ballot language for proposed constitutional amendments, to rewrite the ballot wording drafted for an initiated constitutional amendment because the wording "is in the nature of an argument against adoption of the amendment."[74] Specifically, the court held the word "present," employed in conjunction with "at no cost to the Ohio taxpayers," created the impression that taxpayers would have to bear some of the cost if the amendment were ratified.[75] Similarly, the New Jersey Supreme Court in the same year upheld a ruling by the Appellate Division of the Superior Court that the wording on the November ballot explaining a proposed riparian land constitutional amendment, written by the attorney general's office, was not neutral and would discourage voters' approval.[76] State officials agreed almost immediately to use the court's recommended explanatory statement although such use was not mandatory.

In 1988, the California Court of Appeals addressed the question of whether the attorney general's summary of an initiative proposition — "Insurance Reform and Consumer Protection Act of 1988" — contained any deficiencies. The petitioners complained the summary did not describe specifically the subjects in two proposition sections. The court acknowledged an incomplete title or summary might heighten the possibility for misleading voters, but added:

Assuming, for present purposes only that the omission renders the summary legally inadequate and incomplete, we have been cited to no authority nor are we aware of any holding that an initiative may be struck down as violative of the single subject rule solely because the Attorney General has misdescribed it . . . our determination that sections 11 and 17 satisfy the "reasonably germane" test satisfies the single subject requirement of the constitution and ameliorates any deleterious impact the claimed deficiencies in the Attorney General's summary or description might otherwise have had.[77]

The Maine Supreme Court ruled on a similar question in 1997. The petitioner maintained that the initiated ballot question — "Should spraying pesticides from the air or putting pesticides in Maine's waters be a Class A crime?" — prepared by the secretary of state oversimplified the issue. A Maine statute directs the secretary of state to draft voter initiative propositions "in a simple, clear, concise, and direct manner that best describes the subject matter of the people's veto or direct initiative."[78] The court opined: "Voters are not to rely on the ballot question alone to understand the proposal. . . . The procedure is designed to ensure the voters, who may be reading the question for the first time in the voting booth, will understand the subject matter and the choice presented. It is assumed that the voters have discharged their civic duty to educate themselves about the initiative."[79]

In 1998, a district court judge determined that the Houston City Council prepared ballot language that did not reflect the intent of the sponsors of the initiative to amend the city charter.[80] The proposed amendment stipulated: "The City of Houston shall not discriminate against, or grant preferential treatment, to an individual or group on the basis of race, sex, color, ethnicity, or national origin in the operation of public employment and public contracting." The Council placed the following proposition on the November 1997 referendum ballot: "Shall the charter of the City of Houston be amended to end the use of affirmative action for women and minorities in the operation of the City of Houston employment and contracting, including ending the current program and similar programs in the future?" The proposition was defeated by a vote of 54.5 percent to 45.5 percent.

Federal Preemption

The U.S. Constitution expressly forbids states to take certain actions and allows states to take other specified actions only with the permission of Congress.[81] The Constitution also provides for two types of concurrent powers, which can be exercised by both Congress and states. The first type, including the power to tax, is not subject to formal federal preemption. Concurrent powers of the second type are granted to Congress by the Constitution and not prohibited to states. Should a direct conflict between a state law and a federal law occur involving the second type of concurrent power, the Constitution's supremacy clause ensures the prevalence of the federal law by invalidating the state law.[82] In exercising the second type of concurrent power, Congress often has failed to include an explicit preemption provision.[83] Hence, opponents of state laws based upon this type of concurrent power — including initiated ones — challenge them in the U.S. District Court on the ground they are inconsistent with federal law.

California voters in 1964 approved initiative Proposition 14 repealing the Unruh and Rumford Acts, which prohibited racial discrimination in the sale or rental of private housing containing more than four units. Each owner of real property specifically was guaranteed the right to refuse to sell or rent "property to such person or persons as he, in his absolute discretion, chooses." The constitutionality of the proposition was challenged as violating the equal protection of the laws clause of the Fourteenth Amendment to the U.S. Constitution. In 1967, the U.S. Supreme Court affirmed the judgment of the California Supreme Court in striking down the proposition as unconstitutional.[84]

In 1966, the California Supreme Court upheld a superior court ruling that the voter-approved 1964 initiative declaring pay television to be contrary to the public policy of the state violates freedom of speech as guaranteed by the First and Fourteenth amendments to the U.S. Constitution.[85]

An action initiated in the California Superior Court in 1963 led to a finding in 1970 of *de jure* segregation in the public schools of the City of Los Angeles. While the court was examining alternative pupil reassignment and busing plans, California voters approved Proposition 1 in 1979 stipulating that a state court shall not order mandatory pupil reassignment or busing unless the U.S. District Court "would be permitted under federal decisional law" to take such action to remedy a violation of the equal protection of the laws clause of the Fourteenth Amendment to the U.S. Constitution. Subsequent to the approval of Proposition 1, the school district requested the court to end mandatory reassignment and busing. In 1980, the court rejected the district's application on the ground the proposition was not applicable to the Los Angeles case that involves *de jure* segregation, but the California Court of Appeals reversed the lower court's decision.[86]

The California Supreme Court denied a petition for the issuance of a writ of certiorari. The decision was appealed to the U.S. Supreme Court, which ruled in 1982 that Proposition 1 does not violate the equal protection of the laws clause.[87] The majority opinion held: "Proposition 1 does not inhibit enforcement of any federal law or constitutional requirement. Quite the contrary, by its plain language the proposition seeks only to embrace the requirements of the federal constitution with respect to mandatory school assignments and transportation. It would be paradoxical to conclude that by adopting the equal protection clause of the Fourteenth Amendment, the voters of the state thereby violated it."[88] Justice Marshall entered a strong dissent: "Because I fail to see how a fundamental redefinition of the governmental decision making structure with respect to the same racial issue can be unconstitutional when the state seeks to remove the authority from local school boards, yet constitutional when the state attempts to achieve the same result by limiting the power of its courts, I must dissent from the court's decision to uphold Proposition 1."[89]

In 1982, the U.S. Department of Justice filed suit against the State of Washington challenging the constitutionality of initiative Proposition 394, ratified by the voters in 1981, requiring the approval of the electorate for the issuance of bonds by the Washington Public Power Supply System to obtain revenue to complete construction of three power plants. The suit alleged the initiative violated the contract clause of the U.S. Constitution by impairing contracts entered into a decade ago by the Bonneville Power Administration, a unit of the U.S. Department of Energy, and its preference customers for the construction and operation of the power plants. The suit also alleged the initiative violated the supremacy clause of the

U.S. Constitution and effectively disenfranchised the majority of Bonneville Power Administration's ratepayers throughout the Pacific Northwest. Continental Illinois National Bank & Trust Company also filed suit in the U.S. District Court alleging that the proposition was unconstitutional.

On June 30, 1982, the U.S. District Court for the Western District of Washington found the initiative, as applied to the System's projects 1, 2, and 3, violated the contract clause and therefore was invalid.[90] The court's decision was upheld by the U.S. Court of Appeals for the Ninth Circuit and a petition for the issuance of a writ of certiorari was denied by the U.S. Supreme Court.[91]

On July 15, 1998, U.S. District Court Judge Charles Legge refused to issue a temporary injunction against California initiative Proposition 227 dismantling the state's bilingual education programs by finding the initiative neither discriminated against minorities nor violated a congressional statute requiring schools to overcome students' language barriers.[92]

State Preemption

In common with the U.S. Constitution and statutes, a state constitution or statute can prevent the employment of direct law-making by voters of a local government if the constitution or statute contains restrictions regarding the use of the initiative and the referendum.[93]

The Supreme Court of Utah was called upon in 1954 to determine whether the initiative could be employed by voters to adopt a zoning ordinance. The court decided in the negative. It justified its decision by noting that the constitution granted the state legislature power to enact statutes to protect the owners of real property by establishing procedural, due process requirements in the zoning-enabling statutes, which would apply to the voters as well as the city council.[94]

In 1983, voters in Hinsdale, Illinois, were prevented from employing the initiative to place on the November school board election ballot the question of removing the ban on the sale of alcoholic beverages because state law requires that a liquor referendum question must appear either on a general election or a municipal election ballot.[95] The refusal of the Du Page County Board of Election Commissioners to place the proposition on the referendum ballot was supported by the Illinois Board of Elections. Also in 1983, the California Superior Court ruled invalid a Tehama County initiative proposition, approved by the voters in 1982, stripping the county of its power to regulate land use on the ground an initiated local ordinance cannot preempt the state zoning statute.[96]

The California Supreme Court in 1929 ruled that statutory notice and hearing requirements prior to enactment of municipal zoning and land use ordinances were applicable to initiatives.[97] In 1976, the court was called upon to review the decision of the Superior Court, Alameda County, permanently enjoining enforcement of a City of Livermore zoning ordinance, enacted by the initiative, prohibiting issuance of residential building permits until educational, sewage disposal, and water supply facilities met stipulated standards. Plaintiffs cited the 1929 court decision and alleged the ordinance was an unconstitutional attempt to forbid immigration into the city. The Supreme Court rejected these arguments and announced the 1929 decision "was incorrectly decided; the statutory notice and hearing provisions govern only ordinances enacted by city council action and do not limit the power of municipal electors . . . to enact legislation by initiative."[98]

A residential growth control initiative approved by the voters of the City of Oceanside, however, was invalidated in 1994 by the California Court of Appeals because the initiative conflicted with the city's master plan and the California planning and zoning law.[99]

Limited Constitutional Convention

A 1968 initiative proposition, approved by Massachusetts voters, providing for placing the question of calling a limited constitutional convention on the 1970 referendum ballot was ruled unconstitutional by the Massachusetts Supreme Judicial Court.[100] The General Court did not approve the indirect initiative petition, and proponents collected an additional 95,000 signatures on petitions of which more than 77,700 were certified. The Supreme Judicial Court interpreted the words "law" or "laws" in the constitutional provision authorizing the initiative as not including a proposition that could result in the calling of a constitutional convention.

Excluded Subjects

In 1983, Massachusetts Attorney General Francis X. Bellotti disqualified eight of twenty submitted initiative petitions on the ground the petitions dealt with powers of the courts specifically excluded from the initiative by the Constitution.[101] In the same year, the Supreme Judicial Court invalidated initiative petitions, sponsored by the Coalition for Legislative Reform, to place on the referendum ballot a proposal to change the rules of the General Court. Initiated procedural statutes, according to the Supreme Judicial Court, "are not binding upon the houses; consequently they are not laws in the same sense contemplated in article 48. Either branch, under its exclusive rule-making constitutional prerogatives, is free to disregard or supersede such statutes by unicameral action."[102]

Legislative Reapportionment

Unhappiness with the legislative and congressional reapportionment plans enacted into law by the state legislature controlled by Democrats led California Republican Assemblyman Don Sebastiani, without the support of his party, to conduct a $1 million initiative petition drive to place new reapportionment plans on the referendum ballot.

When sufficient signatures were collected and verified, Republican Governor George Deukmejian on July 17, 1983, called a special election for December 13, 1983; Democrats filed suit challenging the constitutionality of the initiative petition.[103] On September 15, 1983, by a six to one vote, the California Supreme Court ruled the statutory congressional and legislative initiative proposition violated the state constitution, which authorizes reapportionment only once every ten years and the December 1982 reapportionment was valid.[104] This invalidation was the first one in thirty-five years of an initiative proposition before it was submitted to the electorate.

The initiative has been employed in nineteen states to establish term limits for state legislators, and a Utah statute established a similar limit for state legislators. The California term limit was established by Proposition 140 of 1990, but the proposition was invalidated in 1997 by a two to one decision of a three-judge panel of the U.S. Court of Appeals for the Ninth Circuit on the ground the proposition did not provide adequate notice to the electorate that an affirmative vote would establish a lifetime term limit.[105] The court sitting *en banc* subsequently reversed the decision and the U.S. Supreme Court in 1998 refused to hear an appeal of the decision.[106]

Voters in twenty-one states have employed the initiative to limit the number of terms a member of Congress from each of these states can serve, and the Utah State Legislature enacted a term limit statute applicable to members of the state's congressional delegation. In 1995, the U.S. Supreme Court, by a five to four vote, invalidated section 3 of amendment 73 to the Arkansas constitution limiting representatives from the state to the U.S. House of Representatives and Senate to three terms and two terms, respectively.[107]

There is, however, no U.S. constitutional provision prohibiting voters, by means of the initiative, from enacting a statute containing a "moral obligation" provision authorizing candidates to the U.S. House of

Representatives and Senate to file a preprimary pledge to serve only a specified number of terms.

Legislative Organization and Rules

In 1983, Massachusetts Attorney General Francis X. Bellotti refused to certify an initiative petition relating to the selection of the legislature's presiding officers, appointment of leaders and committee chairpersons, and limits on the salaries of members. The attorney general maintained that the initiative petition was not a law and his opinion was upheld by the Supreme Judicial Court, which ruled the petition infringed upon the exclusive unicameral powers of each house of the legislature.[108]

Voter-approved California Proposition 24 of 1984 limits the majority party's control of the state legislature, divides the legislature's appropriations between the two parties according to their respective membership, and curbs the power of the speaker of the assembly by removing his authority to assign members to committees and appoint committee chairpersons.

On November 29, 1984, the Superior Court ruled that the initiated measure was unconstitutional on the ground the state constitution stipulates each house of the state legislature can elect its own officers and adopt procedural rules.[109] The decision was upheld by the California Supreme Court in 1986.[110]

Balanced Federal Budget

In 1984, the California Supreme Court removed from the November referendum ballot initiative Proposition 35 directing the state legislature to memorialize Congress to hold a constitutional convention for the purpose of proposing a balanced federal budget amendment to the U.S. Constitution.[111] The court's majority ruled the proposition violates Article 5 of the U.S. Constitution, which stipulates that only state legislatures, and "not the people through the initiative," can memorialize Congress to call a constitutional convention to propose amendments to the U.S. Constitution. A similar initiative measure was ruled off the Montana ballot for the identical reason by the state supreme court in 1984.[112]

Initiative Campaign Finance

State legislatures and Congress have enacted statutes prohibiting corrupt practices in elections. The early corrupt practices laws prohibit bribery, personation, betting on elections, and the payment of one voter's poll tax by another person. In addition, civil service reform acts specifically forbid the assessing of office holders as a means of raising funds for candidates, political parties, and issue campaigns.

Later corrupt practices statutes have been directed at curbing the excessive use of money in election and referendum campaigns by establishing the maximum permissible amount of campaign contributions and expenditures and often restricting the source of campaign funds. Campaign committees or candidates are required to file periodic reports on campaign contributions, including names and addresses of donors, and expenditures. The enforcement of corrupt practices laws in general leaves much to be desired. Although reports of receipts and disbursements are often incomplete and difficult to understand, persons filing the reports rarely are prosecuted.

The average voter typically is ill-informed regarding the cost of conducting an election or referendum campaign and is apt to be shocked when the total amount of funds expended is published. The plain truth is that in order to make effective appeals to the voters, candidates, political parties, and sponsors of initiatives must spend large sums. Campaign headquarters generally must be rented, staffs must be hired, and campaign literature must be printed and distributed. The advent of radio and television, with their high advertising rates, greatly increased the cost of campaigning. Statewide initiative and referendum campaigns are especially expensive because of the difficulties of obtaining the requisite number of certifiable signatures on petitions and persuading voters to support or reject ballot propositions.

Not surprisingly, initiative propositions affecting business and industry generate the most extensive and expensive campaigns. A study by the Council of Economic Priorities of eighteen initiative and referendum campaigns affecting the interest of corporations revealed that corporations contributed funds to both proponents and opponents in only one campaign — the Colorado proposition to permit branch banking.[113] The study also found that in fourteen campaigns in which "corporate funds dominated, the side with business backing won in eleven cases."[114]

A study by *The Initiative News Report* of initiative campaign spending in the period 1976–83 revealed clearly the importance of money in such campaigns as 80 percent of the propositions were defeated when the opponents outspent the proponents.[115] Thomas E. Cronin in 1989 reported a similar finding.[116]

The U.S. Supreme Court on January 30, 1976, in *Buckley v. Valeo* issued a major ruling related to the restrictions placed on campaign spending by candidates for elective office, which foreshadowed its 1978 decision directly affecting referendum campaign finance.[117] In the *Buckley* case, the court examined the Federal Election Campaign Act of 1971 and its 1974 amendments.[118] The court upheld the individual contribution limits, disclosure and reporting requirements, and public financing provisions, but held "the limitations on expenditures, on independent expenditures by individuals and groups, and on expenditures by a candidate from his personal funds are constitutionally infirm." In particular, the Court ruled that the limitation on personal expenditures by candidates "imposes a substantial restraint on the ability of persons to engage in protected first amendment expression."[119]

Taking a cue from the *Buckley* decision, the California Supreme Court on April 7, 1976, invalidated a provision of the state's Political Reform Act imposing limitations on contributions to referendum campaigns as violative of the freedom of speech guarantee contained in the First Amendment to the U.S. Constitution.[120] Two years later, the U.S. Supreme Court invalidated a Massachusetts statute restricting corporate contributions to referendum campaigns by ruling that a corporation was protected by the First Amendment to the U.S. Constitution and could expend funds to publicize its views relative to a proposed state constitutional amendment authorizing the General Court to levy a graduated income tax.[121]

In 1981, the court examined a City of Berkeley, California, initiated ordinance restricting campaign contributions by any one person to a maximum of $250.[122] The court struck down the ordinance and noted:

The court has long viewed the First Amendment as protecting a market place for the clash of different views and conflicting ideas. That concept has been stated and restated almost since the constitution was drafted. The voters of the City of Berkeley adopted the challenged ordinance which places restrictions on that market place. It is irrelevant that the voters rather than a legislative body enacted § 602, because the voters may no more violate the Constitution by enacting a ballot measure than a legislative body may do so by enacting legislation . . . to place a spartan limit . . . on individuals wishing to band together, while placing none on individuals acting alone, is clearly a restraint on the right of association.[123]

Distinguishing between *Buckley v. Valeo* and the Berkeley case, Mr. Justice White dissented and pointed out that the invalidated Massachusetts statute completely prohibited contributions and expenditures, whereas the Berkeley ordinance allowed contributions up to a maximum of $250.[124] He added: "The role of the initiative in California can not be separated from its purpose of preventing the dominance of special interest.

That is the very history and purpose of the initiative in California and similarly it is the purpose of the ancillary regulations designed to protect it. Both serve to maximize the exchange of political discourse."[125]

California voters on November 5, 1996, sanctioned (61 percent to 39 percent) Proposition 208 limiting a contribution by an individual to a candidate for the state legislature to $250; the limit is increased to $500 if a candidate accepts expenditure limits.[126] The proposition also prohibits one candidate from transferring funds to another candidate and state legislators from soliciting contributions from registered lobbyists. On January 6, 1998, U.S. District Court Judge Lawrence Karlton invalidated the proposition on the ground the expenditure limits were set so low they violated the free speech rights of candidates to communicate with voters.

Chapter 2 noted that eight states had enacted statutes banning paid petition circulators prior to 1976 when the California Supreme Court struck down a provision of a 1974 statute restricting payments for petition signatures to $0.25 per signature.[127] Subsequently, the U.S. District Court in 1982 invalidated Oregon's ban on paid petition circulators, and in 1988 the U.S. Supreme Court applied exacting scrutiny to a Colorado statute prohibiting paid petition circulators.[128]

Federal monies cannot be used to support a campaign for or against an initiated proposition. The Legal Services Corporation Act of 1974, for example, specifically prohibits the use of federal funds to finance a pro or con campaign against a ballot proposition.[129] Nevertheless, a federally financed legal services corporation used federal funds to help defeat California initiative Proposition 9 in 1980, which would have reduced state income sharply.[130] The Comptroller General of the United States reported that "the Western Center for Law and Poverty and certain other unidentified California Legal Services grantees, violated the provision of 42 U.S.C. § 2996e(d)(4) in providing funds and personnel support for the Proposition 9 Task Force that operated a large scale opposition campaign to the Proposition 9 ballot measure during the first half of calendar 1980."[131]

Financial Disclosure

Washington State voters approved initiative proposition 276 in 1972 requiring disclosure of the financial interests of elected officers and lobbyists. The Washington Supreme Court in 1974 rejected challenges to the proposition, maintaining it infringed upon privacy, was impermissively too broad, and infringed on the right of a citizen to seek and hold office and the right of the electorate to choose candidates of their choice.[132] An appeal of this decision was dismissed by the U.S. Supreme Court in the same year.[133]

Required Approval Majority

The Wyoming Constitution stipulates that an initiated measure is approved provided the affirmative vote is in excess of 50 percent of those voting in the preceding general election.[134] An initiative proposition on the 1996 general election ballot encouraged a term limits amendment to the U.S. Constitution.

Voters approved the proposition, but the secretary of state ruled it had been rejected because it did not attain the required affirmative majority vote of those who participated in the 1994 general election. The decision was appealed to the U.S. District Court, which granted summary judgment in favor of the secretary. Plaintiffs appealed, but the decision was upheld by the U.S. Court of Appeals for the Tenth Circuit and the U.S. Supreme Court refused to issue a writ of certiorari.[135]

SUMMARY

The concept of the initiative is a relatively simple one, yet constitutional and statutory provisions authorizing its use have been the subject of a considerable amount of litigation. State and national courts have upheld the constitutionality of the participatory device against the charge that it violates the clause of the U.S. Constitution guaranteeing each state a republican form of government.

When called upon, the highest court in twelve states has interpreted the initiative authorization constitutional or statutory provisions liberally. In general, courts have not looked favorably upon attempts by state legislatures to restrict certain types of petition circulators and have allowed signature solicitation in private shopping malls. Fifteen state constitutions restrict an initiative proposition to a single subject, and, particularly in California, this restriction has generated a relatively large number of suits, alleging a proposition involves more than one subject.

Another common source of court suits is the allegation that the proposition ballot title or summary does not reflect the true goal of the proposition. The courts typically have ruled the title or summary passes the reasonably germane test. A number of important initiative provisions have been invalidated on the ground they violate provisions of the U.S. or state constitution and statutes, particularly preemption ones. These initiatives often involved the issue of civil rights.

Chapter 4 focuses on a number of initiative campaigns covering a wide variety of propositions and raising a number of legal issues examined in Chapter 3. Special attention is paid to those initiative campaigns that have been labeled a tax revolt.

NOTES

1. *The Constitution of the United States*, art. 4; § 4.
2. *Ladderly v. Portland*, 44 Or. 118 at 145, 74 P. 710 at 737 (1903).
3. *Pacific States Telephone and Telegraph Company v. Oregon*, 223 U.S. 118 (1912). See also *Luther v. Borden*, 7 Howard 1 (1849).
4. *Timmons v. Twin Cities Area New Party*, 117 S.Ct. 1364 at 1366 (1997).
5. *Brownlow v. Wunsch*, 103 Colo. 120, 83 P.2d 775 (1938).
6. *Whitman v. Moore*, 49 Ariz. 211, 125 P.2d 445 (1942).
7. *Newsome v. Riley*, 69 Mich.App. 725, 245 N.W.2d 374 (1976).
8. *Citizens for Financially Responsible Government v. City of Spokane*, 99 Wash.2d 339, 662 P.2d 845 (1983).
9. *Rossi v. Brown*, 9 Cal.4th 688, 38 Cal.Rptr.2d 363, 889 P.2d 557 (1995).
10. *Fabec v. Beck*, 922 P.2d 330 (Co. 1996).
11. *Nebraska Revised Statutes*, § 32-705 (1993 Supp.).
12. *Stenberg v. Beermann*, 240 Neb. 754 at 757, 485 N.W.2d 151 at 153 (1992). See also David M. Rahm, "Citizens Versus Legislators — The Continuing Fight to Ensure the Rights of Initiative and Referendum in Nebraska: *State Ex Rel. Stenberg v. Beerman*," *Creighton Law Review*, vol. 26, 1992, pp. 195–220.
13. *Nebraska Revised Statutes*, § 32-629 (1996 Supp.).
14. *Bernbeck v. Moore*, 936 F.Supp. 1543 at 1561 (1996).
15. *Bernbeck v. Moore*, 126 F.3d 1114 at 1117 (8th Cir. 1997).
16. *Colorado Revised Statutes Annotated*, § 1-40-112(1).
17. *American Constitutional Law Foundation v. Meyer*, 870 F.Supp. 995 (1996).
18. *American Constitutional Law Foundation v. Meyer*, 120 F.3d 1092 at 1100 (10th Cir. 1997).
19. *Mississippi Code Annotated*, § 23-17-17(2).
20. *Term Limits Leadership Council, Incorporated v. Clark*, 984 F.Supp. 470 at 475 (S.D. Miss. 1977).
21. *Colorado Revised Statutes*, § 1-40-110 (1980).
22. *Grant v. Meyer*, 741 F.2d 1210 (10th Cir. 1984).
23. *Grant v. Meyer*, 828 F.2d 1446 (10th Cir. 1987).
24. *Meyer v. Grant*, 486 U.S. 414, 108 S.Ct. 1886 (1988).
25. *Ibid.*, 486 U.S. 414 at 421, 108 S.Ct. 1886 at 1892.
26. Daniel H. Lowenstein and Robert M. Stern, "The First Amendment and Paid Initiative Petition Circulators: A Dissenting View and a Proposal," *Hastings Constitutional Law Quarterly*, Fall 1989, p. 185.

27.   *Ibid.*, pp. 187 and 193. See also *State v. Conifer Enterprises*, 82 Wash. 2d 94, 508 P.2d 149 (1973).

28.   *McIntyre v. Ohio Elections Commission*, 115 S.Ct. 1511 (1995).

29.   *Ibid.*, at 1524.

30.   *American Constitutional Law Foundation, Incorporated v. Meyer*, 870 F.995 (1994).

31.   *American Constitutional Law Foundation, Incorporated v. Meyer*, 120 F.3d 1092 at 1101-105 (10th Cir. 1997).

32.   *Buckley v. American Constitutional Law Foundation, Incorporated*, 119 S.Ct. 636 at 662 (1999).

33.   *Term Limits Leadership Council, Incorporated v. Clark*, 984 F.Supp. 470 (S.D. Miss. 1997). See also *Mississippi Code Annotated*, § 23-27-57(3).

34.   *Term Limits Leadership Council, Incorporated v. Clark*, 984 F.Supp. 470 at 475 (S.D. Miss. 1997).

35.   *Pruneyard Shopping Center v. Robins, et al.*, 23 Cal.3d 899, 153 Cal.Rpt. 854 (1979).

36.   *Lloyd Corporation v. Tanner*, 407 U.S. 551 at 569, 92 S.Ct. 2219 at 2228 (1972).

37.   *Pruneyard Shopping Center v. Robins, et al.*, 447 U.S. 74 at 81, 100 S.Ct. 2035 at 2040 (1980).

38.   *Alderwood Associates v. Washington Environment Council*, 96 Wn.2d 230 at 245-46, 635 P.2d 108 at 116-17 (1981).

39.   *Woodland v. Michigan Citizens Lobby*, 423 Mich. 188, 378 N.W.2d 337 (1985).

40.   *H-CHH Associates v. Citizens for Representative Government*, 193 Cal.App.3d 1193, 238 Cal.Rptr. 841 (1987).

41.   *Lloyd Corporation v. Whiffen*, 315 Or. 500, 849 P.2d 446 (1993).

42.   *California Elections Code*, § 29770. This section originally was enacted as § 29256 but was renumbered in 1976.

43.   *Opinions of the California Attorney General*, opinion 37, 1980.

44.   *Bilofsky v. Deukmejian*, 124 Cal.App.3d 825 at 830, 177 Cal.Rptr. 621 at 626 (1981).

45.   *Bilofsky v. Deukmejian*, 456 U.S. 1002, 102 S.Ct. 2287 (1982).

46.   *Constitution of Massachusetts*, amendment 48, general provision, II.

47.   *Massachusetts General Laws*, chap. 214, § 1 and chap. 231A, § 1.

48.   *Massachusetts Public Interest Research Group v. Secretary of the Commonwealth*, 375 Mass. 85 at 94, 375 N.E.2d 1175 at 1183 (1978).

49.   *Ibid.*, 375 Mass. at 91, 375 N.E.2d at 1182.

50.   *Ibid.*, 375 Mass. at 91, 375 N.E.2d at 1180.

51.   *Coalition for Political Honesty v. State Board of Elections*, 83 Ill.2d 236 (1980).

52.   "Tucson Initiative Fails to Make Ballot," *Public Administration Times*, December 15, 1983, p. 1.

53. *Duggan v. Beermann*, 245 Neb. 907 at 915, 515 N.W.2d 788 at 793 (1994).

54. *Dobrovolny v. Moore*, 936 F.Supp. 1536 at 1542 (D.Neb. 1996).

55. *Dobrovolny v. Moore*, 125 F.3d 1111 (8th Cir. 1997).

56. *Massachusetts Acts of 1963*, chap. 506.

57. *Molesworth & Others v. State Ballot Law Commission*, 348 Mass. 23, 200 N.E.2d 583 (1964).

58. "Six in a Bond Drive Indicted for Forged Missouri Petitions," *The New York Times*, September 17, 1972, p. 46.

59. *Constitution of California*, art. 2, § 8(d) (1999).

60. Daniel H. Lowenstein, "California Initiatives and the Single-Subject Rule," *UCLA Law Review*, vol. 30, 1983, pp. 954–55.

61. *Perry v. Jordan*, 34 Cal.2d 87, 207 P.2d 47 (1949). The California Supreme Court prefers to rule on single subject challenges to the initiative "after an election rather than to disrupt the electoral process by preventing the exercise of the people's franchise." See *Brosnahan v. Eu*, 31 Cal.3d1 at 4, 641 P.2d 200 at 201 (1982).

62. *Brosnahan v. Brown*, 32 Cal.3d 236, 186 Cal. Reptr. 30, 651 P.2d 274 (1982).

63. *Ibid.*, 32 Cal.3d 236 at 247, 186 Cal.Rptr. 30 at 36, 651 P.2d 274 at 281.

64. *California Trial Lawyers Association v. Eu*, 200 Cal.App.3d 351, 245 Cal.Rptr. 916 (1988).

65. *Ibid.*, 200 Cal.App.3d 351 at 358, 245 Cal.Rptr. 916 at 919.

66. *Insurance Industry Initiative Campaign Committee et al. v. Eu*, 203 Cal.App.3d 961 at 964, 250 Cal.Rptr. 320 at 321 (1988).

67. *Ibid.*, 203 Cal.App.3d 961 at 967, 250 Cal.Rptr. 320 at 323.

68. *Raven v. Deukmejian*, 52 Cal.3d 336 at 348, 801 P.2d 1077 at 1084 (1990).

69. *Constitution of Mississippi*, art. 15, § 273 (9) and *Massachusetts General Laws*, chap. 53, § 21.

70. *Illinois Compiled Statutes Annotated*, chap. 46, § 28-6.

71. *Georges v. Carney*, 546 F.Supp. 469 (N.D. Ill. 1982).

72. *Ibid.*, at 477. The decision was affirmed by the U.S. Court of Appeals. See *Georges v. Carney*, 691 F.2d 297 (7th Cir. 1982).

73. Linda Greenhouse, "Voters Can Be For and Against a Proposition One in Yonkers," *The New York Times*, November 4, 1972, p. 19.

74. *State ex rel. Bailey v. Celebrezze, Jr.*, 67 Ohio St.2d 516 at 520 (1981).

75. *Ibid.*, at 519-20.

76. *Gormley v. Lan*, 88 N.J. 26, 438 A.2d 519 (1981). See also "Jersey High Court Upholds Ballot Bias Ruling," *The New York Times*, October 7, 1981, p. B5.

77. *Insurance Industry Initiative Campaign Committee et al. v. Eu*, 203 Cal.App.3d 961 at 968, 250 Cal.Rptr. 320 at 324 (1988).

78. *Maine Revised Statutes Annotated*, tit. 21-A, § 906(6)(B).

79. *Olson v. Secretary of State*, 689 A.605 (1997).

80. "District Judge Rules Houston City Council Made Illegal Change in Initiative Language," *Election Administration Reports*, July 20, 1998, p. 3.

81. *U.S. Constitution*, art. I, § 10.

82. *Ibid.*, art. VI, § 2.

83. For details, consult Joseph F. Zimmerman, *Federal Preemption: The Silent Revolution* (Ames: Iowa State University Press, 1991).

84. *Reitman v. Mulkey*, 387 U.S. 369 at 373, 87 S.Ct. 1627 at 1629 (1967).

85. *Weaver v. Jordan*, 64 Cal.2d 235, 49 Cal. 537, 411 P.2d 289 (1966).

86. *Crawford et al. v. Los Angeles Board of Education*, 113 Cal.App.3d 633 (1980).

87. *Crawford et al. v. Los Angeles Board of Education*, 458 U.S. 527, 102 S.Ct. 3211 (1982).

88. *Ibid.*, 458 U.S. 527 at 534-37, 102 S.Ct. 3211 at 3216-217.

89. *Ibid.*, 458 U.S. 527 at 547-48, 102 S.Ct. 3211 at 3223.

90. *Continental Illinois National Bank and Trust Company v. Sterling National Bank*, 565 F.Supp. 101 (W.D. Wash. 1982).

91. *Continental Illinois National Bank and Trust Company v. State of Washington*, 696 F.2d 692 (1983) and *Don't Bankrupt Washington Committee v. Continental Illinois National Bank and Trust Company*, 461 U.S. 950, 103 S.Ct. 1762 (1983).

92. *Valeria v. Wilson*, 12 F.Supp. 2d 1000 (N.D. Cal. 1998). See also "Prop. 227 is Constitutional," *The National Law Journal*, July 27, 1998, p. A8.

93. For details, consult Joseph F. Zimmerman, *State-Local Relations: A Partnership Approach*, 2nd ed. (Westport, CT: Praeger Publishers, 1995).

94. *Dewey v. Dozey-Layton Realty Company*, 3 Utah2d 1 at 6-7, 277 P.2d 805 at 809 (1954).

95. "Hinsdale Won't Vote on Liquor Sales," *Chicago Tribune*, September 2, 1983, sec. 2, p. 2.

96. Rosaline Levenson, "Zoning Initiative Overturned in California," *National Civic Review*, September 1983, p. 442.

97. *Hurst v. City of Burlingame*, 207 Cal. 134, 277 P. 308 (1929).

98. *Associated Home Builders v. City of Livermore*, 18 Cal.3d 582 at 588 (1976). See also David L. Callies et al., "Ballot Box Zoning: Initiative, Referendum, and the Law," *Journal of Urban and Contemporary Law*, vol. 39, 1991, pp. 53–98.

99. *Building Industry Association of San Diego v. City of Oceanside*, 27 Cal.App. 4th 744, 33 Cal.Rptr.2d 137 (Cal. Ct. App. 1994).

100. *Cohen v. Attorney General*, 357 Mass. 564, 259 N.E.2d 539 (1970).

101. *Constitution of Massachusetts*, Articles of Amendment, art. 48, The Initiative, § 2.

102. *Paisner v. Attorney General*, 390 Mass. 593 at 601-02 (1983).

103. Philip Hager, "Remapping Vote Voided by High Court," *Los Angeles Times*, September 15, 1983, pp. 1 and 20. See also Richard W. Gable, "The Sebastiani Initiative," *National Civic Review*, January 1984, pp. 16–23.

104. *Assembly of the State of California v. Deukmejian*, 180 Cal. 297, 639 P.2d 939 (1983). The U.S. Supreme Court denied the petition for issuance of a writ of certiorari. See *Republican National Committee et al. v. Burton*, 456 U.S. 941 (1982). See also *Constitution of California*, art. 21.

105. *Bates v. Jones*, 127 F.3d 839 (9th Cir. 1997).

106. *Bates v. Jones*, 131 F.3d 843 (9th Cir. 1997) and *Bates v. Jones*, 118 S.Ct. 1302 (1998).

107. *U.S. Term Limits, Incorporated v. Thornton*, 115 S.Ct. 1842 (1995).

108. *Paisner v. Attorney General*, 390 Mass. 593 (1983).

109. "California Court Upsets Legislative Initiative," *Public Administration Times*, January 1, 1985, p. 6.

110. *People's Advocate, Incorporated v. Superior Court*, 181 Cal.App.3d 316, 226 Cal.Rptr. 640 (1986).

111. *American Federation of Labor-Congress of Industrial Organizations v. Eu*, 36 Cal.3d 687, 686 P.2d 609, 206 Cal.Rptr. 89 (1984). See also "U.S. Balanced Budget Measure Taken Off Ballot," *The New York Times*, August 28, 1984, p. B20.

112. *Montana v. Waltermire*, 213 Mont. 425, 691 P.2d 826 (1984). See also "Courts Intervene in Initiative Process," *Public Administration Times*, March 1, 1985, p. 3.

113. Steven D. Lydenberg, *Bankrolling Ballots Update 1980* (New York: Council on Economic Priorities, 1981), pp. 1–2.

114. *Ibid.*, p. 2.

115. "INR Campaign Spending Study: Negativism Effective," *The Initiative News Report*, December 2, 1983, p. 1.

116. Thomas E. Cronin, *Direct Democracy: The Politics of Initiative, Referendum, and Recall* (Cambridge: Harvard University Press, 1989), p. 109.

117. *Buckley v. Valeo*, 424 U.S. 1 (1976).

118. *Ibid.* at 143.

119. *Ibid.* at 52.

120. *Citizens for Jobs and Energy v. Fair Political Practices Commission*, 16 Cal.3d 671, 547 P.2d 1386 (1976).

121. *First National Bank of Boston et al. v. Bellotti*, 435 U.S. 765 (1978).

122. *Election Reform Act of 1974*, Berkeley, California, ordinance number 4700-N.S., § 602.

123. *Citizens Against Rent Control v. City of Berkeley*, 454 U.S. 290, 102 S.Ct. 434 (1981).

124. *Ibid.*, 454 U.S. 290 at 302, 102 S.Ct. 434 at 441.

125. *Ibid.*, 454 U.S. 290 at 310, 102 S.Ct. 434 at 445.

126. *California Prolife Council Political Action Committee v. Jan Scully et al.*, 989 F.Supp. 1281 (E.D. Cal. 1998). See also Daniel M. Weintraub and Mark Katches, "Citizen-Set Campaign Limits Too Low, Says Judge," *State Legislatures*, March 1998, p. 30.

127. *Hardie v. Eu*, 18 Ca.3d 971, 556 P.2d 301 (1976).

128. *The Libertarian Party of Oregon v. Paulus*, civil case number 81-521-FR, U.S. District Court, District of Oregon (1982), and *Meyer v. Grant*, 486 U.S. 414 (1988).

129. *Legal Services Corporation Act of 1974*, 88 Stat. 378, 42 U.S.C. § 2996e(d)(4) and 2996f(b)(7).

130. *Letter Report B-210228/B*, dated September 1983, to Representative F. James Sensenbrenner of Wisconsin from the Comptroller General of the United States, pp. 12–16.

131. *Ibid.*, p. 15.

132. *Fritz v. Gordon*, 411 P.2d 911 (1974).

133. *Fritz v. Gordon*, 417 U.S. 902 (1974).

134. *Wyoming Constitution*, art. 3, § 52(f).

135. *Brady v. Ohman*, 153 F.3d 726 (1998) and *Brady v. Ohman*, 119 S.Ct. 619 (1998).

4

Initiative Campaigns

Initiative propositions have been sponsored by a single voter, an *ad hoc* group of voters, national organizations or local chapters of such organizations, reform groups such as good government associations and the League of Women Voters, other permanent organizations of citizens, business firms, and labor unions. The subject matter of a proposition can be a major national issue, a regional issue, a state issue, or a very local issue. It is not uncommon for propositions to be labeled loosely as conservative, liberal, or radical.

Eugene C. Lee, a longtime student of this participatory device, developed a California initiative typology—grassroots, program protection, partisan conflict, self-promotion, self-defense, the Trojan horse, the pork barrel or Christmas tree, logrolling or horse-trading, the poison pill or counter-initiative, shootouts, the campaign against a campaign, the preemptive strike, the "neverendum," and the Hiram Johnson Memorial Initiative.[1] Most of the types are self-explanatory, but a few need a short description.

The program protection type is designed to maintain a preferential funding position for a program such as kindergarten-to-grade 12 education. A self-defense initiative refers to one sponsored by an industry or profession to exercise control over specific government regulations, such as where smoking is permitted. The shootouts type is a proposition sponsored by a special interest group to undermine the position of another special interest. The campaign against a campaign type refers to the threatened placement of an alternative or counter proposition on the referendum ballot to discourage a group from sponsoring a specific proposition. Lee cited the 1994 proposition sponsored by the Philip Morris Company to preempt or remove control of smoking by local governments as an example of the preemptive strike. He classified repeated attempts to amend an approved proposition by new propositions as the neverendum. Lee's last type—The Hiram Johnson Memorial Initiative—is exemplified by "a rail bond measure in 1990, supported by the Southern Pacific Railroad, Hiram Johnson's bête noire, which included construction that would aid the company."[2] Voters rejected the proposition.

There are many reasons why individuals, groups of citizens, business firms, and labor unions sponsor direct initiatives. As noted in Chapter 1, the populist and progressive proponents of this participatory device explained that it would be employed if legislative bodies ignored the wishes of the majority of the voters by refusing to enact bills they favor and by enacting statutes benefiting special interests, such as railroads, that were opposed by most voters. A second reason for the use of the direct initiative is to ensure that the proposed law will be enacted precisely as worded by the sponsoring group and not amended by the state legislature.

As explained in Chapter 2, individuals and organizations desiring to enshrine their proposed statute in a form that will make amendment or repeal nearly impossible will choose the direct initiative in a state such as California whose constitution permits amendment only with the permission of the voters. Although thirteen states permit the state legislature to amend an initiated measure at will, the other initiative states either prohibit amendment without voter permission as in California or place time or super majority affirmative vote requirements on legislative amendments.

A fourth reason for launching an initiative campaign is to exert effective pressure on the legislative body of the state or local government to enact a statute or ordinance promoted by the group. A fifth reason for employment of the initiative is to commence the process of generating public opinion in favor of a sponsor's proposition even though the sponsor is aware there is no possibility in the forthcoming referendum that a majority of the voters will sanction the proposition. A series of campaigns, provided they attract increasing voter support, ultimately might persuade the state or local governing body to enact a measure similar to the initiative proposition. Most legislators pay close attention to public opinion, and circulation of a large number of initiative petitions is an indicator of voter discontent and protest against the unresponsiveness of legislative bodies to the concerns of certain groups of citizens.

Initiated propositions have to compete for voter attention and to share space on the referendum ballot with measures mandated by the state constitution or local charter or referred to the voters by the state legislature or local governing body. A study of initiated propositions and measures referred by the California State Legislature to voters in the period 1911–97 revealed approximately 38 percent of all initiated propositions and 63 percent of referred measures were approved by the electorate.[3] This study also discovered that 73 percent of referred proposals with bipartisan support were endorsed by the voters compared to 58 percent without bipartisan support.[4] A similar pattern, but at significantly lower percentages, applied to initiative propositions with and without bipartisan support, respectively. The study also determined that controversial proposals on the referendum ballot were sanctioned at only one-third the rate of noncontroversial proposals.[5] Not surprisingly, the initiated propositions typically were more controversial than proposals referred to the voters by the state legislature.

A major development involving this participatory device is the professionalization of the signature collection process and the campaign to secure voter approval.[6] Populists and progressives viewed the initiative as a grassroots process involving volunteers and small amounts of money used primarily to print and distribute copies of the proposition and explanatory materials. Although he acknowledged that traditional grassroots petitions could be circulated successfully to collect the required number of certifiable signatures of voters, Eugene C. Lee as early as 1978 wrote, with respect to groups promoting an initiative proposition, "there is no alternative but to seek the services of a professional organization."[7]

A second major development is the use of the alternative or counter initiative proposition designed to compete with and defeat another proposition. Arthur Samish, known as the secret boss of California in the 1930s and 1940s, used a counter initiative successfully on several occasions as described in Chapter 5. A related development is the placement of an alternative proposition on the referendum ballot by the state legislature or local government legislative body. The alternative proposal might have corrected drafting errors in the original proposition or might be a watered down version that, if approved, would be relatively ineffective in achieving the goals of the original proposition.

A third major development is the use of the initiative by governors of states to circumvent their respective state legislature that failed to enact bills favored by the governors. All registered voters, including the governor, in twenty-four states are authorized to circulate petitions to place proposals on the referendum ballot. Increasingly, state governments have become divided by the two major political parties, with the governor from one party and one or both houses of the legislature controlled by the other party. Unless the governor and the opposition legislative leaders can agree on the trade-off of bills each desires to have enacted, a stalemate could result. The initiative offers the governor the opportunity to break a deadlock.

In 1992, the governors of California, Colorado, and Michigan promoted initiative propositions. Governor John Engler of Michigan sponsored a proposition to lower real property taxes by 30 percent and raised approximately $1 million for an advertising campaign to convince voters to endorse the proposition.[8]

A fourth major development is the sharp increase in spending by proponents and opponents of initiative propositions, particularly state ones. Although the cost of employing professional consultants and signature-collecting firms increases spending, the bulk of the increase can be attributed to the advent of television and the high stakes associated with individual propositions. Approximately $200 million were spent by advocates and opponents of eleven propositions on the November 3, 1998, California state ballot.[9] The most expensive campaign involved Proposition 5 allowing video slot machines on California Indian reservations. Total spending was approximately $95 million or 64 percent more than the previous most expensive initiative campaign.[10]

Proponents and opponents of an initiative proposition often conduct their respective campaign in a court of law. Chapter 3 describes court cases involving the scope of the initiative power, handbill circulators, signature solicitation on private property, petition signature requirements, petition fraud, the single subject requirement, and ballot language.

The wording of an initiative proposition on the ballot can affect the probability of the proposition being approved or defeated. The August 1976 primary election ballot in Missouri contained the initiated proposed constitutional amendment 7 removing the constitutional prohibition of state financial assistance for students in private schools. The Missouri attorney general prepared the following ballot title: "Authorizes enactment of laws providing (1) services for handicapped, (2) non-religious textbooks, and (3) transportation for all public and nonpublic elementary and secondary school children."

Opponents of the proposition challenged the ballot wording in court by contending public school children will not receive additional services and hence the ballot wording is misleading, but their challenge was rejected by the court. A post-referendum survey of voters was conducted in Boone

County and revealed that a majority of the interviewees believed approval of the amendment would increase state assistance to private and public schools and "40 percent of the voters correctly understood that aid would be increased only for children in private schools."[11]

Similar confusing wording appeared on the Boone County, Missouri, ballot in April 1975 when voters were faced with the wording "For the termination of county planning and zoning" prepared by the county clerk. Voters in favor of the continuance of such planning and zoning would have to vote no. Exit polls of 583 voters in the City of Columbia revealed "twelve percent of the respondents cast votes inconsistent with their views on the general desirability of planning and zoning . . . but were not misled to the extent that they were by the ballot wording on Amendment Number 7."[12]

Do initiative campaigns increase voter turnout at the polls? Supporters of direct law-making suggest campaigns associated with propositions encourage voters to participate in elections and offer specific examples of sharply increased voter turnout. David H. Everson, who conducted a longitudinal study of voter turnout in initiative and non-initiative states, reported that there was a modest increase in initiative states in presidential and non-presidential election years, and questioned whether the increase was attributable solely to the initiative.[13] He specifically compared the reform traditions in initiative states to southern states and raised the question whether these traditions were responsible for the increased voter participation at the polls. He concluded: "It appears that initiatives will have their greatest impact on turnout under certain conditions. The first is an issue which has broad appeal, on both the pro and con side, in the electorate; the second is the absence of a highly visible candidate election and the third is a situation where previous turnout has dropped off and an initiative can contribute to a return to the norm."[14]

The remaining sections of this chapter are devoted to selected state and local government initiative campaigns. This information and other information are utilized in Chapter 5 to evaluate the arguments of the proponents and opponents of the initiative.

STATE INITIATIVE PROPOSITIONS

The subject matter and the frequency of use of initiative propositions vary to an extent from state to state and have changed over the decade with economic, political, and social changes in the state and local governments. Many of the newer propositions involve subjects that early proponents probably could not have contemplated.

Early Use

The initial proponents sought to make the state legislature more responsive to the citizenry by promoting what they believed to be essential reforms. Oregon voters in 1902, by a margin of eleven to one, amended their state constitution to authorize the initiative and the protest referendum, and first employed the initiative in 1904 to enact a direct primary law that effectively did away with party political conventions controlled by party bosses.[15] The most controversial section of this initiative was that each candidate seeking election to the state legislature would be required to vote for the candidate for U.S. senator who received the largest number of votes in the preceding election. This provision was in effect when the two U.S. senators were elected by the state legislature and became redundant when the Seventeenth Amendment to the U.S. Constitution — providing for the popular election of senators — was ratified by three-fourths of the state legislatures in 1913.

Oregon voters in 1908 approved a second proposition — a corrupt practices act regulating election campaign finance and prohibiting electioneering by candidates on election day.[16] Two years later, a group of Oregon voters placed on the ballot an initiative proposition establishing the right of the electorate to circulate petitions for a special election to determine whether a public officer should be removed from office prior to the expiration of his or her term.[17]

Maine voters in 1908 amended their state constitution to provide for the initiative and the protest referendum (known as the people's veto). In 1911, an initiative signature collection campaign was launched to place on the ballot a proposition providing for the use of the direct primary to nominate candidates for elective office.[18]

California voters in 1911 amended their state constitution to authorize the electorate to employ the initiative, which was used relatively frequently for three decades. Thirty-four propositions, promoted by the Anti-Saloon League and related organizations, related to morals during this period, and prohibition or regulation of alcoholic beverages was the subject matter of fourteen propositions.[19] Boxing, horseracing, and religious practices also appeared relatively frequently on the referendum ballot.[20] Other subjects included antivivisection, compulsory vaccination, usury, Sunday closing, and the eight-hour work day.[21]

Henry George's single tax proposal also was a common early initiative proposal and appeared on the California referendum ballot four times under the sponsorship of the Great Adventure League. Religious groups and business organizations with three major exceptions — alcoholic beverages firms, horseracing, and prizefight promoters — made very little use of the initiative.

Two new subjects appeared in California initiative propositions in the 1920s. Supporters of public schools placed a proposed constitutional amendment on the referendum ballot specifying the amount of money to be appropriated for public schools, and reformers initiated a constitutional executive budget amendment and a statute establishing a state athletic commission. Voters in 1922 approved a proposition creating boards to license chiropractors and osteopaths, despite the strenuous opposition of the medical associations.

With ratification of the Twenty-First Amendment to the U.S. Constitution, national prohibition was repealed in 1933. California voters approved an initiated constitutional amendment expanding the jurisdiction of the board of equalization to include the regulation of alcoholic beverages, and several other propositions relating to the regulation of such beverages appeared on the referendum ballot in the 1930s. During the same time period, voters approved initiative propositions amending the state civil service provisions and granting the attorney general supervisory powers over district attorneys and county sheriffs.

Supporters of old-age pension plans turned to the initiative and placed a proposal on the 1938 and 1939 ballots. Both were defeated. Pension plan initiative proposals appeared on the California referendum ballot again commencing in 1948 and their supporters were known as the "ham and eggs" group. The 1948 constitutional amendment proposition, entitled the "California Bill of Rights," was approximately 2,100 words in length, dealt with a wide variety of topics, and was ruled off the referendum ballot by the unanimous decision of the state supreme court.

Proposition 4 of 1948, however, was approved and established a state pension plan, removed from office the director of the state department of social welfare (provided the voters would select one of three named persons to be the new director), removed the requirement that relatives are responsible for the care of aged family members, and stipulated that the costs of the pension program were a first priority lien on the state general fund. A new proposition repealing Proposition 4 was placed on the ballot by the Federation of Women Clubs, State Council of the Blind, League of Women Voters, and other organizations. Voters approved the repealer in 1949.

Joseph G. LaPalombara and Charles B. Hagan examined initiative propositions that qualified for the Oregon ballot in the period 1938–48.[22] A 1938 initiated constitutional amendment proposition would have made it legal for the state to license bank nights, bridge studios, charitable bazaars, dog and horse racing, pinball machines, pool and billiard halls, raffles, and vending machines. Officially sponsored by the Oregon Merchants Legislative League, Inc., the accusation was advanced that cigar stand operators, beer hall proprietors, labor union officers, and leaders of Townsend Clubs were the guiding spirits behind the initiative, whose primary purpose allegedly was to generate state revenue for old-age pensions. The proposed constitutional amendment was rejected by the electorate.

Appearing on the same ballot was an initiated statutory proposition creating a state commission to solve water purification problems and, interestingly, no opposition arguments were published in the voters' information pamphlet. The measure was approved by an overwhelming vote. Another proposition, initiated by the Anti-Liquor League of Oregon, would include beer and unfortified wines under the state's monopoly control of alcoholic beverages. The Oregon Hop Growers and the Law and Temperance League of Oregon launched a campaign against the proposition, and it was defeated by the voters.

The electorate in 1940 was presented with an initiated 10,000-word constitutional amendment, drafted by the Oregon Merchants Legislative League, reducing state gambling restrictions. Labeled the punchboard bill, the measure also would legalize bank nights, bingo, dog and horse racing, several types of lotteries, and pinball machines. The stated purpose of the proposition was to reduce the real estate tax and generate revenue for assistance to senior citizens. The proposition did not receive a favorable vote in a single county.

The second initiative proposal would repeal the 1933 state milk-control statute designed to assist the fluid milk industry. Proponents maintained that the statute in effect created a monopoly for 24,000 persons. In a hotly contested campaign, the measure was defeated. The only initiative proposition on the 1942 referendum ballot was sponsored by teachers convinced that school districts needed additional state financial aid. The measure was approved.

A 1944 proposed constitutional amendment, initiated by the Oregon State Teachers Association, would add a new section to the state constitution requiring the state legislature to establish a new state fund in addition to the existing common school fund. Opponents were successful in persuading the electorate that the proposed amendment failed to include a provision for raising the required additional revenue and, if the state income tax did not produce adequate revenue to support the proposed program, a special levy would be placed on real property owners. The proposition was rejected. A second initiated constitutional amendment, sponsored by Townsendites, authorized monthly annuities for senior citizens financed by a 3 percent gross income tax and required annuitants to spend the funds within thirty days. Critics pointed out the cost of the program would be excessive, and the proposed gross income tax in effect would be a regressive sales tax. Voters in only six of the state's thirty-six counties endorsed the proposal.

Two initiated propositions appeared on the 1946 referendum ballot. The first, initiated by teachers, provided for the levy of an annual state school tax to generate $50 per capita to be used as supplemental revenue for schools, but the two mill real property tax levy for the state elementary school fund would be repealed. Although the electorate in twenty-seven counties rejected the proposition, it was approved by a 6,000-vote margin because of overwhelming support in Multnomah County (Portland area). The second measure was initiated by Townsendites and differed only in details from the 1944 measure. The 1946 proposal was rejected by an overwhelming margin.

In 1948, one proposed constitutional amendment and three initiated proposals appeared on the general election ballot. The proposed amendment would create bonded indebtedness to raise funds to pay cash bonuses to Oregon residents who served in World War II outside the continental limits of the nation. Poorly drafted, the proposition restricted the payments to veterans who entered active duty service prior to December 7, 1942. Opposed by veterans' organizations, the proposal was rejected.

The first initiated statutory proposition was sponsored by fishermen who use gill nets to catch salmon. The measure would make it illegal for any person (other types of commercial fishermen) to use any fixed appliance, such as set nets or fishwheels, to catch salmon in the Columbia River and its tributaries. This proposition would give the gill netters a monopoly, yet it was approved by the voters.

A second statutory initiative proposition, sponsored by the Oregon State Federation of Labor, would allow the sale of hard liquor by the glass and permit licensed clubs, hotels, common carriers of passengers, and restaurants to serve alcoholic liquor with or without food. Proponents maintained that serving intoxicating liquor by the glass was more temperate than the sale of bottled liquor. The Oregon Church Council led a successful campaign to defeat the proposition.

Townsendites sponsored the third statutory initiative proposition declaring it was the policy of the state to provide a pension of $50 per month for men over the age of sixty-five and women over the age of sixty. The proposition also directed the state legislature to appropriate the necessary funds for a permanent program and to establish an Old Age

Pension Commission to administer the payments. Voters registered their approval at the polls. Fearing the state would be unable to finance the program, the attorney general was requested to rule on the constitutionality of the proposition. Attorney General George Neuner in his formal opinion interpreted the proposition as simply advising the legislature to appropriate funds for the program and, hence, the necessary appropriations were not mandated.

More Recent Use

The Congressional Research Service of the Library of Congress conducted a study of initiative proposals qualifying for state referendum ballots in the period 1976–92 and reported 216 (43.6 percent) of the 495 propositions were approved (see Table 4.1).[23] Proposals relating to borrowing, spending, and taxation far outnumbered any other type, and 55 (41 percent) of the 134 proposals received the sanction of the electorate. The next most common type related to nuclear power and hazardous waste (37) and was followed by lotteries (31) and crime and punishment (27).

The Congressional Research Service report also revealed the number of initiative proposals appearing on the ballot each year increased by close to 300 percent compared to the number of such proposals on referendum ballots in the period 1904–75 (see Figure 4.1).[24] Similarly, the approval rate for propositions increased from 38.7 percent in the period 1904–75 to 43.6 percent in the period 1976–92.[25] Initiated constitutional amendments had the highest approval rate in both time periods.

Constitutional amendments proposed by the initiative during the period 1976–92 totaled forty-one in Colorado, twenty-nine in California, eighteen in Oregon, and seventeen in Ohio.[26] The largest number of statutory initiative propositions appeared on the referendum ballot in Oregon (39), followed by Massachusetts (21), Montana (20), and Washington (19). Only nine statutory initiative propositions appeared on the Colorado referendum ballot in sharp contrast to the forty-one constitutional initiative propositions.

Environmental Protection

As the environmental movement gained strength in the 1960s, activists took advantage of the initiative in the states and local governments where the participatory device is authorized. Bottle and can deposit propositions commonly were placed on the initiative ballot in states where the state legislature failed to enact deposit statutes.

TABLE 4.1
Number of Initiatives by Type, 1976–92

		Passed	
Issue	Total	Number	Rate (%)
Abortion (abo)	12	3	25.0
Beverage Containers, Recycling (bev)	15	1	6.7
Budgets, Spending, Taxes, Bonds (bud)	134	55	41.0
Campaign, Lobbying Laws (cam)	10	8	80.0
Consumer, Auto Insurance (con)	11	2	18.2
Crime and Punishment (cri)	27	17	63.0
Educational Standards, Operations (edu)	11	2	18.2
English as Official Language (eng)	5	5	100.0
Health Care Financing (hea)	10	1	10.0
Lottery, Gambling (lot)	31	11	35.5
Nuclear weapons (nw)	10	7	70.0
Nuclear Power, Hazardous Waste (np)	37	16	43.2
Redistricting, Legislative Powers (red)	20	11	55.0
Sexuality and Gender/AIDS (sex)	8	2	25.0
Term Limitations (ter)	20	18	90.0
Voting Rights, Registration, Elections (vot)	15	10	66.7
Utilities: Rates, Commissions (uti)	16	7	43.7
Other Issues (oth)	103	40	33.8
Total	495	261	43.6

Source: Lisa Oakley and Thomas H. Neale, *Citizen Initiative Proposals Appearing on State Ballots, 1976–1992* (Washington, DC: Congressional Research Service, 1995), p. 3.

Initiated environmental propositions often generate strenuous opposition by industries that would be affected by proposed environmental regulations or taxes. California voters on November 4, 1986, approved (62 percent to 38 percent) Proposition 65 (Safe Drinking Water and Toxic Enforcement Initiative of 1986) guaranteeing the following rights of citizens:

(a) To protect themselves and the water they drink against chemicals that cause cancer, birth defects, or other reproductive harm.
(b) To be informed about exposure to chemicals that cause cancer, birth defects, and other reproductive harm.

(c) To secure strict enforcement of the laws controlling hazardous chemicals and
     deter actions that threaten public health and safety.
(d) To shift the cost of hazardous waste cleanup more onto offenders and less
     onto law-abiding taxpayers.

FIGURE 4.1
Number of Initiatives and Passage Rate, 1904–92

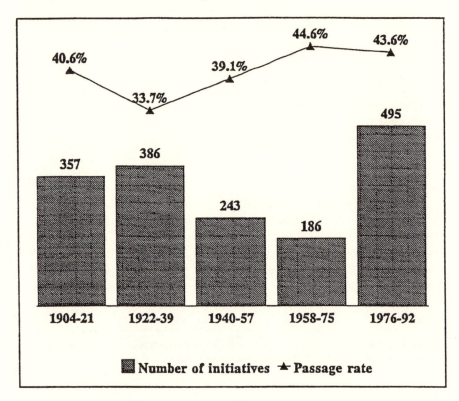

Source: Lisa Oakley and Thomas H. Neale, *Citizen Initiative Proposals Appearing on State Ballots,*
1976–1992 (Washington, DC: Congressional Research Service, 1995), p. 6.

The success of Proposition 65 encouraged environmentalists to place
three propositions on the 1988 referendum ballot: Proposition 81 (Safe
Drinking Water Bond Law), Proposition 82 (Water Conservation Bond
Law), and Proposition 83 (Water Reclamation Bond Law). Voters
approved the propositions.[27]

The two environmental initiative propositions on the Massachusetts
November 5, 1988, referendum ballot were rejected by identical margins

(59 percent to 41 percent).[28] Question 3, supported by environmental and state government leaders, was designed to reduce wasteful packaging of products. Its supporters contended that the proposed standards would encourage manufacturers to purchase additional recycled materials for packaging. Landfill space would be saved as the market for discarded milk jugs, newspapers, and other recyclable materials collected by cities and towns increased. Opponents, particularly paper and plastic firms, spent $5 million in an overwhelming television campaign alleging that approval of the proposal would result in higher consumer prices, costing the typical family an additional $230 annually and engulfing supermarkets in red tape. Question 4 would have taxed chemicals and industrial oil to raise funds for hazardous waste cleanups.

Oregon voters in the same year were asked to pass upon Measure #6 (Indoor Clean Air Act) and Measure #7 (Rivers Initiatives). Measure #6 would have prohibited most designated smoking areas and smoking in public buildings and in private ones open to the public. The measure was defeated by a six to four margin. Measure #7 proposed adding 500 miles of natural waterways to the scenic rivers system and was approved (63 percent to 37 percent).

The South Dakota electorate in 1988 acted upon Measure #1 (Large-Scale Metallic Mineral Mining and Reclamation Act) and Measure #2 (Large-Scale Metallic Mineral Mining Tax Act). The two initiative campaigns pitted economic development objectives against environmental protection, and the voters chose the former.

Washington state voters in 1988 acted on three alternative questions: Initiative Measure 97 establishing a hazardous substances cleanup program, Alternative Measure 97B providing for a smaller program, and neither proposal should be adopted. The oil industry promoted 97B as an alternative to measure 97 that would authorize imposition of larger fines on polluters, but voters approved Measure 97 by a large margin.

Environmentalists placed on the November 6, 1990, referendum ballot Proposition 128 (California Environmental Protection Act) popularly known as "Big Green."[29] The proposition dealt with coastal pollution, chlorofluorocarbon emissions, pesticides, and a new state environmental protection agency. A public opinion poll revealed strong support for "Big Green." The principal authors of the proposition were Attorney General John Van de Kampf, Campaign California, the Natural Resources Defense Council, and the Sierra Club, and they were supported subsequently by the California League of Conservation Voters, Citizens for a

Better Environment, California Public Interest Research Group, Green-peace, and the National Toxic Campaign.

There were political risks for proponents in placing four proposals in a single initiative proposition as each proposal might mobilize a different opposition group. Furthermore, the detailed nature of several provisions in the proposition and broad discretionary authority of implementing agencies provided an opening for the charge the proposition involved micromanagement of environmental regulation. Opponents stressed the costs that would be imposed by the initiative. In assessing the initiative campaign, John Tweedy, Jr., concluded there were "three weaknesses in the Proposition 128 campaign — insufficient grassroots work in local communities, failure to court independent opinionmakers, and a failure to undermine the credibility of the opposition."[30]

A group of Maine environmentalists collected 58,000 signatures to place on the November 5, 1996, ballot an initiative proposition prohibiting clear-cutting of forests and restricting other logging activities.[31] Public opinion polls revealed strong support for the proposition and induced the timber companies to join with two moderate environmental groups — The Maine Audubon Society and the Natural Resources Council of Maine — and Governor Angus King to draft a twenty-seven page Compact for Maine's Forest that was placed on the ballot by the state legislature. The compact would reduce the size of a clear-cut area from 250 to 75 acres and place a limit on the total acreage a single landowner could clear-cut in one year. Forty-eight percent of the voters favored the compact and, as a consequence, the compact was placed on the November 4, 1997, ballot.[32] The compact was rejected with approximately $1.2 million spent by proponents and $892,000 spent by opponents.

The use of cyanide to separate gold and silver from ore in new mines and expanded ones was banned by voter approval of an initiative proposition on the November 3, 1998, Montana referendum ballot. The Montana Mining Association led the opposition and warned that jobs would be lost and mining communities would be devastated if the proposition was approved.

Legislative Procedures

The initiative somewhat surprisingly has been little used to attempt to change legislative procedures to make state legislatures more responsive to the wishes of the voters. In 1984, however, California voters approved Proposition 24 granting more power to the minority party in the state legislature by changing procedures.

Most of the provisions of this proposition, however, were ruled unconstitutional by a Superior Court judge who opined that the proposition was *ultra vires* because it exceeded the powers of the statutory initiative.[33] In upholding the lower court decision, the Court of Appeals wrote that each house of the state legislature under the state constitution possesses the exclusive power to adopt rules for selecting officers and conducting business.[34]

In reviewing this initiative's origin, campaign, and court challenge, James E. Castello concluded that the proposition's real sponsors were Republican members of the Assembly and not Paul Gann, the purported sponsor.[35]

Term Limits

Initiative proponents of term limits for state legislators are convinced these representatives tend to become less accountable and responsive to voters and more responsive to special interest groups that provide campaign funds and other favors. The remedy for this problem, according to term limits proponents, is to limit the number of years legislators can serve to ensure they will be citizen legislators and not professional legislators.

The United States has had experience with term limits for elected officers dating to the Articles of Confederation and Perpetual Union (1781–89) that provided for annual elections and limited members of the unicameral Congress to no more than three years of service during a six-year period.[36] In addition, a number of states and cities have had considerable experience with tenure restrictions as illustrated by a constitutional single four-year limit for the governor in Virginia and a city charter two-term limit for the Atlanta, Georgia, mayor.[37]

Currently, nineteen states have term limits for state legislators. All the limits, except the Utah statutory limit, were adopted by means of the initiative and referendum.[38] Courts in Massachusetts and Washington invalidated term limit statutes by opining that such a limit can be adopted only by a constitutional amendment. As explained in Chapter 3, California Proposition 140 of 1990 established a term limit for members of the state legislature and was upheld as constitutional when the U.S. Supreme Court in 1998 refused to hear an appeal from the decision of the U.S. Court of Appeals for the Ninth Circuit.[39]

The initiative has been employed in twenty-one states to limit the number of terms a member of Congress from each of these states can serve, and the Utah State Legislature enacted a term limit statute applicable to members of the state's congressional delegation. State term limits for members of congressional delegations are not binding, and only an amendment of the U.S. constitution could impose a limit. In 1995, the U.S. Supreme Court, by a five to four vote, invalidated section 3 of amendment 73 to the Arkansas constitution limiting representatives from the state to the U.S. House of Representatives and Senate to three terms and two terms, respectively.[40] Nevertheless, there is no U.S constitutional provision forbidding a state legislature or voters by means of the initiative or referendum processes from enacting a statute containing a moral obligation provision authorizing candidates to the U.S. House of Representatives and Senate to file a preprimary pledge to serve only a specified number of terms. The 1973 Arizona State Legislature enacted a statute containing a moral obligation resignation clause that authorizes candidates for seats in the U.S. Congress to file a preprimary pledge to resign their seats should they lose a recall election.[41]

The electorate in fourteen states in 1996 acted upon initiated propositions labeling candidates "for seats in Congress who did not pledge to seek a constitutional amendment establishing term limits for members of Congress."[42] Such propositions were approved in nine states — Alaska, Arkansas, Colorado, Idaho, Maine, Missouri, Nebraska, Nevada, and South Dakota — and rejected in five states — Montana, North Dakota, Oregon, Washington, and Wyoming.

Term limit initiatives support the hypothesis that legislative bodies seldom will adopt a major reform in the governance system affecting the direct interest of members. Critics of term limits, however, argue legislatures are making sound decisions in defeating term limit bills because they (1) make it difficult for members to gain sufficient experience to be effective lawmakers, (2) enhance the power position of the chief executive, (3) result in unhealthy staff influence over members, and (4) facilitate the effectiveness of lobbyists. Opponents also cited a 1997 survey — by the Council of State Governments of legislators, their staff, and government relations professionals — revealing approximately two-thirds of the persons surveyed reported legislators facing the maximum term limit in the next election are less accountable to constituents.[43]

In 1998, Henry Flores raised a new objection against municipal term limits by arguing a "high degree of racial polarization combined with a small pool of potential city council candidates makes term limitations a candidate for inclusion as a dilutive mechanism under section 5 of the VRA" [Voting Rights Act].[44] Flores is convinced that term limits are a barrier to the election of members of a racial minority to public office and reported the Texas cities included in his study that had been sued under the Voting

Rights Act had instituted term limits that appear to be a strategy "to prevent Hispanics from holding office for too long a term."[45]

Tax Limits

Voters in New England towns with the open town meeting always have had the direct opportunity to reject borrowing and spending proposals.[46] In 1842, Rhode Island voters amended their state constitution to include the first requirement for a referendum on proposed state government borrowing. This was followed by a number of other states whose constitutions stipulate that the state legislature can enact a conditional bill authorizing the borrowing of funds and pledging the full faith and credit of the government subject to a popular referendum. Furthermore, bond referenda are held in numerous municipalities under state or local charter requirements. California cities, counties, and school districts, for example, can issue general obligation bonds only if two-thirds of those casting ballots on the proposed borrowing give their consent.[47]

The West Virginia constitution stipulates political subdivisions can borrow funds or exceed constitutional tax limits only with an affirmative majority of 60 percent of the voters participating in a referendum. Based upon the U.S. Supreme Court's 1963 one-person, one-vote dictum employed to strike down legislative districts unequal in population, many observers assumed the court would extend its dictum to extra-majority affirmative vote requirements in borrowing and taxation referenda because a negative vote carries more weight than a positive vote.[48] The court in 1971, however, upheld the West Virginia constitutional requirement for an extra-majority approval requirement.[49] The court could not identify a section of the population that would be fenced out from the franchise by the votes they cast in such a referendum and opined that the extra-majority affirmative vote requirement was reasonable with respect to bond issues because the credit of children and unborn generations would be affected.

With the exceptions of the open town meetings in New England, the initiative was not employed on a regular basis to restrict state and local government spending until the 1970s. The success at the polls of California Proposition 13 on June 6, 1978, stimulated interest in the employment of the initiative to limit the property tax. Similar propositions were approved by Idaho and Nevada voters on November 8, 1978, and Massachusetts voters in 1980 sanctioned initiative Proposition $2\frac{1}{2}$. The California electorate in 1979 endorsed the Gann-sponsored Proposition 4, which limits increases in spending by the state and its political subdivisions to the percentage increase in the cost of living and population. Voters in

Anchorage, Alaska, in 1983, approved a proposal similar to the Gann's proposition.

The tax revolt began to lose momentum in the 1980s as Oregon voters in 1982 defeated initiated ballot Measure 3, which would have limited local property taxes to 1.5 percent of the full value of property in 1979. Ohio voters in 1983 defeated propositions to cut nearly in half the state income tax and require a three-fifths vote of each house of the state legislature to approve a tax increase.[50] In 1985, tax limitation initiatives were defeated in California, Louisiana, Michigan, Nevada, and Oregon.[51]

The Colorado electorate on November 3, 1992, approved an initiated proposition amending the state constitution by placing limits on income, property, and other taxes, and requiring voter approval for specified state and local tax increases. Similar initiative propositions over the previous twenty years failed to receive voter approval on seven occasions. Oklahoma voters, by a two to one margin, in 1996 rejected State Question 669, an initiative proposition designed to reduce property taxes to their 1993 levels and to allow property tax increases of up to 3 percent each year provided three-fifths of those voting on the proposed increased agreed.[52] However, Montana voters in 1998 approved a constitutional amendment forbidding the state legislature and counties and municipalities to increase taxes without voter approval.

Proposition 13. This proposition, a constitutional initiative, was sponsored by Howard A. Jarvis and Paul Gann. The former had been working actively to lower property taxes for fifteen years and stated in 1978 "government is the biggest growth industry in this country" and "the only way to cut the cost of government is not to give them money in the first place."[53] The latter commented: "The thing I am proudest of is that the voters have turned out and told the government that we have had enough. The government has tried to become uncle, mother, and father and we simply can not afford it any more."[54]

The most common explanations for the two-to-one affirmative vote for Proposition 13 are the sharp increase in the property tax, a highly visible tax, and voter distrust of government. David O. Sears and Jack Citrin maintained the early part of the Proposition 13 movement "incorporated important elements of a populist crusade against established political and economic institutions. . . . Whatever mass character the tax revolt possesses, then, appears to be largely a function of generalized political cynicism."[55]

This proposition stipulates "the maximum amount of any *ad valorem* tax on real property shall not exceed one percent (1%) of the full cash value of such property."[56] However, the restriction does "not apply to *ad valorem* taxes or special assessments to pay the interest and redemption charges of any indebtedness approved by the voters prior to the time this section becomes effective."[57] Furthermore, Proposition 13 permits the reassessment of property only when it is sold.

The authority of the state legislature to levy taxes also is limited by the proposition. Changes in tax laws designed to increase revenues require the approval of two-thirds of all members elected to each house. No new real property tax or property sales transaction taxes, however, can be levied. Cities, counties, and special districts also are restricted in their taxing power as they, "by a two-thirds vote of the qualified electors of such district, may impose special taxes on such district, except *ad valorem* taxes on real property or a transaction tax or sales tax on the sale of real property within such city, county, or special district."[58]

Relatively minor amendments to the proposition were made by Proposition 8 (November 7, 1978), Proposition 7 (November 4, 1980), and Proposition 3 (June 9, 1982). These amendments deal with assessment of property and the definition of the term change of ownership of property.

In 1978, the California Supreme Court upheld the constitutionality of Proposition 13.[59] Proponents, however, have been disturbed by several court decisions. In 1979, the California Court of Appeals ruled the 1 percent tax limitation on property taxes does not apply to various special assessments authorized by state law.[60] The following year, the same court held that special taxes referred to in Proposition 13 do not include fees for various land use regulatory activities."[61] In 1981, the California Court of Appeals opined a City of Oxnard ordinance levying a school impact fee was not a prohibited "special tax."[62]

The California Supreme Court in 1982 upheld the imposition of a sales tax levied by the Los Angeles County Transportation Commission and approved by 54 percent of the voters in 1980 on the ground the sales tax was adopted by a body lacking the authority to impose property taxes and that was not seeking to replace lost property tax revenues.[63] Hence, the sales tax imposition did not violate the provision of Proposition 13 banning the levy of a special tax by a special district without the affirmative vote of two-thirds of the qualified electors. Critics charged that the series of court decisions weaken the effectiveness of Proposition 13. Harly Cole, vice president of the American Tax Reduction Movement and an associate of Howard Jarvis, described the decision as "an end run," and predicted "they'll come up with special taxes for police and fire protection in high-crime areas."[64] In common with Massachusetts Proposition 2½, described in a subsequent section, Proposition 13 has had intended and unintended effects.

Although the property tax revenues of local governments decreased by approximately $7 billion during the first year Proposition 13 was in effect, local governments were not affected as dramatically as had been predicted for two major reasons. First, municipalities reduced personnel and relied more heavily upon user charges to raise revenues. Second, the state government distributed in excess of $4 billion of its approximately $7 billion surplus to local governments. This loss of revenue, because of the limit placed upon the property tax, was reduced to approximately $3 billion. In the period to June 1984, the state government distributed $32 billion in extra financial assistance to local governments.[65] Furthermore, the statewide revenue total produced by the property tax increased relatively sharply after the approval of the proposition because of new construction. This proposition also created an equity problem in real property taxation because property can be reassessed only when it is sold, which results in new owners paying more in property taxes than long-term owners.

Unintended consequences include the levying of new user charges and the increasing of existing user charges. Cities and towns in parts of the state have been imposing fees of up to $25,000 per unit on developers of homes and business buildings.[66] The fees are factored into mortgages and are used to finance new streets, schools, sewer and water lines, and other infrastructure facilities. A corollary effect has been the great reliance placed upon special district governments to provide services. These governments typically are not subject to the same degree of voter control as municipalities.

The supporters of Proposition 13, particularly Mr. Gans, were conservatives favoring broader discretionary authority for local governments. An unintended consequence has been the increased state government control of education, with approximately 90 percent of the funds coming from the state. Rural counties, mandated by the state to provide many services — medical, criminal justice, and welfare are examples — have lost much of their discretionary authority and have become heavily dependent upon state financial assistance.[67]

The U.S. Supreme Court in 1992 opined that Proposition 13 does not violate the equal protection of the laws clause of the Fourteenth Amendment to the U.S. Constitution and makes no distinction between the two classes of property owners with respect to the tax rate and the annual assessments adjustment rates.[68] The court noted the proposition makes a distinction between the two classes of property owners only with respect to the initial assessment of their respective properties but offered the following rationale for the constitutionality of the difference:

First, the State has a legitimate interest in local neighborhood preservation, continuity, and stability. . . . The State therefore legitimately can decide to structure its tax system to discourage rapid turnover in ownership of homes.

Second, the State legitimately can conclude that a new owner at the time of acquiring his property does not have the same reliance interest warranting protection against higher taxes as does an existing owner. The State may deny a new owner at the point of purchase the right to "lock in" to the same assessed value as is enjoyed by an existing owner of comparable property because an existing owner rationally may be thought to have vested expectations in his property or home that are more deserving of protection than the anticipatory expectations of a new owner at the point of purchase.[69]

Proposition 2^1/$_2$. The general property tax rates in Massachusetts were 70 percent higher than the national average in the late 1970s, and citizen concern with the tax had been increasing for many years. In 1978, voters approved, by a three to one margin, an advisory referendum proposition that the General Court (state legislature) should act to reduce property taxes, increase state aid to cities and towns, and limit increases in state and local taxes.

In 1980, Citizens for Limited Taxation secured the necessary signatures to place Proposition 2^1/$_2$ on the November referendum ballot, and the electorate, by nearly a three to two margin, approved the proposition that sought to reduce property taxes by an average of 40 percent for a total of approximately $385 million effective January 1, 1981. The state government, in contrast to California, did not have a budgetary surplus.

The proposition is named after its major provision limiting the municipal general property tax levy to 2.5 percent of the full and fair cash value of property located in a city or town. In 1980, approximately one-third of the cities and towns were assessing property at full and fair cash value even though a 1971 Supreme Judicial Court decision required assessment at 100 percent of full and fair cash value.[70]

If the property tax levy exceeds 2.5 percent in a city or town, the levy must be decreased by 15 percent annually until the allowable maximum is reached. A total of 182 of the Commonwealth's 351 cities and towns exceeded the limit and generally were the larger municipalities. If the rate was below 2.5 percent, the rate was lowered to the 1979 level, and future increases were restricted to 2.5 percent annually. The 2.5 percent limit could be exceeded by a two-thirds vote of the local electorate provided the

General Court placed the override question on a state election ballot in a city or town.

The General Court in 1981 approved a bill amending Proposition 2½.[71] Effective July 1, 1982, the board of selectmen or council in a town and a city council by a two-thirds vote can place on the referendum ballot at any time the question whether the 2.5 percent limit should be exceeded.

A two-thirds vote of the electorate is required for approval of the question only if the referendum proposal is to override the limit by more than 2.5 percent or a total exceeding 5 percent. In other cases, only a majority vote is required. In addition, only a majority vote is required to reduce the 15 percent reduction in the general property tax rate in one year to 7.5 percent in cities and towns exceeding the 2.5 percent limit. Under no circumstances, however, can a city or town under the 2.5 percent cap exceed the cap in any given year. To date, town voters have been reluctant to override the limit established by the initiative proposition.

Proposition 2½ rapidly achieved its major objective as the revenue raised by the general property tax decreased from 43 to 32 percent between 1975 and 1982.[72] In part, the reduction was due to increased state financial assistance that enabled cities and towns to reduce their spending cuts, as required by the proposition, by nearly 50 percent. The major spending cuts were made in the area of capital improvements.

Cities and towns have become more dependent upon state financial assistance with a consequent loss of some local discretionary authority. Mayor Carlton M. Viveiros of Fall River, for example, stated in 1989 "we are now essentially a creature of the state."[73]

In towns with a general property tax rate near the maximum allowable rate, the ability of the town meeting attendee to influence spending decisions has been curtailed greatly and the influence of the finance committee increased correspondingly. In order to win support for spending exceeding the financial committee's recommendations or to add an item to the committee's budget, a citizen or citizen group must convince the meeting to delete an item(s) from the committee's recommended budget. Some selectmen complain the finance committee has been attempting to act as a "super board of selectmen."

The Association of Town Finance Committees recognized the adverse impact of Proposition 2½ on the town meeting in many towns and offered the following advice to its members.

To repeal sage counsel — try not to recommend a budget which presses all the way to the levy limit. This results in a budget so rigid that no item can be increased unless one or several inoffensive items are cut an equivalent amount.

The voter who favors such an increase must either get in his licks before the budget is set in stone, find a soft spot in the budget or, more likely, give up and stay silent or even stay home. The town meeting will still have zoning and nonfinancial matters to consider but attendance will suffer badly unless there is some leeway for town meeting fiscal action. Perhaps 1 percent or 2 percent of the levy will be enough slack so that its appropriation will be worth the time and attention of a quorum.[74]

Cigarette Excise Tax

The initiative can be viewed by many citizens as an anti-tax weapon in the light of Proposition 13 and its progeny, yet California Proposition 10 of 1998 raised the state excise tax on a package of cigarettes by $0.50 to $0.87.[75]

The sponsors of the proposition were movie director Rob Reiner, a conservative Democrat, movie actor Charlton Heston, and Republican millionaire Michael Huffington. Reiner has little in common with the other two regarding numerous issues and policies, but teamed up with them to enable the state to raise funds for early childhood development and prenatal care programs and to discourage smoking by teenagers.[76]

Proponents, who spent approximately $7.8 million, were outspent by tobacco industry expenditures of $28.5 million.[77] The tobacco industry waged an aggressive campaign and used the same arguments it employed against a proposed 1998 national settlement of suits brought by forty state attorneys general against five large tobacco firms — the tax increase adds to the regressiveness of the existing state tobacco excise tax and burdens low income and minority groups.[78] The proposition was approved.

Homosexual Rights

Colorado voters in 1992 endorsed proposed constitutional amendment 2 barring special legal protections for homosexuals. The amendment was stimulated by ordinances adopted in several cities — including Aspen, Boulder, and Denver — banning discrimination on the basis of sexual orientation. The proposition was challenged immediately. The Colorado District Court for the City and County of Denver issued a permanent injunction enjoining enforcement of the amendment, and its decision was affirmed by the Colorado Supreme Court.[79]

On appeal, the U.S. Supreme Court in 1996, by a six to three vote, held the proposition violated the equal protection of the laws clause of the Fourteenth Amendment to the U.S. Constitution and rejected the argument the amendment "does no more than deny homosexuals special rights."[80]

In 1998, however, the U.S. Supreme Court denied a petition for the issuance of a writ of certiorari relative to a 1997 decision of the U.S. Court of Appeals for the Sixth Circuit upholding as constitutional an initiated Cincinnati city charter amendment denying gay persons and lesbians any special legal rights.[81] The group that sponsored Issue 3 on the 1993 Cincinnati referendum ballot was Equal Rights, Not Special Rights. Issue 3 stipulates:

The City of Cincinnati and its various Boards and Commissions may not enact, adopt, enforce, or administer any ordinance, regulation, rule, or policy which provides that homosexual, lesbian, or bisexual orientation status, conduct, or relationship constitutes, entitles, or otherwise provides a person with the basis to have any claim of minority or protected status, quota preference, or other preferential treatment. This provision of the City Charter shall in all respects be self-executing. Any ordinance, regulation, rule or policy enacted before this amendment is adopted that violates the foregoing prohibition shall be null and void and of no force or effect.

On the surface, the Supreme Court's denial of the petition for issuance of a writ of certiorari suggests the court was reversing its 1996 Colorado decision. Justice Stevens, in an unusual action, issued an opinion emphasizing that the denial of the petition should not be interpreted as a ruling on the merits of the issues in the case. He explained;

Sometimes such an order reflects nothing more than a conclusion that a particular case may not constitute an appropriate forum in which to decide a significant issue. In this case, the Sixth Circuit held that the city charter "merely removed municipally enacted special protection from gays and lesbians." This construction differs significantly, although perhaps not dispositively, from the reading advocated by the petitioners. They construe the charter as an enactment that "bars antidiscrimination protections only for gay, lesbian, and bisexual citizens."

This Court does not normally make an independent examination of state law questions that have been resolved by a court of appeals. . . . Thus, the confusion over the proper construction of the city charter counsels against granting the petition for certiorari. The Court's actions . . . should not be interpreted either as an independent construction of the charter or as an expression of its views about the underlying issues that the parties have debated at length.[82]

On November 3, 1998, Colorado voters rejected a proposition that would grant homosexuals civil rights protection against discrimination.

Undocumented Immigrants

California voters, by 59 percent to 41 percent, approved Proposition 187 of 1994 denying a range of state social services benefits, including education and health care, to undocumented immigrants, which cost the state an estimated $3 billion annually.[83] The constitutionality of the proposition was challenged almost immediately in the U.S. District Court by the American Civil Liberties Union of Southern California, Mexican-American Legal Defense and Education Fund, and other organizations. U.S. District Court Judge Mariana R. Pfaelzer issued a preliminary injunction and in 1997 opined that the key provisions of the proposition were invalid because of constitutional flaws and its supersession by national immigration statutes and regulations.[84] Governor Pete Wilson included approval of Proposition 187 in his reelection campaign platform and expressed his dismay with the court decision.

In 1998, Judge Pfaelzer reconfirmed her earlier decision and ruled the Personal Responsibility and Work Opportunity Reconciliation Act of 1996 by denying welfare benefits to illegal immigrants that made it clear a state legislature or voters could not enact a statute regulating immigration.[85] The only provisions of Proposition 187 the judge did not invalidate related to criminal penalties for the manufacture, use, and sale of documents concealing an individual's immigration status. Governor Wilson announced the decision would be appealed to the U.S. Court of Appeals for the Ninth Circuit.

Assisted Suicide

Americans Against Human Suffering was organized in 1986 to promote enactment of laws allowing physician-assisted suicide and, in 1992, qualified an initiative proposition for the California ballot that was rejected (54 percent to 46 percent) by the electorate.

Oregon voters approved (51 percent to 49 percent) a 1994 initiative petition — Death with Dignity Act — allowing physician-assisted suicide for terminally ill persons. The proposition was challenged by four medical doctors, a nonprofit organization, and three terminally ill persons, who feared they might be persuaded to commit suicide.

To take advantage of the law, a medical doctor must conclude that a terminally ill person has less than six months to live, and the person must make a written request, witnessed by two persons, for suicide medication. A second physician decides whether the patient is mentally competent. The patient making the written request also must orally request the prescription.

Judge Michael R. Hogan of the U.S. District Court issued a preliminary injunction against the enforcement of the initiated statute and subsequently held the law was unconstitutional because there were inadequate safeguards to protect mentally incompetent, terminally ill persons.[86] On February 27, 1997, the U.S. Court of Appeals for the Ninth Circuit dismissed the lawsuit on the ground the plaintiffs lacked standing.[87] The U.S. Supreme Court on October 14, 1997, rejected an appeal of the decision of the appellate court.[88] Earlier in 1997, the Supreme Court opined there was no constitutional right to die and upheld the validity of a Washington state statute prohibiting assisted suicide against the charge the statute violated the due process of law clause of the Fourteenth Amendment to the U.S. Constitution.[89]

The 1997 Oregon State Legislature decided to place the question of the repeal of the Death with Dignity Act on the November 4, 1997, referendum ballot. A major campaign was launched by the Roman Catholic Church, which spent close to $2 million to persuade voters to repeal the law, and repeal opponents spent approximately $600,000.[90] The electorate (60 percent to 40 percent) decided not to repeal the initiated proposition.[91]

Michigan voters on November 3, 1998, rejected Proposition B that would have legalized physician-assisted suicide.

Medical Use of Marijuana

The Alaska Supreme Court in 1975 interpreted the state constitutional guarantee of privacy rights as allowing the possession of up to four ounces of cannabis or marijuana in a home for personal use, but the initiative was used in 1990 to amend the constitution and reverse the court's decision by a 55 percent to 45 percent margin. On November 3, 1998, Alaskan voters utilized the initiative again to legalize the use of marijuana for medical purposes and were joined by voters in Arizona, Nevada, Oregon, and Washington who approved similar initiative propositions.[92] The Washington electorate had rejected an identical proposition in 1997. Federal law, however, does not allow such use.

In 1996, Arizona voters approved Proposition 200 and California voters approved Proposition 215 legalizing the use of marijuana for medical purposes. The California Medical Association supported the proposition as did multimillionaire George Soros and his foundation. Proponents spent a large sum for an advertising campaign appealing to the compassion of the electorate for ill persons. Governor Pete Wilson earlier vetoed two bills enacted by the state legislature legalizing the medical use of marijuana.

The 1997 Arizona State Legislature enacted statutes that effectively repealed the initiative proposition. The state's voters in 1998, however, approved two initiated propositions restoring the language of the 1996 proposition. Similarly, the 1997 Oregon State Legislature made possession of marijuana a criminal offense, but voters in 1998, by a two to one margin, reduced possession of cannabis to a violation and approved a second initiated proposition authorizing the medical use of marijuana.

General Barry R. McCaffrey, Director of the Office of National Drug Control Policy, made an indirect reference to Mr. Soros by stating before a Senate Committee "there is a carefully camouflaged, exorbitantly funded well-heeled elitist group whose ultimate goal is to legalize drug use in the United States."[93] Commenting on the November 3, 1998, voter approval of marijuana initiative proposals in five states, he stressed the initiatives "in no way alter the status of marijuana under federal laws."[94]

Affirmative Action

African-American businessman Ward Connerly headed the successful drive that collected approximately 1.1 million signatures to place Proposition 209 — a proposed constitutional amendment — on the November 5, 1996, California ballot. The proposition forbids the state government or a local government to "discriminate against or grant preferential treatment to any individual or group on the basis of race, sex, color, ethnicity, or national origin" and was endorsed by a 54 percent to 46 percent margin.

Connerly has been described as a moderate Republican who is conservative on economic issues and liberal on social ones. Governor Pete Wilson appointed Connerly to the Board of Regents of the University of California and he investigated racial preferences in the university system. Connerly explained: "I used to believe affirmative action involved widening the pool of applicants so that the best person could be selected. What I found is that these programs amount to pure racial nepotism — the functional equivalent of quotas."[95]

The initiative campaign was a highly charged emotional one with name calling a prominent feature. Connerly was disturbed greatly by a newspaper cartoon depicting him dressed in a Ku Klux Klan robe while burning a church with the caption "Connerly and Company, Ethnic Cleansers."[96] Opponents of the proposition sought and obtained a U.S. District Court preliminary injunction preventing enforcement of the proposition. On appeal, the U.S. Court of Appeals for the Ninth Circuit rejected the lower court's conclusion that the plaintiffs demonstrated a probability of success on their equal protection of the law claim and their claim that the proposition was preempted by Title VII of the *Civil Rights Act of 1964*.[97] The

U.S. Supreme Court on November 3, 1997, rejected a petition for the issuance of a writ of certiorari and did not rule on the merits of the case.[98]

A group of voters in Washington State in 1998 employed the initiative process to place a similar ban on affirmative action programs on the November 3, 1998, ballot. In common with the California campaign, the Washington state campaign was a highly emotional one that ended with voters (58 percent to 42 percent) approving the proposition.

Proposition opponents included national civil rights leaders Julian Bond and Jesse L. Jackson, who came to the state to urge the electorate to retain the affirmative action programs. Governor Gary Locke, a Chinese American and a Democrat, maintained the proposition would "hurt real people."[99] Other critics attempted to explain the major beneficiaries of such programs were not minorities but women. Following the approval of the Washington proposition, Connerly announced he would promote a similar initiative proposition in Arizona, Michigan, or Nebraska.

Bilingual Education

The large influx of non–English-speaking immigrants in recent years generated pressure for the establishment of bilingual education programs to ensure immigrant students would become proficient in core subjects while increasing gradually their skill in the use of the English language. Proponents of such programs assert it is exceptionally difficult for students to learn core subjects simultaneously with their efforts to learn English.

The failure of large numbers of students in bilingual programs to make significant progress in schools led to a reaction in the form of a movement for English-only instruction. Douglas Lasken, a fifth-grade teacher of non-native English speakers in Los Angeles wrote an op-ed article for *The New York Times* in which he noted he had "watched hundreds of Spanish-speaking children, fully capable of mastering English within a year, denied meaningful English instruction" because "everything is taught in Spanish" and a "mere 90 minutes a day is allocated for English in Los Angeles Schools."[100]

Ron Unz, a political conservative and multimillionaire, organized "English for the Children," whose objective is to terminate most state financial support for bilingual education. His group collected the required 433,000 petition signatures to place Proposition 227 on the June 2, 1998, California primary election ballot. The proposition had broad support in the Hispanic community due in part to Fernando Vega, a Latino leader, who agreed to be honorary chairman of the campaign.

Voters approved the proposition by a two to one majority, and schools were faced with dismantling bilingual education programs and preparing to offer all courses overwhelming in English, with limited exceptions, commencing in September 1998. Proposition 227 directs schools to offer intensive English instruction for students with little skill in the English language for a period of one year.[101] Furthermore, parents are provided with three choices for their children: (1) intensive English, (2) regular classes taught in English, or (3) request a waiver to allow their children to continue in bilingual classes. Complicating the implementation of the proposition are court desegregation orders in San Francisco and San Jose requiring courses to be bilingual.[102]

Gambling

As noted in a preceding section, gambling often was the topic of initiative propositions during the early years of the participatory device. Today, gambling remains a common initiative proposition. Voters in seven states on November 5, 1996, were given the opportunity to decide whether specific types of gambling should be legal in their respective states.[103]

Arkansas voters in 1964 and 1984 rejected casino gambling propositions and in 1996 rejected a proposed constitutional amendment authorizing three casinos in Hot Springs, bingo, and a lottery. Proponents, including the owner of the Hot Springs horse track, spent approximately six times the amount spent by opponents. The bulk of the opponents' funds were donated by Mississippi casinos, which did not want competition from Arkansas casinos.

In 1996, Governor George V. Voinovich of Ohio was a leader in the successful campaign to reject a proposal permitting operation of eight riverboat casinos by organizing the support of many businessmen, churches, and educators. Colorado and Nebraska voters rejected proposals allowing a limited expansion of gambling, but voters in Arizona and West Virginia approved similar proposals. Michigan voters, by a 3 percent margin, approved casinos for Detroit. The proposition was supported by Mayor Dennis Archer as a counter attraction to a new casino in nearby Ontario province.

In 1998, Missouri voters sanctioned proposed constitutional amendment 9 — "Boats in Moats" — as additional sites for gambling on riverboats authorized by voters in 1992.[104] Gambling interests spent more than $8 million to promote the proposition as a result of a 1997 Missouri Supreme Court decision that games of chance could be offered on riverboats only in the main channel of a river. The proposition amended the constitutional definition of a river to include "artificial spaces that contain water and that are within 1000 feet" of a river. Failure of voters to approve the proposal would have resulted in eleven of fifteen casinos losing their licenses to operate games of chance, including slot machines that are major revenue generators. Casino operators maintained there was heavy boat traffic on the rivers that often flooded and the safety of passengers would be placed in jeopardy if the riverboats cruise on the rivers.

Congress enacted the Indian Gaming Regulatory Act of 1988, which classifies gaming on Indian reservations as Class I, II, and III.[105] Class I games are social ones conducted for prizes of low value and are part of tribal celebrations and ceremonies. Tribal governments regulate Class II games, such as bingo and lotto, with oversight by the National Indian Gaming Commission. Class III games are regulated by concerned state and tribal governments under provisions of a state-tribal compact negotiated by tribal leaders with the state governor. More than 100 tribal-state compacts, involving 19 states and 78 tribes, have been negotiated.

Governor Pete Wilson of California refused to negotiate a compact with any Indian tribe that engaged in slot machine gambling on their reservations. In the spring of 1998 he reached an agreement on a gambling compact with the Pala Band of Mission Indians authorizing video slot machine gambling but forbidding their use by gambling tribes currently using the machines.[106] Subsequently, the compact was approved by the state legislature in August 1998, and ten additional tribes signed the compact limiting each tribe to a total of 199 video slot machines.

The bulk of the Indian tribes complained that the governor did not negotiate with the tribes in good faith and worked to place Proposition 5 on the November 3, 1998, ballot mandating the state must enter into a compact allowing use of slot machines on any reservation if the Indian tribe desires to use such machines. The California Labor Federation, United Farm Workers, church groups, and Nevada casinos, which feared competition from such gambling would reduce their revenues, opposed the proposition. The proposition was approved (63% to 37%) and campaign expenditures for and against the initiative proposition were approximately $95 million, 64 percent higher than the previous record.[107]

Gun Control

The National Rifle Association and other gun organizations have exercised considerable influence in Congress and blunted efforts to enact strict gun control statutes. A federal system of government allows individual states to take action to solve a problem if congressional action is inadequate or not taken, provided state actions are not preempted by the U.S. Constitution, statutes, or court decisions.[108]

Gun control advocates in 1997 decided to focus on toughening state laws and organized an initiative campaign to place Proposition 676 on the November 4, 1997, referendum ballot in the State of Washington. The proposition would require safety tests for owners of handguns to obtain a license and trigger locks on all new and used handguns offered for sale.

The National Rifle Association mobilized its approximately 80,000 members in the state, spent approximately $3.5 million for billboard and television advertising, and called upon its prominent members, such as movie actor Charlton Heston, for assistance. Opponents argued the initiative was an attack on the personal freedom of citizens and the right to bear arms guaranteed by the Second Amendment to the U.S. Constitution, and would make it extremely difficult for the owners of handguns to defend themselves against an intruder who enters their homes because of the time required to remove the trigger lock.[109] Many police organizations opposed the proposition because of added duties that would be imposed on police, including record keeping.

Proposition supporters, primarily Washington Citizens for Handgun Safety and National Handgun Control, Inc., argued that the trigger locks would prevent the accidental deaths of children; 30 children were killed and 211 were injured by firearms in the state in the period 1991–95.[110] Proponents spent less than $1 million in their campaign to convince voters to approve the proposition.

The proposed measure was defeated by a large margin, and the defeat was attributed in part to the proposition's complexity with two dozen provisions and the failure to secure the support of most law-enforcement organizations that were highlighted by the National Rifle Association.[111]

Campaign Finance

The failure of the U.S. Congress to enact a rigorous campaign finance statute and the U.S. Supreme Court decisions striking down campaign finance reform statutes and ordinances generated increased support for public financing of election campaigns of candidates agreeing to limit their expenditures.

Maine voters on November 5, 1996, approved an initiated proposition providing for a system of public financing of election campaigns, and the 1997 Vermont State Legislature enacted a similar law.[112] The Arizona electorate on November 3, 1998, endorsed Proposition 200 establishing public financing of elections, and the Massachusetts electorate sanctioned Proposition 2 establishing a similar system.

A major argument employed by opponents of such initiatives is the cost of the program to taxpayers. The Arizona proposition negated this argument by increasing the registration fee of lobbyists from $25 to $100, adding a 20 percent surcharge to civil and criminal fines, and dedicating the revenue to financing the program. The proposition also provides for a voluntary checkoff on the income tax returns of taxpayers and public financing for candidates for state offices receiving a specified number of $5 contributions provided they agree to accept voluntary campaign spending limits.

Massachusetts Proposition 2 of 1998 — the Clean Elections Initiative — provides for public financing of campaigns by means of state legislative appropriations and the voluntary checkoff on income tax returns. Opponents estimated the proposition will cost taxpayers $56 million over a four-year period and proponents responded by indicating the appropriation of public funds is limited to 0.1 percent of state appropriations or approximately $4 per year for each taxpayer. A very important provision of Proposition 2 prohibits the transfer of funds (soft money) from a national political party to its state party.

In a related action, California voters on June 2, 1998, rejected (53 percent to 47 percent) Proposition 226, which would allow the deduction of union dues from a worker's paycheck for political purposes only with the annual written permission of the member.[113]

LOCAL INITIATIVE PROPOSITIONS

As noted in Chapter 1, local government voters first were authorized to use the initiative by the 1898 voter-approved San Francisco charter. Many early and current initiative propositions appearing on local government referendum ballots mirror propositions appearing on state referendum ballots, but there are significant differences.

North Carolina lacks a constitutional or statutory provision empowering all local government voters to employ the initiative, but the state legislature authorized voters in ten cities to place propositions on the referendum ballot; six special acts exclude the annual budget from the initiative.[114] Greensboro voters employed the device in 1946 to place on the ballot a proposition forbidding the city council to sell a site initially intended as a war memorial and dedicating the site to public use. The proposal was rejected by a vote of 1,361 to 1,123. Twelve years later, the initiative was utilized to place the question of fluoridation of the drinking water supply on the ballot, but the measure was defeated by a vote of 7,441 to 5,013. In 1989, the device was used successfully to enact, by a vote of 14,991 to 14,818, an ordinance restricting smoking in public places. Two years later, union workers at cigarette manufacturing plants placed on the ballot a proposed ordinance making compliance with the smoking restriction ordinance voluntary instead of mandatory. The proposal was rejected overwhelmingly by a vote of 1,871 in favor to 9,585 in opposition.

The indirect initiative was employed by group of Raleigh voters in 1982 who presented to the city council a petition signed by more than 18,000 registered voters directing the city manager to petition annually the President of the United States to propose to the Soviet Union a nuclear arms freeze. The council approved the proposal. A second indirect initiative petition achieved its purpose in 1982 when the city council enacted an ordinance opening the process of selecting a cable television franchiser to competition, including a group of local investors. In 1991, an initiative proposal appeared on the ballot that would prohibit construction of a proposed 1.4-mile extension of a major city boulevard. The measure was defeated by a narrow margin.

A group of Wilmington voters in 1982 collected the required number of signatures to place on the referendum ballot a proposed zoning ordinance prohibiting coal transfer facilities in light manufacturing zones. The proposition was approved by a vote of 3,239 to 1,799. Voters in 1984 presented more than 11,000 signatures on petitions to the city council calling for the repeal of the Sunday closing ordinance, and the council enacted such a repeal.

A dispute over the awarding of a community antenna television system in Asheville in 1967 involved a franchise agreement, between the city and a community antenna television provider, which the council placed on the March referendum ballot. A competing provider successfully led a campaign against the agreement and subsequently circulated petitions to place its own franchise agreement on the referendum ballot. The electorate approved the proposition granting the franchise for a period of thirty-five years.

The Morganton City Council in 1986 decided not to renew its expiring twenty-year cable television franchise with the current operator and to provide the service directly. The operator unsuccessfully brought lawsuits in U.S. and state courts and subsequently decided to place on the ballot, via the initiative, the awarding of a new franchise to the operator. Voters rejected the proposal.

Rapid growth of suburban municipalities induced a movement to adopt new zoning ordinances to limit building permits to slow the rate of growth. Voters in the City of Livermore, California, on April 11, 1972, approved an initiative ordinance that found the excessive issuance of residential building permits had resulted in sewage pollution, school overcrowding, and water rationing, and prohibited issuance of permits until specified standards were met relating to educational, sewage disposal, and water supply facilities.[115]

The initiated ordinance was challenged by an association of home builders and Judge Lyles E. Cook of the Superior Court for Alameda County issued an injunction enjoining enforcement of the ordinance. The state supreme court reversed the lower court decision and ruled that state statutes requiring notice and a hearing prior to enactment of municipal zoning and land use ordinances do not apply to initiated ordinances incorporating standards, and the ordinance was not unconstitutionally vague. A 1987 study of initiated California growth control measures in the period 1971–86 identified 106 and noted the use of such initiative propositions was increasing annually.[116]

Napa County, California, voters endorsed an initiative proposition that seeks to preserve agricultural land and allows amendments only by the voters. Opponents challenged the constitutionality of the proposition on the ground it frustrates the purposes of the state planning law because the county legislative body is powerless to amend or repeal the initiative. The California Supreme Court rejected this argument and upheld the use of the initiative to amend general plans because of the constitutional right of voters to employ the initiative and the large state grant of authority to general-purpose local governments to regulate land use.[117]

The trend involving use of the initiative to enact growth control ordinances continued in 1998 as voters in local governments approved close to 200 such propositions.[118] To cite only one example, Ventura County, California, voters approved a proposition removing from the board of supervisors the authority to approve new subdivisions and making each proposed subdivision subject to a referendum.

In 1993, the electorate in four Oregon counties — Douglas, Josephine, Klamath, and Linn — and two towns — Canby and Linn — endorsed initiative propositions prohibiting the concerned governments from promoting homosexuality and laws designed to protect gays and lesbians from discrimination. The following year, the electorate in Austin, Texas, approved Proposition 22 that amended the city charter and reversed a city ordinance extending insurance benefits to domestic partners of city employees by limiting benefits to husbands, wives, and other immediate relatives of city employees.

New York City voters in 1993 approved (60 percent to 40 percent) an initiative proposition limiting city elected officers to two terms or a total of eight years.[119] The measure, sponsored by New Yorkers for Term

Limits, was designed to ensure elected officers serving in 1993 would be required to leave office on December 31, 2001.

A conservative group in Houston, Texas, used wording in the Civil Rights Act of 1964 to frame an initiative proposition and succeeded in collecting the required 20,000 petition signatures to place the proposition on the November 4, 1997, ballot. Proposition A stipulated: "The City of Houston shall not discriminate against, or grant preferential treatment of an individual or group on the basis of race, sex, color, ethnicity, or national origin in the operation of public employment and public contracting." Public opinion polls indicated 70 percent of the interviewees favored the proposition.[120]

Proposition A was opposed by Mayor Bob Lanier and the majority of the city council members. The council changed the ballot language to: "Shall the charter of the City of Houston be amended to end the use of affirmative action for women and minorities in the operation of City of Houston employment and contracting, including ending the current program and similar programs in the future?" On referendum day, voters rejected (55 percent to 45 percent) the reworded proposition. Edward Blum, a businessman, spearheaded the drive to collect signatures to place Proposition A on the ballot and commented after the referendum "the language was so misleading and frightening and confusing that that, in our opinion, was the primary reason we lost."[121]

A supporter of the original Proposition A challenged the validity of the referendum in view of the city council's rewording of the proposition. In July 1998, a Texas District Court judge agreed with the contention of the plaintiff and nullified the referendum on the ground the rewording of the proposition by the city council did not represent accurately the proposed city charter amendment.[122]

Voters in thirty-three of Louisiana's sixty-four parishes (counties) in 1996 rejected video poker propositions but approved casinos for New Orleans and riverboats.

The Cleveland (Ohio) Teachers Union and other opponents of tax abatements charged they were diverting approximately $10 million annually from public schools and launched a drive to collect signatures on initiative petitions to place on the referendum ballot in 1997 Issue 1, which would require tax abatement recipients or the city government to pay the Cleveland School District the share of the abatement that in its absence would have been received by the district.[123]

The opposition to the proposal was led by Mayor Michael White who maintained tax abatements had preserved jobs for city residents and resulted in a strong city tax base. *The Plain Dealer* and *Crain's Cleveland*

Business also opposed the proposition. Only 13 percent of the registered voters participated in the August referendum and the proposal was defeated (58 percent to 42 percent).

South Portland, Maine, voters on November 3, 1998, approved an initiated ordinance banning discrimination based on sexual orientation, but similar measures were defeated in the City of Fayetteville, Arkansas, City of Fort Collins, Colorado, and Town of Ogunquit, Maine.[124] Neighbors in the Town of Newport, Maine, were disturbed by a woman who mowed her lawn without wearing a shirt and employed the initiative to place a proposed ordinance on the November 3, 1998, referendum ballot subjecting women who display their breasts in public to punishment.[125] The proposal was rejected.

SUMMARY

This review of selected state and local government initiative propositions appearing on referendum ballots since 1904 reveals that this participatory instrument is an important tool used by reformers in several states and numerous local governments to bring proposed solutions to public problems to the electorate for their determination. There has been a significant change in topics over the years although certain topics — such as campaign finance and gambling — have appeared regularly on the referendum ballot since 1908. Certain initiative propositions in recent years — physician-assisted suicide, special rights for homosexuals — have involved new moral issues and other propositions — affirmative action — have involved minority rights.

Proponents of the initiative frequently fault the state legislature for failing to enact needed reforms. One must agree that the legislature should have tightened campaign finance statutes, provided relief for homeowners from the inequitable property tax, and taken other actions. Nevertheless, it is difficult to fault a state legislature for refusing to enact a statute legalizing the use of marijuana for medicinal purposes and physician-assisted suicide.

One of the greatest concerns raised by the initiative in states with a large population, California in particular, is the excessive sums paid to professional signature-gathering firms, political consultants, and radio and television stations to promote the approval or rejection of specific propositions. U.S. Supreme Court decisions unfortunately prevent a state legislature or local government legislative body to establish reasonable campaign expenditure limits (see Chapter 3).

Chapter 5 evaluates the initiative as a participatory instrument by examining in detail the arguments of the proponents and opponents.

NOTES

1. Eugene C. Lee, "The Initiative Boom: An Excess of Democracy" in Gerald C. Lubenow and Bruce E. Cain, eds., *Governing California* (Berkeley, CA: Institute of Governmental Studies Press, 1997), pp. 6–8.

2. *Ibid.*, p. 8.

3. Tina Curatolo and Jason Teel, "Want to Pass an Initiative?" *Public Affairs Report*, July 1998, p. 15.

4. *Ibid.*, p. 16.

5. *Ibid.*

6. David McCuan, Shaun Bowler, Todd Donovan, and Ken Fernandez, "California's Political Warriors: Campaign Professionals and the Initiative Process" in Shaun Bowler, Todd Donovan, and Carolina J. Tolbert, eds., *Citizens as Legislators: Direct Democracy in the United States* (Columbus: Ohio State University Press, 1998), pp. 55–79.

7. Eugene C. Lee, "The Initiative Process in California," a paper presented at the 84th National Conference on Government, Louisville, Kentucky, November 12–15, 1978, p. 9.

8. Michael deCourcy Hinds, "Frustrated Governors Bypass Legislators with Voter Initiatives," *The New York Times*, October 16, 1992, p. A10.

9. Mary L. Vellinga, "Initiative Races' Tab : $200 Million," *Sacramento Bee*, November 5, 1998, p. A15.

10. *Ibid.*

11. Roger Gafke and David Leuthold, "The Effect on Voters of Misleading, Confusing, and Difficult Ballot Titles," *Public Opinion Quarterly*, Fall 1979, p. 396.

12. *Ibid.*, p. 398.

13. David H. Everson, "The Effects of Initiatives on Voter Turnout: A Comparative State Analysis," *Western Political Quarterly*, vol. 34, 1981, pp. 420–24.

14. *Ibid.*, p. 424.

15. Allen H. Eaton, *The Oregon System: The Story of Direct Legislation in Oregon* (Chicago: A.C. McClurg & Company, 1912), p. 4.

16. *Ibid.*, p. 5.

17. *The Historical Development and Use of the Recall in Oregon* (Salem: Legislative Research, 1976), pp. 1–2. See also Joseph F. Zimmerman, *The Recall: Tribunal of the People* (Westport, CT: Praeger Publishers, 1997).

18. J. William Black, "Maine's Experience with the Initiative and Referendum," *The Annals of the American Academy of Political and Social Science*, September 1912, pp. 174–75.

19. John Allswang, *California Initiatives and Referendums: 1912–1990*

(Los Angeles: Institute of Public Affairs, California State University, 1991), p. 12.

20. *Ibid.*

21. Winston W. Crouch, *The Initiative and Referendum in California* (Los Angeles: The Haynes Foundation, 1950), p. 7. Material in the following five paragraphs is derived from this source, pp. 7–10, and V.O. Key, Jr. and Winston W. Crouch, *The Initiative and the Referendum in California* (Los Angeles: University of California at Los Angeles, 1939), pp. 44–47.

22. Joseph G. LaPalombara and Charles B. Hagan, *The Initiative and Referendum in Oregon: 1938–1948* (Corvalis: Oregon State College Press, 1950). Information in this paragraph and the following four paragraphs is derived from this source.

23. Lisa Oakley and Thomas H. Neale, *Citizen Initiative Proposals Appearing on State Ballots, 1976–1992* (Washington, DC: Congressional Research Service, 1995), p. 3.

24. *Ibid.*, p. 4.

25. *Ibid.*

26. *Ibid.*, pp. 44–79.

27. R. Steven Brown and John M. Johnson, "Four State Environmental Protection Initiatives for the 1990s," *The Book of the States 1990–91* (Lexington, KY: The Council of State Governments, 1990), pp. 504–6.

28. Scott Allen, "Question 3 Backers to Push Case on Hill," *The Boston Globe*, November 5, 1992, p. 43.

29. Information in this paragraph is derived from John Tweedy, Jr., "Coalition Building and the Defeat of California Proposition 128," *Stanford Environmental Law Journal*, vol. 11, 1992, pp. 114–48.

30. *Ibid.*, p. 147.

31. Sara Rimer, "In Clear-Cutting Vote, Maine Will Define Itself," *The New York Times*, September 25, 1996, p. 1.

32. Carey Goldberg, "Logging Debate in Maine Turns into Babbling," *The New York Times*, October 31, 1997, p. 14.

33. *People's Advocate, Incorporated v. California Legislature*, No. 324111 (Superior Court for Sacramento County, December 11, 1984).

34. *People's Advocate Incorporated v. Superior Court*, 181 Cal.App.3d 316, 226 Cal.Rptr. 640 (1986).

35. James E. Castello, "The Limits of Popular Sovereignty: Using the Initiative Power to Control Legislative Procedure," *California Law Review*, January 1986, p. 499.

36. *Articles of Confederation and Perpetual Union*, art. V.

37. Tarri Renner and Victor S. DeSantis, "Municipal Form of Government: Issues and Trends," *The Municipal Year Book 1998* (Washington, DC: International City/County Management Association, 1998), p. 38.

38. "Who's Next?" *State Government News*, December 1997, p. 16.

39. *Bates v. Jones*, 118 S.Ct. 1302 (1998).

40. *U.S. Term Limits, Incorporated v. Thornton*, 115 S.Ct. 1842 (1995).

41. Arizona Laws of 1973, chap. 159, *Arizona Revised Statutes*, §§ 19-221, 19-222.

42. Elaine Stuart, "Voters Make Laws," *State Government News*, December 1996, p. 31.

43. Drew Leatherby, "The Truth About Term Limits," *State Government News*, December 1997, pp. 14–16.

44. Henry Flores, "Term Limits and the Voting Rights Act: The Case of San Antonio, Texas," a paper presented at the 1998 annual meeting of The American Political Science Association, Boston, Massachusetts, September 5, 1998, pp. 9–10.

45. *Ibid.*, pp. 17–18.

46. Joseph F. Zimmerman, *The New England Town Meeting: Democracy in Action* (Westport, CT: Praeger Publishers, 1999).

47. *Constitution of California*, art. 16, § 18.

48. *Sanders v. Gray*, 372 U.S. 368 at 381 (1963).

49. *Gordon v. Lance*, 403 U.S. 1 (1971).

50. "Ohio Rejects Tax Repeal," *The New York Times*, November 10, 1983, p. D26.

51. William C. Mathewson, "Michigan, Five Other States Reject Rollback Proposals," *Michigan Municipal Review*, March 1985, p. 35.

52. Richard R. Johnson, "The Continuing Evolution of the Direct Initiative in Oklahoma," *Comparative State Politics*, June 1996, pp. 6–7.

53. "Generals of the California Taxpayers' Revolt," *The New York Times*, June 8, 1978, p. 25.

54. *Ibid.*

55. David O. Sears and Jack Citrin, *Tax Revolt: Something for Nothing in California* (Cambridge, MA: Harvard University Press, 1982), p. 8.

56. *Constitution of California*, art. 13A, § 1.

57. *Ibid.*, § 3.

58. *Ibid.*, § 4.

59. *Amador Valley Joint Union High School District v. State Board of Equalization*, 22 Cal.3d 208, 583 P.2d 1281 (1978).

60. *County of Fresno v. Malmstrom*, 94 Cal.App.3d 974 (1979).

61. *Mills v. County of Trinity*, 108 Cal.App.3d 656 (1980).

62. *Trent Meredith, Incorporated v. City of Oxnard*, 114 Cal.App.3d 317 (1981).

63. *Los Angeles County Transportation Commission v. Richmond*, 31 Cal.3d 197, 643 P.2d 941 (1982).

64. Judith Cummings, "Ruling on Transit Stirs Coast Hopes," *The New York Times*, May 8, 1982, p. 8.

65. Charles Bell, "California's Continuing Budget Conflict," *Comparative State Politics Newsletter*, October 1983, p. 9.

66.   Robert Reinhold, "10 Years Later, Voters in California are Asked to Make Up for Lost Taxes," *The New York Times*, June 5, 1988, p. 24.

67.   Katherine Bishop, "Rural Counties are Still Gasping from California's Tax Revolt," *The New York Times*, August 18, 1988, p. A16.

68.   *Nordlinger v. Hahn*, 112 S.Ct. 2326 at 2332 (1992).

69.   *Ibid.*, p. 2333.

70.   *First National Stores Incorporated v. Board of Assessors of Somerville*, 358 Mass. 554, 266 N.E.2d 848 (1971).

71.   *Massachusetts Laws of 1981*, chap. 782; *Massachusetts General Laws*, chap. 4B; chap. 59, § 21(a-d); chap. 62, § 3(B)(9); and chap. 71, § 34. Relative to sewer and water districts, see *Massachusetts Acts of 1982*, chap. 82.

72.   Governor Edward J. King, *Testimony Before the Joint Economic Committee* (Boston: Massachusetts Executive Department, February 24, 1982), p. 4.

73.   Frederic M. Biddle, "Filling the Gap Created by Proposition $2^1/_2$," *The Boston Globe*, February 24, 1989, p. 1.

74.   *Memorandum to All Finance Committee Chairmen & Secretaries* (Boston: Association of Town Finance Committees, April 1, 1983), p. 2.

75.   "Increase in Cigarette Tax is Approved in California," *The New York Times*, November 13, 1998, p. A28.

76.   Don Terry, "Cigarette Tax Supported by Unlikely Coalition," *The New York Times*, October 18, 1998, p. 20.

77.   Vellinga, "Initiative Races' Tab: $200 Million," p. A15.

78.   Joseph F. Zimmerman, "Interstate Cooperation: The Roles of the State Attorneys General," *Publius*, Winter 1998, pp. 71–89.

79.   *Evans v. Romer*, 882 P.2d 1335 (Colo. 1994).

80.   *Romer v. Evans*, 116 S.Ct. 1620 at 1624 (1996).

81.   *Equality Foundation of Greater Cincinnati v. City of Cincinnati*, 128 F.3d 289 (C.A.6 1997) and *Equality Foundation of Greater Cincinnati v. City of Cincinnati*, 119 S.Ct. 365 (1998).

82.   *Equality Foundation of Greater Cincinnati v. City of Cincinnati*, 119 S.Ct. 365 at 365-66 (1998).

83.   B. Drummond Ayres, Jr., "Court Blocks California on Alien Rules," *The New York Times*, November 17, 1994, p. A16.

84.   Don Terry, "Strong Blow is Delivered to State Law on Aliens," *The New York Times*, March 19, 1997, p. A8.

85.   Todd S. Purdum, "Judge Nullifies Most of California Immigrant Law," *The New York Times*, March 19, 1998, p. A12. See also the *Personal Responsibility and Work Opportunity Reconciliation Act of 1996*, 110 Stat. 2110, 42 U.S.C. § 601 note.

86.   *Lee v. State of Oregon*, 891 F.Supp. 1429 (1996).

87.   *Lee v. State of Oregon*, 107 F.3d 1382 (1997). See also "Suicide Law Withstands a Challenge," *The New York Times*, February 28, 1997, p. A20.

88.   *Lee v. Harcleroad*, 118 S.Ct. 328 (1997).

89.   *Washington v. Glucksberg*, 117 S.Ct. 2258 (1997).

90. Timothy Egan, "Assisted Suicide Comes Full Circle to Oregon," *The New York Times*, October 26, 1997, pp. 1 and 25.

91. Timothy Egan, "In Oregon, Opening a New Front in the World of Medicine," *The New York Times*, November 6, 1997, p. A26.

92. James Brooke, "5 States Vote Medical Use of Marijuana," *The New York Times*, November 5, 1998, p. B10.

93. *Ibid.*

94. *Ibid.*

95. Dinesh D'Souza, "The Education of Ward Connerly," *Forbes*, May 5, 1997, p. 90.

96. *Ibid.*

97. *Coalition for Economic Equity v. Wilson*, 110 F.3d 1431 (1997). Opinion amended and superseded on denial of a rehearing, 122 F.3d 692 (C.A.9-Cal. 1997).

98. *Coalition for Economic Equity v. Wilson*, 118 S.Ct. 397 (1997).

99. William Booth, "The Ballot Battle," *The Washington Post*, November 5, 1998, p. A33.

100. Douglas Laskin, "It's Time to Abandon Bilingual Education," *The New York Times*, January 13, 1998, p. 21.

101. John Ritter, "English Only, Ready or Not," *USA Today*, August 3, 1998, p. 2A.

102. *Ibid.*

103. Information in this paragraph and the following two paragraphs is derived from Adam Nossiter, "Ballot Losses Signal End of Gambling's Lucky Run," *The New York Times*, November 19, 1996, p. A22.

104. Brett Pully, "Casinos Widen Rivers to Increase Business," *The New York Times*, October 30, 1998, p. A16.

105. *Indian Gaming Regulation Act of 1988*, 102 Stat. 1467, 25 U.S.C. § 2710.

106. Todd S. Purdum, "Costly Fight Rages in California Over Indian Gambling Measure," *The New York Times*, October 13, 1998, p. 1.

107. Mary L. Velling, "Initiative Races' Tab: $100 Million," *Sacramento Bee*, November 5, 1998, p. A15.

108. Consult Joseph F. Zimmerman, *Federal Preemption; The Silent Revolution* (Ames: Iowa State University Press, 1991).

109. Timothy Egan, "Struggle Over Gun Control Laws Shifts to States and Tests N.R.A., *The New York Times*, October 13, 1997, p. B6.

110. *Ibid.*

111. B. Drummond Ayres, Jr., "Gun-Control Measure is Decisively Rejected," *The New York Times*, November 6, 1997, p. A28.

112. Information in this paragraph and the following two paragraphs is derived from Carey Goldberg, "2 States Consider Boldly Revamping Campaign Finance," *The New York Times*, October 19, 1998, p. A12.

113. Tara Getty and John Culver, "Initiative Policymaking in California," *Comparative State Politics*, October 1998, pp. 13–16.

114. Information is derived from David M. Lawrence, "Initiative, Referendum, and Recall in North Carolina," *Popular Government*, Fall 1997, pp. 8–18.

115. *Associated Home Builders of the Greater Eastbay v. City of Livermore*, 18 Cal.3d 582, 135 Cal.Rptr. 41, 557 P.2d 473.

116. Madelyn Glickfeld, LeRoy Graymer, and Kerry Morrison, "Trends in Local Growth Control Ballot Measures in California," *Journal of Environmental Law*, vol. 6, 1987, pp. 114 and 116.

117. *DeVita v. County of Napa*, 9 Cal.4th 763, 38 Cal. Rptr.2d 699, 889 P.2d 1019 (Cal. 1995).

118. Timothy Egan, "The New Politics of Urban Sprawl," *The New York Times*, November 15, 1998, p. 3.

119. Vivian S. Toy, "Foes of Ballot Proposal to Ease Council-Term Limits Law Begin TV Campaign," *The New York Times*, October 16, 1996, p. B3.

120. Sam H. Verhovek, "Houston to Vote on Repeal of Affirmative Action," *The New York Times*, November 2, 1997, p. 28.

121. Sam H. Verhovek, "Referendum in Houston Shows Complexity of Preferences Issue," *The New York Times*, November 6, 1997, p. A26.

122. "District Judge Rules Houston City Council Made Illegal Change in Initiative Language," *Election Administration Reports*, July 20, 1998, p. 3.

123. James P. Melcher, "Abatements Unabated: Cleveland's Historic Vote and the Dilemma of Tax Abatements," *Comparative State Politics*, December 1997, pp. 19–25.

124. Sam H. Verhovek, "From Same-Sex Marriages to Gambling, Voters Speak," *The New York Times*, November 5, 1998, p. B10.

125. *Ibid.*

5

An Evaluation

The initiative is a significant modification of conventional, representative government based upon the leadership-feedback theory, which limits the role of voters primarily to electing, periodically, government officers who provide leadership in public affairs by proposing policies. This law-making model is reflected in the due process requirement for public hearings on many types of proposed or requested governmental actions. Citizen feedback on proposals might induce elected officers to modify proposals prior to their enactment into law. Decision-making responsibility, however, remains with the legislators.

The delegate theory of representation posits that elected officers in making decisions reflect the will of the people, and it is well-known that candidates for elective state and local government offices express in their campaigns deference to the opinions of voters on issues. Once elected to office, however, they are confronted on occasion with the question of whether they should follow the wishes of a majority of their respective constituents when voting on a major divisive issue or vote their conscience that might be at odds with the popular view on the issue. If a legislator digresses too far from the thinking of most constituents, they could reject the legislator's reelection bid or employ the recall, where authorized, to call a special election for the purpose of removing the legislator from office. Of course, it is possible the threat of an initiative or recall campaign could persuade the solon to change his or her position on the issue.

Direct voter law-making was viewed initially with trepidation by legislators and supporters of Republican government, who often used emotional arguments in their campaigns to persuade voters to abandon or not adopt the initiative or to sanction changes that make using the device more difficult.

This chapter evaluates the initiative and its associated referendum by summarizing and analyzing the arguments of proponents and opponents in the light of experience with the device in state and local governments. The earliest arguments date to the 1890s and are employed today along with newer arguments generated by experience with citizen law-making by the initiative. Several arguments for and against this participatory device apply more fully to the direct as opposed to the indirect initiative.

Conclusions about the desirability and efficacy of the initiative are drawn and are utilized to develop in Chapter 6 model initiative provisions for state and local governments that decide to adopt the device or to modify existing constitutional, statutory, or charter initiative provisions.

ARGUMENTS IN FAVOR

Seven major interrelated arguments have been developed and forcibly advanced in support of the initiative by its early proponents who were populists, progressives, and municipal reformers seeking to make state and local legislative bodies more fully representative and responsive to the voters. Not surprisingly, several of these arguments also were advanced in support of the protest referendum and the recall that often were promoted jointly with the initiative as reform measures, particularly in local governments.

The Sovereign Citizen

The early initiative advocates were convinced that the governmental system should ensure the citizen is sovereign and popular law-making is the most legitimate form of law-making. Citing the initiative as a reform device to empower sovereign citizens, Martin Rittinghausen in 1897 stressed, with reference to legislators, "these so-called superior minds can not reform anything whatever, for the reason, that their own interests are opposed to any reform the objective of which is the interest of the collective masses of the people."[1]

In 1899, James H. Hyslop criticized legislators for pretending to reflect public opinion while ignoring it whenever possible, accused them of voting "submissively in obedience to a 'boss,'" and added: "The consequence is that our assemblies have come to pass where they must either cease to be deliberative bodies and put themselves under the "sovereign" power of the Speaker, a petty pass for democracy, or place themselves at the mercy of the unscrupulous minority."[2]

Delos F. Wilcox, a strong initiative proponent, argued in 1912 that voters should have authority to enact statutes and not have to rely upon legislators whom he described as intermediaries. He also wrote that this participatory device would free voters "from the domination of their own representatives" and allow the electorate to solve major problems directly.[3] This view was endorsed three years later by Benjamin P. De Witt, who explained "where the initiative is in force, the people are not entirely dependent upon the state legislatures.[4] In other words, voters can circumvent legislatures whenever they are dissatisfied with the legislative process.

Supporters of the initiative note it can check corruption of legislators by special interest groups and also correct errors made by sincere legislators who misinterpret the electorate's views on a policy issue without the need to recall legislators or vote them out of office at the next general election.

U.S. Senator Mark O. Hatfield of Oregon in 1979 was convinced "the initiative is an actualization of the citizens' First Amendment right to petition the Government for redress of grievances."[5] In 1989, David D. Schmidt went beyond viewing the initiative as an extension of citizens' right to petition governments by describing it as capable of preventing the overconcentration of political power and noted: "American history is rife with instances of corruption and misrule, but even under an honest government, political power in a given city or state can fall into the hands of an individual, a small group, or a single party. With the initiative process, however, the people retain the ultimate authority, thus preventing any monopoly power, even when an individual party controls the legislative, executive, and judicial branches of government."[6]

Voter sovereignty can be placed in another light by citing numerous good government reforms in state and local governments that are products of the initiative overcoming the opposition of representative law-making bodies to the reforms.

More Representative Legislative Bodies

A consistent theme of initiative supporters is the pressure it places on legislators to be representatives of the citizenry and its ability to neutralize the influence of the bosses and special interests. This participatory device allows the electorate to help establish the legislative agenda, circumvents inertia, makes legislative bodies more sensitive to voters' concerns, and comports with the principles of electoral democracy.

Woodrow Wilson in 1911, while serving as Governor of New Jersey, decried the complex governmental machines that "made it so difficult, so full of ambushes and hiding places, so indirect, that, instead of having true representative government, we have a great inextricable jungle of organizations intervening between the people and the processes of their government; so that by stages, without intending it, without being aware of it, we have lost the purity and directiveness of representative government."[7]

Wilson believed the initiative and the protest referendum would help to restore genuine representative government, urged they be considered in the light of existing conditions in legislatures instead of theoretical representative government, and stressed no one would be proposing these devices if the theoretical model in fact existed in the state legislatures.[8]

In 1912, Lewis J. Johnson unequivocally argued that the initiative and the referendum would make legislatures "cease to be attractive objects for bribery and secret influence," which will make seats "unattractive to grafters," and will make them "more attractive to high-minded, public-spirited citizens" who will not be corrupted.[9] Henry J. Ford in the same year attributed the lack of action on reform proposals by state legislatures to the fact they are divided into committees, with each committee possessing "the power of frustrating or perverting action on the public business."[10] Five years later, John R. Haynes in a similar vein asserted that the California experience revealed that the initiative and the protest referendum made legislators more responsible to the voters and improved the quality of legislation.[11] A long-time student of the initiative, William B. Munro, wrote in 1937: "The people want their laws to fit the age, and they grow impatient with legislatures which move haltingly because of constitutional restrictions, checks and balances, long debates, the retarding influence of vested interests, the blight of bossism, and the wariness of the lawmakers."[12] Munro concluded that the initiative allowed the voters to enact the laws they want and need, and also to prod the legislature to be more responsive to the general will of the people. Claudius O. Johnson in a 1945 article agreed with Munro and wrote that the twin participatory devices generally had altered legislative policies by making them "conform more closely to the will of the electors.'[13]

A 1980 survey by the New York State Senate Subcommittee on the Initiative and Referendum revealed eighteen of twenty-nine respondents in states with the initiative believed "the legislature does often or occasionally act on various issues because of pressure resulting from a possible initiative."[14] Confirming Munro's 1937 judgment, the filing of 145,170 signatures on indirect initiative petitions providing for the prohibition of the use of cats and dogs from pounds for medical research prompted the 1983 Massachusetts General Court (state legislature) to enact the petition into law within a fortnight.[15]

Schmidt in his 1989 book emphasized that the initiative pressures legislators to act, which he termed "an increase in government accountability" representing a "quantum leap in the power of self-government."[16] Reporting in 1996 on a study of states with the initiative and the issue of parental consent for abortions for women under the age of eighteen, Elisabeth R. Gerber concluded that the threat of an initiative campaign encourages legislators to move "away from the initial positions" and "when the threat of initiatives moves legislative outcomes away from their initial positions, different groups may benefit."[17] She noted, however, groups amply represented in the legislature might discover "their interests [are] less well represented" when activists use the threat of initiatives.[18]

The California Commission on Campaign Financing in 1992 referred to the effectiveness of the initiative in pressuring the state legislature to be more responsible by citing the circulation of a 1974 campaign finance and ethics initiative that generated interest in the subjects by the legislature. This initiative led to enactment of major campaign finance and ethics laws, and the threat of an initiative campaign in 1991 that pressured the governor and the legislature to reach a compromise in the form of a forest preservation statute.[19]

Facilitates Major Reforms

If the threat of the use of the initiative fails to persuade the legislative body to enact major reforms opposed by special interest groups, the participatory device can be employed to enact the reforms. Examples abound of the use of the initiative to provide relief to property taxpayers, more stringent regulation of election campaign finance and lobbying, and greater environmental protection among other policy changes. The California Commission on Campaign Finance reported Los Angeles area voters had "used it to retool land-use planning processes, establish district-by-district elections, and enact term limits on local officials" and a number of other major state government reforms.[20]

Enhanced Citizen Participation Opportunities

Lewis J. Johnson wrote that direct legislation offers "an attractive field of usefulness for citizens [who] do not care to give up their whole time to public life."[21] Reviewing initiative and referendum experience in California, Winston W. Crouch in 1950 stressed as very significant that voter participation on initiated propositions is considerably higher than such participation on proposals placed on the referendum ballot by the state legislature.[22]

David D. Schmidt examined employment of the initiative in all states where its use is authorized and concluded that in a period "when political activity is more and more dominated by big-money fund-raising and 30-second television ads, initiative campaigns are one sector of politics where the efforts of ordinary individuals still make a difference.[23] Voters, according to Schmidt, are aware that their participation can produce a desired policy outcome, and their desire to go to the polls to support propositions increases the number of ballots cast because they also vote for candidates.[24]

Increased Citizen Interest in Public Affairs

Eugene C. Lee of the University of California, Berkeley, commented in 1978, that in his state, "the vote on initiatives—reflecting their more controversial nature—almost always exceed by several percentage points the vote for constitutional amendments proposed by the legislature."[25] In the same year, *The New York Times* editorialized: "Direct democracy offers another benefit: It is a powerful stimulus to political participation. Nobody said democracy has to be dull. People are more likely to vote when issues capture their interest. Consider Oregon's experience. Elsewhere there were complaints of voter turnout as low as 30 percent. In Oregon, which had a half-dozen hot ballot measures, the turnout was 65 percent. Use of the referendum and initiative is not the only explanation, but it's a good one."[26]

John S. Shockley's monograph on initiated propositions in Colorado in 1976 revealed that citizens were not "apathetic, cynical, or ignorant in their approach to the initiatives" and were very interested in propositions.[27] He also reported a larger number of people throughout the state voted for the more controversial propositions than voted for candidates for seats in the state legislature.[28]

Writing in 1989, Julian N. Eule acknowledged that the initiative process in California has defects and there is a need "for a greater judicial checking role." However, he expressed concern that removing the ability of voters to participate in making public policy will lead to a loss of interest in issues and reinforce distrust of government and political alienation.[29] Initiative propositions, in his judgment, stimulate the interest of registered voters "and provide an escape valve against a seemingly unresponsive government."[30] The California Commission on Campaign Financing reported "voter drop-off rates for initiatives in recent years have been consistently low . . . and more voters voted on Proposition 134 [alcohol tax] than on the contest for state insurance commissioner in 1990."[31]

Educational Function

In common with the protest referendum, the initiative performs an important civic educational function. Admittedly, the public can be misinformed and some groups who utilize the device are aware that the proposition will not receive voter approval but are convinced that the campaign will have a long-term beneficial educational effect, which will lead to legislative action.

William B. Munro in 1912 placed particular stress on the promotion of the civic education of the voters by their involvement in the initiative process and distribution by the concerned state or local government of an informational pamphlet containing the proposition and a neutral summary of the arguments of proponents and opponents.[32]

James K. Pollock studied the Michigan experience with the initiative and was of the opinion in 1940 that the educational value of proposition campaigns had been unsatisfactory and limited to a degree but, nevertheless, forced numerous voters to ruminate over questions they would not have directed their attention to in the absence of the initiative.[33] He attributed the responsibility for the limited educational impact of the initiative to certain government officers who failed to promote education of the public on governmental matters in general and ballot propositions in particular.[34]

In 1989, Thomas E. Cronin, although not denying the educational value of direct democracy, pointed out that proponents always have overstated this value.[35] In the same year, Schmidt explained that an initiative campaign generates a public debate, which educates voters on the issue and affords candidates for elective office "an opportunity to make an issue-based appeal to the voters that goes beyond campaign promises."[36]

Shorter Constitutions and Charters

Voter disappointment in the integrity of many state legislatures and local governments in the nineteenth century led to constitutional and char-ter amendments forbidding the legislative body to initiate specified actions and mandating precise procedures be followed in taking other specified actions. The initiative, in common with the mandatory and peti-tion referenda, generates public support for brief state constitutions and local government charters confined to fundamentals because voters know they can initiate action as well as reverse the decisions made by legisla-tive bodies. Armed with the initiative, protest referendum, and recall, the electorate does not need restrictive constitutional and charter provisions to protect the public's interest.

Many constitutional and charter prohibitions and restrictions add to the cost of government and generally have been ineffective with respect to their stipulated objectives because legislators and chief executives have found ways to circumvent the prohibitions and restrictions. Similarly, the two-year term is designed to promote voter control of elected officers but has the undesirable effect of forcing officers to raise funds and campaign for reelection continuously, thereby taking time away from their official duties. Authorization of the use of the above participatory devices encour-ages voters to approve constitutional amendments lengthening the term of office of state legislators to four years.

ARGUMENTS IN OPPOSITION

Sixteen major interrelated arguments have been developed by early and current critics of the initiative, who also use several of these arguments in opposition to the protest referendum and the recall. The reader should be aware that most of the critical comments are directed at the direct initia-tive and many of the most negative comments on the initiative process during the past quarter century are based principally on California's expe-rience, which does not apply to the use of the device in the typical initia-tive state.

An Undemocratic Process

The argument that the initiative involves an undemocratic process that could lead to anarchy facially appears to be an invalid one, but in drawing a conclusion relative to the argument's validity one must examine it carefully on the basis of available evidence.

James Boyle in 1912 focused on the direct initiative and held it is undemocratic to allow a minority of the voters, by petitions, to initiate constitutional amendments and statutes, and to determine the exact wording to be placed on the referendum ballot without affording the electorate the opportunity to amend the propositions.[37] He particularly objected to the fact that a "proposition, though concocted in secret by a cabal, club, or caucus, and no matter how crude or vicious, or how little understood by the majority, or how new in principle, can be forced to popular vote by an insignificant minority."[38]

Charles M. Hollingworth concluded in the same year that progressive reforms were introducing an era of political disorganization similar to what occurred in the Roman Republic and would lead to anarchy.[39] He continued his opposition to the device by writing that the submission of propositions to the voters increases "the opportunities for widespread corruption among the 'people' in whose name they are advocated," subjects the governmental system to continuous, undesirable, capricious changes, and discourages the most competent men from seeking election to office.[40]

In 1914, Albert M. Kales asserted that the initiative and protest referendum enable "the extra-legal government . . . to secure the passage of undesirable laws or to defeat good ones and to insist for a time at least that this is 'the judgment of the people.'"[41] In 1997, Lee wrote that the initiative in California had lost its democratic character:

Important aspects of the state's political agenda are being set, not by its elected leaders, but by unaccountable, single-interest groups operating in a fragmented, uncoordinated, and frequently contradictory manner. . . . It is the impact of all those that appear on the ballot forcing attention, time, and energy onto those few measures that attracted signatures (for a price) and providing an excuse for legislators and governors to abdicate their leadership roles in deference to a spurious "voice of the people."[42]

Lee described the voice of the people as "a voice dominated by million-dollar campaigns," heavy use of short television advertisements, and a declining rate of voter participation.[43]

Destruction of Distinction between Constitutional and Statutory Law

In the view of former President William H. Taft the major objection to the initiative is the destruction of the distinction between the fundamental law, the state constitution, and an ordinary statute because initiated statutes can be amended or repealed only by the process utilized for adoption of constitutional amendments and repeal of constitutional provisions.[44] In his judgment, this obliteration of the distinction between the two types of law endangers individual rights because there is no protection against "the unjust aggression of the majority of the electorate."[45]

Two Coordinate Law-Making Bodies

Constitutional authorization of the initiative permits *ad hoc* establishment of a second law-making body, which lacks a continuing responsibility to the general public that is a hallmark of a permanent legislative body. Opponents allege it discourages energetic and innovative individuals from seeking election as legislators because their law-making function can be superseded by voter use of the initiative and associated referendum. Writing in 1912, Walter E. Weyl contended: "A high-spirited statesman, placed in a position where he may be checked, halted, thwarted—often most unreasonably—when an appeal lies from his every action, where even his tenure depends upon his 'giving satisfaction,' is tempted to withdraw from the important eminence of office; if, he remain, he may suffer in initiative, courage, and self-esteem."[46]

The following year, Taft wrote in a similar vein that the initiative and referendum reduce the importance and powers of a legislative body and act as a deterrent to competent individuals who agree to be candidates for election to the body.[47] More recent California experience suggests that the restraints placed on legislative bodies with respect to raising revenues—such as Proposition 2 of 1989 in Pasadena, California, and California's Proposition 13 of 1978—make it exceedingly difficult for elected officers to solve critical problems.[48] Furthermore, critics charge that the initiative process encourages legislators to avoid their responsibilities by allowing voters to determine governmental policies. Gerber in 1995 wrote that responsibility for governmental policies in California is not clear-cut and voters are unable to "electorally reward or punish lawmakers when they either can not identify the lawmakers or are the lawmakers themselves."[49]

Poorly Drafted Laws

A major indictment of initiated laws is that some are poorly drafted by amateurs and create implementation problems. Referring in 1911 to the recently approved constitutional initiative provision in Oregon, Frederick V. Holman described initiated statutes as distinguished by "careless and loose phraseology" creating ambiguities that must be resolved by the state supreme court.[50] This view was endorsed the next year by Boyle who judged propositions submitted to the voters as crude ones that either must be accepted or rejected without opportunity for amendment.[51]

An editorial in *The New York Times* in 1978 explained the defeat of a California proposition limiting smoking in public places in the following terms: "It lost heavily, people on both sides agree, not simply because of an expensive campaign by the tobacco industry but because it was poorly drafted. Opponents were able, with reason, to ridicule the proposition for permitting smoking at rock concerts but not a jazz concert. A legislature could have clarified or compromised on language. But the terms of a proposition are frozen and must be voted on, yes or no."[52]

The California Court of Appeals in 1986 highlighted the difficulty of interpreting proposition 51 (Fair Responsibility Act) by opining it had to "engage in the often Delphic exercise of divining legislative intent, a process made more difficult by the need to assess the collective intent of millions of voters rather than a legislative body" that maintains records of hearings held by committees on a bill.[53]

Referring to crudely drafted propositions, the California Commission on Campaign Finance noted three of twenty-one statewide approved propositions in the period since 1980 had been struck down totally by courts and another eight propositions had sections invalidated.[54] Poor draftsmanship also can result in initiated measures having unintended consequences that disappoint even the proponents.[55]

Legislators Make Better Laws

Elected legislators, according to initiative opponents, produce better laws than initiated ones, in part because legislators are supported by professional staff and in time become experts in various areas of the law.[56] A Massachusetts Special Committee in 1932 stressed that "many public issues . . . are not vivid and clear cut as to be readily capable of clear presentation. Still others are so intricate in their nature and so full of detail that it is hard to explain their salient features in terms intelligible to the voting public. The initiative and referendum, like the franchise itself, imply an interest in and knowledge of public affairs which the average voter does not always possess."[57]

Munro in 1937 described the submission of a complicated or technical issue to the voters as referring "the decision to a Supreme Court of ignorance."[58] The Citizens League of the Twin Cities area of Minnesota concluded in 1979 that "a 'saturation point' is quickly reached, after which the number of persons who inform themselves on the issues does not increase, regardless of the length or intensity of the education campaign."[59]

Cynthia L. Fountaine endorsed the above view in 1988 and advanced another reason why voters are not well informed; that is, they "are bombarded with political advertising designed to manipulate opinions by appealing to the voters' emotions rather than to provide useful information on the issues."[60]

Proponents of the legislative process emphasize it improves a bill through input from citizens and interest groups at public hearings and by written communications, floor debates, and research by professional staff. Furthermore, opponents of a bill are afforded the opportunity to explain its defects and to suggest remedial amendments. Such an opportunity is lacking during the initiative process.

Propositions Poorly Coordinated with Other Statutes

The failure of authors of an initiative proposition to examine carefully existing statutes related to the proposition inadvertently can cause implementation problems if it is not coordinated with the statutes. In 1979, the Citizens League in the Twin Cities area of Minnesota pointed out that "Minnesota's tax policy is expressed through many laws, including those governing income tax rates, deductions and credits, property classification, sales tax rates, school aids, tax base sharing, and tax increment finance. An initiative or referendum could address any of these items singly, and throw the whole system out of balance."[61] Alan Rosenthal in 1995 reached the same conclusions and explained: "While legislatures may sometimes neglect relationships between one policy and another and how policies interact, the Initiative is oblivious to such relationships. Voters choose initiatives separately, ignoring policies that are interrelated or contradictory."[62]

Focus on Single Issues

Single-issue politics is a product of the initiative process and has a number of undesirable consequences, according to critics. Proponents are accused of being concerned with their respective special issue and failing to consider or to be aware of the impact of their separate propositions on other public policies.[63]

Critics also assert the single-shot approach to public policy-making inhibits the ability of elected officers to develop coherent policies in the best long-term interests of a state or a local government. Legislators, for example, in favor of a specific policy change respond to a charge their bill will affect other policies adversely by entering into negotiations to modify the bill to eliminate the adverse consequences and recognize they might have to compromise to develop the most effective statute.

Oversimplification of Issues

A major charge against direct citizen law-making is it oversimplifies complex issues. According to its detractors, the initiative is based upon the unrealistic assumption that there is a simple yes or no answer to each question and sets up a confrontation between supporters and opponents of a proposition who through the legislative process might be able to draft a compromise bill agreeable to all concerned parties.

Campaigns Mislead the Public

An initiative campaign involving a major proposition can lead proponents and opponents to be unethical in their media campaigns and mislead the electorate. There is no denying the possibility such campaigns might misrepresent the nature of an issue and the misrepresentation might be the product of an attempt to influence voters by means of thirty- and sixty-second television advertisements.

Confusing Proposition Wording

The wording of an initiated proposition on the ballot can confuse voters who cast an affirmative vote believing they voted in favor of a given policy whereas in fact a yes vote is against the policy. Referring to Florida's employment of the initiative, Robert J. Lowe reported in 1992 "most ballot summaries heighten misunderstanding rather than enlighten voters" because the average voter cannot understand the wording.[64] Similarly, John Jacobs in 1997 reported only 5 percent of interviewees in California stated all propositions could be understood by the average voter.[65]

Use by Special Interests

Perhaps the most damning criticism of the initiative is its use by special interest groups whose stranglehold on state legislatures was intended to be broken by voter employment of the device. In 1914, Herbert Croly recognized a potential danger relative to the initiative:

The ordinary mechanism of the initiative operates so as to give to a small percentage of the voters the right to force the electorate either to accept or reject a
specific legislative measure. This is an extremely valuable privilege, because the
right to force a vote on specific legislative projects . . . places an enormous power
in the hands of a skillful and persistent minority. The initiators might frequently
be able to wear down or circumvent the opposition of a less able and tenacious
majority.[66]

The fear often is expressed that well-financed, special interest groups
will overwhelm the voters with a sophisticated media campaign, particularly in view of the U.S. Supreme Court's decision in *First National Bank
of Boston v. Bellotti*, described in Chapter 3. The decision struck down
state laws prohibiting or limiting corporate spending to influence the outcome of initiative and referendum campaigns.[67] As pointed out in Chapter
4, corporations in most instances react to rather than initiate propositions.

John S. Shockley reported in 1980 that Colorado opponents of "four
liberal or consumer oriented" propositions received contributions totaling
$1.292 million, whereas proponents' contributions were only $169,000.[68]
He also noted the defeat of each initiative opposed strongly by corporate
interests.[69] In 1978, the tobacco industry spent $5.6 million in a success-
ful campaign to defeat a California initiative proposition prohibiting
smoking in most enclosed places, and out-of-town developers contributed
a major part of the $550,000 raised to help defeat San Francisco's Propo-
sition M in 1983, which would have required developers to share benefits
of the building boom with city residents.[70]

Betty H. Zisk, a long-time student of the initiative, wrote in 1987 "the
most damning of all my findings, from the progressive reform perspective, is the obvious success of the well-financed media campaigns in
defeating so many proposals initiated by *ad hoc* groups of concerned
citizens."[71]

The California Commission on Campaign Financing decried the fact
that committees promoting an initiative in a local government in the Los
Angeles area frequently spend more money than all candidates seeking
election to the city council.[72] In 1988, spending for and against a proposition relative to allowing Pacific Palisades oil drilling in the City of Los
Angeles totaled about $8.227 million.[73]

Spending by special interests to persuade voters to approve or reject
propositions continues to escalate. The gambling industry has become a
major source of funding in a growing number of states. California
Proposition 5 of 1998, which would legalize casino gambling on Indian

reservations, was opposed by Nevada casino operators who spent in excess of $71 million in an unsuccessful effort to defeat it.[74]

The initiative process has become professionalized in certain states with proponents of a proposition raising millions of dollars to pay petition circulators, professionals who advise proponents about political strategy and use of the media, and the print, radio, and television media for advertisements promoting the proposition. In California, the process at the state level and in the larger cities and counties no longer is a grassroots process.

Arthur Samish was considered by many political observers in the 1930s and 1940s to be the unelected "boss" of California because of the wide influence he exercised in the establishment of state policies. Samish, who was employed by major interest groups, explained in a 1971 book that the use of an alternative or counter initiative as an effective tactic to defeat a proposition he opposed and his influence with Secretary of State Frank Jordan resulted in his proposition appearing near the top of the ballot and the opposition proposition appearing in a much lower position.[75] He added: "When you get such a high 'no' vote for any measure, the other propositions are going to suffer too. Proposition Number Two was also defeated. But I didn't give a damn. I had only put it up to wipe out Number Twelve."[76]

David R. Lagasse in 1995 concluded that corporations readily can raise large amounts of funds to hire professional advisers and launch a massive media campaign that "need only muddy the public's perceptions of the initiative and its impact."[77] After studying twenty-eight initiative campaigns in Massachusetts and Oregon, James H. Gallagher in 1995 concluded "direct democracy can not be considered a viable way of changing public policy when corporate interests are at stake" because business groups have such a great financial advantage over grassroots organizations that the business message dominates the media advertising.[78]

Kenneth Mulligan in 1997 reported that the evidence from initiative campaigns revealed proponents who vastly outspent opponents increased significantly the prospects that voters would approve the proposition.[79] Also in 1997, Jacobs highlighted the growth of the professional initiative industry in California and the fact that voters "are forced to choose between competing versions of unvetted bad policy and hidden agendas, often dress up as populist reforms by entrenched interests who don't have a populist bone in their collective bodies."[80]

There has been at least one instance of a petition signature-gathering firm in California promoting an initiative campaign to generate revenue for the firm. In 1984, Kelly Kimball sponsored a state lottery initiative and his target was "Scientific Games, Incorporated, a Georgia based lottery equipment company," which pumped more than $2.1 million into a successful campaign to persuade voters to approve the initiative.[81] The company subsequently was awarded a $40 million state contract to print game tickets, provide advice, and develop a computer system, and Mr. Kimball's firm was paid approximately $200,000 to organize the collection of petition signatures.

Adverse Impact on Minorities

Critics cite examples of propositions designed to have a negative impact on minorities and low-income persons. A related objection is the "tyranny of the majority" argument that the initiative might be used to deprive minorities of some of their basic rights. Derrick A. Bell, Jr. argued in 1978 that the initiative and referendum involve at-large elections on issues and in common with multi-member district elections can dilute the voting strength of a minority group.[82] Noting that conservative politicians, after election to public office, are under pressure to become more moderate, Bell asserted there are no similar pressures on voters to take a more moderate stand on an issue because they vote in the privacy of the polling booth and can express fully their biases.[83] Eugene C. Lee, in the same year, also expressed the view that the initiative facilitated prejudice.[84]

Fountaine, a strong opponent of direct legislation, wrote in 1988: "Representative government is superior to direct democracy in protecting minority rights because the delegation of government responsibilities to a small number of elected representatives allows a more thorough evaluation of the issues and a determination of the entire electorate's best interests. As the legislature engages in give-and-take debate on the merits of both sides of an issue, solutions can be formulated which fuse minority majority interests."[85]

Barbara S. Gamble in 1997 expressed the view that direct democracy has been employed by the majority to deprive minorities of their rights and added "the record shows that American voters readily repeal existing civil rights protections and enthusiastically enact laws that bar their elected representatives from passing new ones."[86] In 1998, Peter Schrag reached a similar conclusion about California's initiative experience and wrote that the device seldom authorizes spending that benefits other than proponents "and is rarely respectful of minority rights."[87]

Impact on Non-Participants

Initiative opponents argue that law-making by elected representatives more accurately reflects the views of all citizens and ensures the interests of those who do not go to the polls to vote on propositions will be protected fully.[88] The turnout of voters on Election Day has been declining for several decades, and the selection of public officers often is made by a minority of the electorate. Furthermore, opponents suggest that, when faced by a long ballot containing numerous initiated and referred propositions, voters become fatigued and will not cast a ballot on all propositions, thereby allowing a small percentage of the electorate to make important policy decisions.

A Cluttered Ballot

The electorate, according to initiative critics, often is faced with a ballot containing a large number of minor as well as emotional propositions diverting attention from the important questions on the ballot. As explained in Chapter 2, only Illinois and Mississippi restrict the number of questions that can appear on a referendum ballot. Edwin A. Cottrell reported as early as 1939 that the long list of questions appearing on California election ballots makes it impossible "for any great percentage of the voters to be informed adequately on all of them" and, consequently, voters tend to concentrate on the major issues and to avoid the minor questions.[89] On November 5, 1996, California voters were faced with twelve initiated constitutional amendments and statutes plus three proposed bond acts.[90]

Inflexible Laws

A successful initiative campaign can produce inflexibility as statutes enacted by the voters cannot be amended or repealed by the state legislatures in eleven states. In Arkansas, Florida, and Nevada there are time or other restrictions on amendments or repeals as noted in Chapter 2.[91]

In 1980, Louis J. Sirico, Jr. expressed concern about majoritarian voting and its potential for abuse and wrote: "Depending on the state, a deplorable measure may prove legally irreversible by the legislature or state executive."[92]

Increased Taxpayer Costs

All initiative propositions increase taxpayers' costs because of the equipment and staffs needed to review and certify petition signatures, publish a voter information pamphlet, and count the ballots. Additional costs are involved if propositions are voted on at a special election. Fountaine endorsed complaints about the governmental costs involved with the process and added "a fourth inefficiency which results from direct democracy is that time and money are wasted on ballot measures which are subsequently declared unconstitutional."[93]

CONCLUSIONS

A careful weighing of the evidence marshaled over the years by initiative proponents and opponents leads to a conclusion generally favoring the former but also acknowledges that this process of popular law-making occasionally has exhibited shortcomings.

Circulation of a large number of initiative petitions is an indicator of voter discontent and protest against the unresponsiveness of legislative bodies to the concerns of certain groups of citizens. As noted, legislative sins of omissions are correctable by the successful employment of the initiative. I agree with Hugh A. Bone's 1974 conclusion: "The persistence of initiatives as against demanded referenda appears to be a reflection of legislative inaction. This is especially true in areas of reapportionment, liquor policies, and political-governmental reform. Special interests have frequently been successful in bottling up proposals for change in committees or defeating them on the floor of the legislature."[94]

With respect to the sovereign citizen argument, there can be no denying that the initiative empowers voters, provided the authorizing provisions do not restrict severely applicable subjects or establish an exceptionally high signature threshold, to place a proposition on the referendum ballot. The initiative tends to make the legislative body more responsive to the opinion of voters. The threat of an initiative campaign or the collection of the required number of certifiable signatures has prodded the state legislature to enact a statute activists had been seeking, and a direct initiative campaign on occasion is terminated if the organizers are satisfied with the enacted statute.

The existence of concurrent powers in the U.S. federal system offers states the opportunity to address a serious national problem when Congress fails to act, and the initiative allows voters to enact a statute to solve such a problem should the legislature fail to take effective action. It is difficult to quarrel with a 1998 editorial in *The New York Times*: "The demise of national tobacco control legislation puts the burden on states to find new strategies to reduce smoking and its harmful consequences. The California Children and Families Initiative, which will be on the November ballot as Proposition 10, provides a model that other states could emulate."[95]

Evidence also supports the third affirmative argument that this participatory device can produce needed governmental reforms that legislative bodies, under pressure from special interest groups, had refused to approve. The same conclusion was reached by another student of the initiative, Betty H. Zisk, who referred in 1987 to the "broadening of the public agenda" and forcing voter action on proposals state legislatures ignore.[96] With respect to the heavily criticized California system, Charles M. Price, a long-time student of direct democracy, concluded in 1997: "If the state did not have initiatives, popular laws such as campaign finance and lobby reform, tobacco-tax increase, property-tax relief, the open primary, and the state lottery probably never would have made it out of the Legislature."[97]

One also must not overlook the well-established trend for voters to provide for divided political party control of state government with the governor of one party and the legislature or one house controlled by the other major party. Stalemate can be a product of such divided control and can be broken by voter use of the initiative process as in California in the period 1983–99.

Ipso facto, the initiative increases opportunities for voter participation in the policymaking process, and results in a higher turnout at the polls of eligible voters who also cast ballots for candidates. Critics do not disagree with this conclusion. This direct democracy process also allows citizens with a special interest in a subject to play a greater individual role in the law-making process by helping to draft a proposition, collect the necessary signatures, and campaign to persuade the electorate to approve the proposed constitutional or charter amendment or statute. Furthermore, citizen distrust of government can be reduced by the success of grassroots campaigns for changes in governmental policies.

The initiative process is an educational one for interested citizens as major propositions are brought to their attention, debated with respect to their respective merits, and information on each is provided by proponents, opponents, voter information pamphlets, and nonpartisan organizations such as the League of Women Voters. Admittedly, the educational process has been abused, particularly by special interest groups financing numerous thirty- or sixty-second television advertisements oversimplifying complicated issues and containing half-truths. As citizens and groups become informed about propositions, many voters will question candidates for elective office and ask for their positions on the various initiative propositions.

The initiative, in conjunction with the protest referendum and the recall, has helped to persuade the electorate to remove several prohibitions and restrictions on the legislative branch in state constitutions and local government charters. Voter loss of faith in the ability of law-making bodies to act responsibly in the nineteenth century led to adoption of the prohibitions and restrictions that lengthen the fundamental document, increase governmental costs, and are subject to circumvention.

Drawing conclusions as to the merits of the proponents' arguments is a much simpler task than drawing conclusions with respect to the critics' arguments. The initiative process has been abused on occasions and such abuse has occurred most frequently in California where the device often is employed. A review of the critical literature uncovers the fact that much of it is derived from California's experience and many of these negative conclusions might not apply to the use of the device in other states.

In theory, a representative law-making body examines each bill carefully, conducts necessary research, and holds public hearings to solicit input into the legislative process. In practice, state legislatures tend not to be deliberative bodies. Many bills enacted did not benefit from the theoretical legislative process and were enacted with little consideration that they were the products of logrolling or in response to directions from party leaders or major campaign fund contributors. It is not unusual for several hundred bills to be approved during the last night of a state legislative session, with several bills not printed at the time of approval as in New York.

The charge that the initiative process is an undemocratic one is supported to a limited degree by evidence that special interests employing multimillion-dollar media campaigns have been able to defeat on occasion citizen-sponsored propositions. Corporate interest groups have been more successful in defeating citizen-sponsored initiatives than in enacting their own propositions. In general, corporate interest groups tend to be reactors to and not initiators of propositions. It is also important to consider that special interest groups spend large sums of money lobbying legislators, governors, and administrators, and appear to have equal or more influence on legislative decisions than they do on voter decisions.

Eugene C. Lee, an expert on the California initiative process, increasingly has become disillusioned with it. In 1997, he wrote: "Turned on its head, 'direct democracy' is no longer democratic. Important aspects of the state's political agenda are being set, not by its elected leaders, but by unaccountable, single-interest groups operating in a fragmented, uncoordinated, and frequently contradictory manner."[98] He also lamented the courts paying homage to a "voice of the people" whose opinions have been influenced by expensive media campaigns and reflect a turnout of voters at the polls that is declining.[99]

The charge that the existence of two coordinate law-making bodies discourages capable men and women from seeking election to legislative bodies is unsupported by experience. Highly qualified individuals might be deterred from seeking elective offices, but there is no evidence that the initiative is the only major reason these individuals do not seek election to a legislative body. In California, seats in the state legislature are contested strenuously, and candidates spend large sums in their campaigns.

Determining whether the initiative changes the behavior of legislators is a difficult task, yet experience indicates they do not shirk their duties because dissatisfied citizens can place propositions on the referendum ballot. Legislators, of course, are free to educate the citizenry about the complexities of certain issues and the need for compromises that can be fashioned more effectively through the legislative process than the popular law-making process.

In effect, many critics contend that the initiative process undermines representative government. After an extensive study, Thomas E. Cronin concluded in 1989 "the initiative, referendum, and recall have been no more of a threat to the representative principle than has judicial review or the executive veto."[100] Dennis Polhill reached a similar judgment in 1998 and explained legislatures are still important and their roles have been changed by the initiative that allows voters to address directly issues, such as conflicts-of-interest, that these bodies will avoid.[101]

The reader should be aware that opponents overemphasize the value of legislative debates in improving bills because relatively few bills are debated extensively, especially in states with a constitutional limit on the length of the legislative session. Gilbert Hahn III and Stephen C. Morton in 1997 judged the quality of the initiated and legislative-enacted statutes as approximately equal and wrote "the electorate probably should be credited with being able to recognize and reject unintelligent proposals consistently."[102]

Charles A. Beard and Birl E. Shultz explained: "Undoubtedly one may imagine a group of ignoramuses drawing together and drafting a legal monstrosity; but in view of the fact that, under the initiative and referendum, private persons do not initiate bills unless they are deeply interested in the success of their particular measures, there is every reason for supposing that they will take proper precautions to employ that legal talent which is necessary to secure technical formality."[103]

A review of initiated statutes reveals that a small number have been poorly drafted, resulted in unintended consequences, failed to achieve stated objectives, or created the need for judicial interpretation of intent. These problems are not confined to initiated statutes. A small number of bills annually enacted by state legislatures suffer from the same problems and often are vetoed by the governor. Initiative proponents have major incentives to exercise great care in drafting a proposition because wording problems can be utilized by opponents to persuade the electorate to reject the proposal, and voter approval automatically will produce court challenges. As noted in Chapter 2, Colorado, Idaho, Washington, and Wyoming have statutes providing for conferences of petition filers and state officers where the latter can explain drafting problems and suggest language to overcome the problems.

The average legislator generally is better informed on all issues than the average voter. This fact, however, does not necessarily mean legislators are better informed, possess more wisdom, or have given more consideration than voters to the subject of an initiative proposition, particularly if it is the only one on the referendum ballot. Polhill answered the charge that the initiative leads to undesirable Colorado laws by explaining "tax limits failed eight times before it became a good idea. It became a good idea because it eventually became clear that the issue would not be addressed by the legislature."[104]

Initiative campaigns can inform and also misinform voters because of the desire of the two sides to simplify the issue or to win support for their respective position on a proposition. The same conclusion applies to campaigns associated with questions referred by the state legislature or local government legislative body to the voters and contests for election to office.

The charge that the wording of an initiated measure question on the ballot can be confusing contains some merit relative to a few measures. The charge in fairness should not be directed against the process as the responsibility for determining the wording is confined to a state or local government officer. Should the officer be under the influence of a boss, such as Arthur Samish, the chosen wording might be designed purposely to confuse voters to vote yes in the belief they are casting a ballot in favor of a proposition, when the result is really a negative one.

A special interest group, by spending huge sums of money, is able to defeat a citizen-initiated proposition and also can persuade the majority of the electorate to endorse its counter proposition. These groups, however, have had less success in winning voter approval for propositions they have placed on the ballot through the initiative process. Polhill suggested the standard for determining whether the process is a tool of special interests is the degree to which these interests successfully exert influence in the legislature and added the initiative process is feared by special interests "because it is a mechanism for expressing the public will."[105]

Campaigns associated with citizen propositions, in common with election campaigns, allow voters to express their prejudices with respect to minority groups in the privacy of the voting booth. What had been labeled by opponents as an anti-civil rights initiative proposition depends upon the perspective of the individual citizen. The use of the initiative to outlaw affirmative action programs in California has been described as an attack on the civil rights of blacks and Hispanics. Proponents, however, argued that such programs discriminate against the non-protected classes of citizens who are deprived of their equal protection of the laws' rights.

Barbara S. Gamble in 1997, under the heading "Tyranny of the Ballot Box," directed one of the strongest attacks on the initiative by criticizing voter approved propositions "that constituted a defeat of minority interests."[106] She focused in particular on initiative propositions relating to housing and accommodation, school desegregation, gay rights, English as the only official language, and AIDS. She acknowledged the courts had struck down as unconstitutional the most blatant discriminatory propositions, but failed to examine carefully the nondiscriminatory reason(s) advanced by initiative supporters.

Proponents of the neighborhood schools, for example, have supported propositions banning the busing of school children to achieve racial desegregation of public schools. Gamble made no reference to the nondiscriminatory reasons for a proposition she labeled anti-civil rights. Supporters of the proposition place great value on neighborhood schools that allow children to walk or take a short bus ride to their respective school, which also serves as a community-uniting institution. Gamble also did not note that black parents of school-age children in increasing numbers support neighborhood schools and do not want their children riding on a bus many miles to and from a distant school to achieve the social purpose of racial integration.

Similarly, Gamble failed to examine the nondiscriminatory reasons why English as the only official language propositions have been placed on referendum ballots by the initiative and described such a 1980 proposition as one "that sought to restrict the rights of language minorities."[107] Members of such groups still have the right to speak their respective native language; publish newspapers, magazines, and other materials in their native language; and to broadcast radio and television programs in their native language. Foreign language organizations often urge their members to learn English because their prospects for advancement in the United States will be limited if they lack skill in this language.

In 1964, California voters repealed statutes prohibiting racial discrimination in the rental or sale of private housing containing more than four units. As explained in Chapter 3, the U.S. Supreme Court in 1967 upheld the decision of the state supreme court invalidating Proposition 14 as violative of the Fourteenth Amendment's guarantee of equal protection of the laws.[108] The above and other decisions reveal national and state courts have been capable of striking down an approved initiative proposition if it clearly violates the constitutional rights of a group of citizens.

We concur with Lee's conclusion that "the initiative will continue to permit 'flashes of prejudice and emotion to sweep legislation onto or off the statute books,' but the increased role of the courts in ruling on the constitutionality of such measures would appear to provide a protection against the dangers of such actions with respect to questions of civil liberties and civil rights."[109]

The charge that individuals who shun the polls have their views represented better by legislative bodies is of questionable validity. These individuals, a majority of voters in many elections, might have to suffer certain consequences for their failure to participate in the electoral process. It is reasonable to assume legislators might not be particularly responsive to nonvoters on policy issues.

The ballot in certain states, highlighted by California, has become more cluttered with propositions during the last three decades of the twentieth century. Depending on the state, the clutter is as much the responsibility of the state legislature as the initiative process because the legislature commonly refers questions to voters for decisions. Nevertheless, the ballot becomes very cluttered if initiative petitions generate counter initiatives either by the legislative body or opponents of grassroots propositions. Ballot clutter could be reduced by limiting the number of referrals to the voters by the legislative body and the number of initiative propositions. The key question involves determining a limit that would not place an insurmountable obstacle in front of the legislature desiring to refer measures and voters desiring to utilize the initiative process. The limit in Illinois, for example, has not created a major problem because the participatory device is not used often.

The inflexibility produced in state and local governments by constitutional provisions prohibiting legislative amendment or repeal of approved initiated propositions has not been a serious problem. The early proponents believed it was absolutely essential to prohibit legislative amendment or repeal of approved propositions because state legislatures were controlled by special interests that the device was designed to circumvent.

The charge of inflexibility also can be directed against laws enacted by state and local government legislative bodies. In fact, the initiative was developed because representative bodies enacted statutes, often benefiting special interests, which prove to be impervious to attempts to amend or repeal them. Similarly, courts tend to be inflexible in their decisions and only on rare occasions reverse a precedent.

Initiated propositions increase governmental costs, but the increase is not significant when measured as a percentage of total spending by a state or a local government. In fact, the increase might be a trifling amount when the legislative body has referred questions to the voters, and the product is limited primarily to the cost of reviewing and certifying petition signatures and the materials included in the information pamphlet. Litigation involving an initiated statute obviously raises governmental expenses, but it must be remembered that statutes enacted by representative bodies also are challenged in court and increase governmental costs.

Concluding Comments

The evidence suggests that the initiative generally has been a salutary device that has educated citizens with respect to important public policy issues, and the electorate has been discriminating in examining the pro and con arguments about a proposition before deciding how to vote. The evidence also supports the thesis that voter employment of the initiative results in the enactment of *pro bono publico* constitutional amendments and statutes, and on occasions has helped to reinvigorate representative law-making by acting as a sword of Damocles by persuading legislators to enact statutes they had opposed. Furthermore, special interests have not captured control of the initiative process as they have captured control of legislative decision-making on certain subjects, although these interests on occasion are able to defeat needed grassroots initiatives.

Experience with the participatory device and its associated referendum supports the Aristotelian concept of the collective wisdom of the electorate.[110] Furthermore, voters have not been enthralled with the rhetoric of ideologues on the right or the left, as noted in an editorial in *The New York Times:* "If California voters show themselves to be conservative by reviving the death penalty, then what do they show themselves to be upholding the right of homosexuals to teach in public schools? Such mixed results are evident in other states and in other years and nullify fears that the process would invite ideological triumph for the right — or the left."[111]

A major advantage of the initiative is that it makes the operation of interest groups more visible in comparison with their lobbying activities in a state legislature and a local legislative body. Furthermore, the availability of the initiative increases the citizen's stake in the government.

Nevertheless, the older, better educated, and wealthier voters participate to a much greater extent in the initiated referenda with the result that decisions tend to be made by what can be labeled an elite group. Although one can deplore the failure of younger, lower income, and less formally educated citizens to exercise the franchise as fully as others, there is little evidence the process produces significant special benefits for only the elite group of voters.

The indirect initiative is a useful adjunct or complement to the conventional law-making process and preferable to the direct initiative. The former takes advantage of the legislative process, which allows for the incorporation, modification, and deletion of language to improve a proposition before its enactment either by the legislative body or the voters. Support for the indirect initiative does not suggest it should be employed frequently. It should be a reserved power or last-resort weapon, and the relative need for its use depends upon the degree of responsibility, representativeness, and responsiveness of legislative bodies to the voters.

Would populists and progressives of the late nineteenth and early twentieth centuries be pleased with their initiative legacy? Although they probably still would espouse faith in the average voter, they undoubtedly would be disturbed by the large sums spent by corporate interests in attempts to defeat grassroots initiatives. They also would not comprehend the logic of the U.S. Supreme Court in striking down key provisions of state corrupt practices acts that prohibit unlimited corporate spending in initiative campaigns. Yet their trust in the common sense of the average citizen would be undaunted.

NOTES

1.   Martin Rittinghausen, *Direct Legislation by the People* (New York: The Humboldt Library, 1897), p. 51.

2.   James H. Hyslop, *Democracy: A Study of Government* (New York: Charles Scribner's Sons, 1899), p. 127.

3.   Delos F. Wilcox, *Government by All the People* (New York: The Macmillan Company, 1912), p. 119.

4. Benjamin P. De Witt, *The Progressive Movement* (New York: The Macmillan Company, 1915), p. 221.

5. Mark O. Hatfield, "Voter Initiative Amendment," *Congressional Record,* February 5, 1979, p. S. 1062.

6. David D. Schmidt, *Citizen Lawmakers: The Ballot Initiative Revolution* (Philadelphia: Temple University Press, 1989), p. 29.

7. Woodrow Wilson, "The Issues of Reform," *Case and Comment,* November 1911, p. 307.

8. *Ibid.*

9. Lewis J. Johnson, "Direct Legislation as an Ally of Representative Government" in William B. Munro, ed., *The Initiative, Referendum, and Recall* (New York: D. Appleton and Company, 1912), p. 247.

10. Henry J. Ford, "Direct Legislation and the Recall," *The Annals of the American Academy of Political & Social Science,* September 1912, p. 71.

11. John R. Haynes, *Direct Government in California* (Washington, DC: Government Printing Office, 1917), p. 8.

12. William B. Munro, *The Government of the United States,* 4th ed. (New York: The Macmillan Company, 1937), p. 610.

13. Claudius O. Johnson, "The Initiative and Referendum in Washington, *Pacific Northwest Quarterly,* January 1945, p. 50.

14. *Report of the Subcommittee on Initiative and Referendum to the Majority Leader of the New York State Senate* (Albany: New York State Senate, 1980), p. 23.

15. *Massachusetts Laws of 1983,* chap. 631.

16. Schmidt, *Citizen Lawmakers,* p. 26.

17. Elisabeth R. Gerber, "Legislative Response to the Threat of Initiatives," *American Journal of Political Science,* February 1996, p. 125.

18. *Ibid.*

19. *To Govern Ourselves: Ballot Initiatives in the Los Angeles Area* (Los Angeles: California Commission on Campaign Finances, 1992), pp. 66–67.

20. *Ibid.,* pp. 65–66.

21. Johnson, "Direct Legislation as an Ally," p. 151.

22. Winston W. Crouch, *The Initiative and Referendum in California* (Los Angeles: The Haynes Foundation, 1950), p. 32.

23. Schmidt, *Citizen Lawmakers,* pp. 26–27.

24. *Ibid.,* p. 27.

25. Eugene C. Lee, "California" in David Butler and Austin Ranney, eds., *Referendums: A Comparative Study of Practice and Theory* (Washington, DC: American Enterprise Institute for Public Policy Research, 1978), p. 108.

26. "Making Democracy More Interesting," *The New York Times,* November 17, 1978, p. A18.

27. John S. Shockley, *The Initiative Process in Colorado Politics: An Assessment* (Boulder: Bureau of Governmental Research and Service, University of Colorado, 1980), p. 45.

28.   *Ibid.*, p. 47.

29.   Julian N. Eule, "Checking California's Plebiscite," *Hastings Constitutional Law Quarterly,* Fall 1989, p. 157.

30.   *Ibid.*

31.   *To Govern Ourselves,* p. 66

32.   William B. Munro, ed., *The Initiative, Referendum, and Recall* (New York: D. Appleton and Company, 1912), p. 21.

33.   James K. Pollock, *The Initiative and Referendum in Michigan* (Ann Arbor: University of Michigan Press, 1940), p. 67.

34.   *Ibid.*

35.   Thomas E. Cronin, *Direct Democracy: The Politics of Initiative, Referendum, and Recall* (Cambridge: Harvard University Press, 1989), p. 198.

36.   Schmidt, *Citizen Lawmakers,* pp. 27–28.

37.   James Boyle, *The Initiative and Referendum: Its Folly, Fallacies, and Failure,* 3rd ed. (Columbus, OH: A. H. Smythe, 1912), pp. 20–21.

38.   *Ibid.*

39.   Charles M. Hollingworth, "The So-Called Progressive Movement: Its Real Nature, Causes, and Significance," *The Annals of the American Academy of Political & Social Science,* September 1912, p. 43.

40.   *Ibid.*

41.   Albert M. Kales, *Unpopular Government in the United States* (Chicago: University of Chicago Press, 1914), p. 121.

42.   Eugene C. Lee, "The Initiative Boom: An Excess of Democracy" in Gerald C. Lubenow and Bruce E. Cain, eds., *Governing California* (Berkeley: Institute of Governmental Studies Press, 1997), p. 18.

43.   *Ibid.*, p. 19.

44.   William H. Taft, *Popular Government* (New Haven: Yale University Press, 1913), p. 64.

45.   *Ibid.*

46.   Walter E. Weyl, *The New Democracy: An Essay on Certain Political and Economic Tendencies in the United States* (New York: The Macmillan Company, 1912), p. 307.

47.   Taft, *Popular Government,* p. 64.

48.   *To Govern Ourselves,* pp. 57–58.

49.   Elisabeth R. Gerber, "Reforming California Initiative Process: A Proposal to Increase Flexibility and Legislative Accountability" in Bruce E. Cain and Roger G. Neil, eds., *Constitutional Reform in California: Making State Government More Effective and Responsive* (Berkeley: Institute of Governmental Studies, University of California, 1995), p. 298.

50.   Frederick V. Holman, "Results in Oregon" in *Dangers of the Initiative and Referendum* (Chicago: Civic Federation of Chicago Bulletin, no. 5, 1911), p. 12.

51.   Boyle, *The Initiative and Referendum,* pp. 47–48.

52.   "Making Democracy More Interesting, *The New York Times*, November 27, 1978, p. A18.

53.   *Russell v. Superior Court*, 185 Cal.App.3d 810 at 817-18, 230 Cal.Reptr. 102 at 107 (1986).

54.   *To Govern Ourselves*, p. 59.

55.   See Gerber, "Reforming the California Initiative Process," p. 298.

56.   Priscilla F. Gunn, "Initiatives and Referendums: Direct Democracy and Minority Interests," *Urban Law Annual*, vol. 22, 1981, p. 136.

57.   *Report of the Special Commission to Make an Investigation with a View to Improving the Procedure under which the Initiative and Referendum Provisions of the Constitution for the Purpose of Rendering Questions Submitted thereunder More Understandable to the Voters and of Eliminating Certain Inconsistencies in Said Provisions* (Boston: Wright & Potter Printing Company, 1932), p. 15.

58.   Munro, *The Government of the United States,* p. 617.

59.   *Initiative and Referendum..."No" for Minnesota* (Minneapolis: Citizens League, 1979), p. 10.

60.   Cynthia L. Fountaine, "Lousy Law-making: Questioning the Desirability and Constitutionality of Legislating by Initiative," *Southern California Law Review*, March 1988, p. 741.

61.   *Initiative and Referendum..."No" for Minnesota,* p. 27.

62.   Alan Rosenthal, "Sloppy Democracy," *State Government News*, January 1995, p. 20.

63.   *To Govern Ourselves*, p. 62.

64.   Robert J. Lowe, Jr., "Solving the Dispute Over Direct Democracy in Florida: Are Ballot Summaries Half-Empty or Half-Full?" *Stetson Law Review*, Spring 1992, p. 586.

65.   John Jacobs, "Poll: Voters Like the Initiative Process, But Want It Fixed," *The Sacramento Bee*, December 9, 1997, p. B7.

66.   Herbert Croly, *Progressive Democracy* (New York: The Macmillan Company, 1914), p. 307.

67.   *First National Bank v. Bellotti*, 435 U.S. 765 (1978).

68.   Shockley, *The Initiative Process in Colorado Politics,* p. 9.

69.   *Ibid.*, p. 10.

70.   John Herbers, "13 States Curb Taxes on Spending: A Variety of Other Initiatives Fail," *The New York Times,* November 9, 1978, p. A20 and Judith Cummings, "San Francisco's Absentees Decide Smoking and Building Measures," *The New York Times*, November 10, 1983, p. D26.

71.   Betty H. Zisk, *Money, Media, and the Grass Roots: State Ballot Issues and the Electoral Process* (Beverly Hills, CA: Sage Publications, 1987), p. 251.

72.   *To Govern Ourselves*, p. 11.

73.   *Ibid.*, p. 223.

74.   Betty Pulley, "Gambling Proponents Bet $85 Million on Election," *The New York Times*, October 31, 1998, p. A11.

75.   Arthur H. Samish and Bob Thomas, *The Secret Boss of California* (New York: Crown Publishers, Incorporated, 1971), p. 68.

76.   *Ibid.*, pp. 68–69.

77.   David R. Lagasse, "Undue Influence: Corporate Political Speech, Power, and the Initiative Process," *Brooklyn Law Review*, Winter 1995, p. 1395.

78.   James H. Gallagher, *Corporate Influence on Initiative Campaigns in Massachusetts and Oregon, 1962–1992* (Boston: Unpublished PhD. Dissertation, Boston University, 1995), p. 184.

79.   Kenneth Mulligan, *The Effects of Campaign Spending on Voting on Ballot Elections* (Washington, DC: Unpublished Master of Arts Thesis, George Washington University, 1997), p. 124.

80.   John Jacobs, "How Special Interests Captured the Initiative Process," *The Sacramento Bee*, October 12, 1997, Forum, p. 5.

81.   Dan Bernstein, "Lottery Initiative was One Consultant's Roll of the Dice," *The Sacramento Bee*, August 5, 1996, p. 1.

82.   Derrick A. Bell, Jr., "The Referendum: Democracy's Barrier to Racial Equality," *Washington Law Review*, no. 1, 1978, p. 25.

83.   *Ibid.*, p. 14.

84.   Lee, "California," p. 188.

85.   Fountaine, "Lousy Law-making," p. 749.

86.   Barbara S. Gamble, "Putting Civil Rights to a Popular Vote," *American Journal of Political Science*, January 1997, p. 262.

87.   Peter Schrag, *Paradise Lost: California's Experience, America's Future* (New York: The New Press, 1998), p. 224.

88.   "A Tool of Democracy?" *National Civic Review*, September 1978, p. 353.

89.   Edwin A. Cottrell, "Twenty-Five Years of Direct Legislation in California," *The Public Opinion Quarterly*, January 1939, p. 37.

90.   *California Ballot Pamphlet* (Sacramento: Office of the California Secretary of State, 1996), p. 3.

91.   Jonathan Bourne, Jr., "A Defence of Direct Legislation" in Munro, ed. *The Initiative, Referendum, and Recall*, p. 209.

92.   Louis J. Sirico, Jr., "The Constitutionality of the Initiative and Referendum," *Iowa Law Review*, vol. 65, 1980, p. 676.

93.   Fountaine, "Lousy Law-making," p. 753.

94.   Hugh A. Bone, "The Initiative in Washington: 1914–1917," *Washington Public Policy Notes*, October 1974, p. 2.

95.   "California's Tobacco Initiative," *The New York Times*, October 8, 1998, p. A34.

96.   Zisk, *Money, Media, and The Grass Roots*, p. 251.

97.   Charles M. Price, "Direct Democracy Works," *State Government News*, June/July 1997, p. 35.

98.   Lee, "The Initiative Boom: An Excess of Democracy," p. 18.

99.   *Ibid.*, p. 19.

100.   Cronin, *Direct Democracy*, p. 198.

101.   Dennis Polhill, "Are Coloradans Fit to Make Their Own Laws?" *Independence Issue Paper* (Independence Institute, Golden, CO.), October 25, 1996, p. 14.

102.   Gilbert Hahn III and Stephen C. Morton, "Initiative and Referendum — Do They Encourage or Impair Better State Government?" *Florida State University Law Review,* vol. 5, 1997, p. 946.

103.   Charles A. Beard and Birl E. Shultz, *Documents on the State-Wide Initiative, Referendum, and Recall* (New York: The Macmillan Company, 1912), p. 34.

104.   Polhill, "Are Coloradans Fit to Make Their Own Laws?" p. 9.

105.   *Ibid.*, p. 4.

106.   Gamble, "Putting Civil Rights to a Popular Vote," p. 254.

107.   *Ibid.*, p. 260.

108.   *Reitman v. Mulkey*, 387 U.S. 369 at 373 (1967).

109.   Lee, "California," p. 118.

110.   Benjamin Jowett, trans., *Aristotle's Politics* (New York: Carlton House, n.d.), pp. 45–46.

111.   "Making Democracy More Interesting," p. A18.

6

A Model for
Direct Voter Law-Making

The problems flowing from centralization of policymaking power in representative law-making bodies, based upon the leadership-feedback theory, have been well documented in the political science literature and need no recitation here. Various changes in legislative structure and procedures have been made, yet voter dissatisfaction with these institutions remains high and there is a widespread perception that the "invisible government" has not disappeared. This perception is promoted by large campaign contributions made by corporate, labor, and other political action committees, suggesting there might be a quid pro quo arrangement between certain legislators and contributors. The frequent use of the direct initiative and its obligatory referendum in several states, most noticeably California and Oregon, appears to be due in part to this perception. Chapter 1 explains that the initiative, protest referendum, and recall were adopted primarily in response to legislative bodies controlled by special interests, and these participatory devices were designed to help ensure that state statutes and local ordinances reflect the views of the majority of the electorate.

Chapter 5 reviews and evaluates the criticisms of the initiative with emphasis upon the direct type. Nearly one century of experience with the use of this participatory device, since its first employment in 1904, makes it possible to identify the most effective legal authorization provisions and those that create problems. There is innate danger to democracy, direct and representative, posed by monied interests contributing large sums to campaigns to elect candidates and convince voters to approve or reject initiative propositions. This danger, however, cannot be removed by amending state constitutions, state statutes, and local government charters because of two important U.S. Supreme Court decisions.

In 1976, the court ruled, relative to the 1974 amendments to the Federal Election Campaign Act of 1971, "that the limitations on expenditures, on independent expenditures by individuals and groups, and on expenditures by a candidate from his personal funds are constitutionally infirm."[1] The court in 1978 invalidated the Massachusetts corrupt practices act provisions prohibiting or limiting the amount of money that can be spent by corporations, and by extension labor unions and other organizations, in an initiative-referendum campaign.[2]

This chapter draws on Chapters 2–5 to develop model constitutional, statutory, and local government charter provisions to assist jurisdictions and their voters contemplating adoption of the initiative or amendment of current constitutional, statutory, and charter initiative provisions.[3] Included in the model are additional provisions to reduce the need for the electorate to utilize the law-making device that should be viewed as a last resort device employed by voters who have been unable to persuade the assembly to follow their wishes concerning enactment of a bill.

MODEL PROVISIONS

The model provisions address drafting self-executing state constitutional and local government charter provisions, application process, signature collection and verification, ballot question title and summary, authorization of a legislative alternative for each initiated proposition, voter information pamphlet, referendum, and amendment or repeal of approved propositions.

It is essential that constitutional, statutory, or charter initiative provisions be drafted by a nonpartisan citizen commission to ensure that legislators, who otherwise might draft implementing provisions, do not place a large number of exemptions in the authorizing provisions or a high signature threshold. The extensive list of subject matters exempted from the initiative by the Massachusetts Constitution is undesirable and one can make a persuasive case that propositions should be allowed on all matters other than designating a person to hold a specific office, deletions of rights in the bill of rights, and possibly the judiciary. The case for exempting the judiciary is not a strong one because the electorate should be empowered to change the system of selecting judges.

State voters must be allowed to use both the constitutional initiative and the statutory initiative. Limiting the initiative to constitutional amendments, as in Florida and Mississippi, could result in statutory-type propositions being incorporated into the constitution.[4]

All statutory provisions and rules and regulations applicable to general elections are applicable to the initiative and its associated referendum. The statutory initiative provisions specifically must make it a criminal offense for an individual to interfere with the circulation of a petition. In addition, a statutory provision should make it a misdemeanor for a person to offer to pay a voter money or anything of value to persuade a voter to sign or refrain from signing a petition.

Constitutional and charter initiative provisions may be self-executing or require enabling statutes or ordinances. Experience reveals the desirability of a self-executing provision to guard against the possibility of a hostile legislative body refusing to enact the necessary implementing legislation or including obstacles to initiative use in such laws. The Arkansas Constitution contains a provision that could serve as a model.[5] If the constitutional initiative provision is a brief one, which directs the state legislature to enact implementing provisions, the constitution should stipulate explicitly that the legislature should not enact any statute that restricts or impairs the right of the initiative.

Opponents of an initiative petition commonly challenge it in a judicial forum as part of a strategy to defeat the proposition. No constitutional initiative provision currently contains a liberal interpretation directive, but a South Dakota statutory provision that could serve as a model stipulates "petitions . . . shall be liberally construed, so that the real intention of the petitioners may not be defeated by a mere technicality."[6] Lacking a constitutional liberal interpretation provision, the initiative might be rendered less effective if the enabling provisions are interpreted narrowly by partisan-elected judges beholden to legislative leaders. The constitutional initiative provisions also should stipulate that the device could be used to revise and to amend the state constitution to address the problem of a court disallowing an initiative proposition on the ground the proposal revises rather than amends the state constitution.

It is essential to include the single-subject rule in the constitutional or charter initiative provisions even though experience reveals such a rule often needs judicial clarification. Inclusion of diverse matters in a single proposition can confuse many voters or offer them no choice other than to vote for a proposition containing policies voters oppose in order to promote adoption of a specific policy they favor.

Voter fatigue can be caused by a long ballot containing candidates for numerous offices or referenda questions and typically is reflected in a small percentage of the electorate expressing their preferences on questions near the bottom of the ballot or voting machine. Hence, the number of referenda questions on a single ballot should be limited to the first six to qualify with a proviso that an additional one could be placed on the ballot by a petition containing 50 percent more signatures than the percent required for the first six propositions. Alternatively, propositions qualifying for the ballot after the first six can be given preference on the next referendum ballot. To reduce ballot clutter, a provision could be included in the constitution or charter prohibiting a defeated proposition or a substantially similar one from appearing on the ballot for a period of two years, a subject examined in more detail in a subsequent section. Initiative propositions mandating spending must contain a cost estimate and provide specifically for the raising of revenues needed for full implementation or be subject to a supermajority affirmative approval requirement.

In our considered judgment, the indirect statutory initiative is preferable to the direct initiative because the former enjoys the potential benefits of study by expert legislative committees and floor debate that can result in an improved bill acceptable to initiative sponsors. Hidden consequences — the Trojan horse — and unanticipated ones can be discovered by means of committee public hearings and deliberations, and debate on the floor of legislative bodies.

Use of the indirect initiative could be encouraged by requiring voter signatures to activate the process of only 5 percent of those who cast ballots for governor in the previous general election and 10 percent if the direct type is to be employed. In either case, the signature threshold needs to be kept reasonably low to encourage grassroots citizen groups lacking adequate financial resources to collect a large number of signatures.

The general decline in the percentage of registered voters participating in California elections and referenda has led to the suggestion that the signature requirement be based upon a percentage of the total number of such voters and not the percentage who cast ballots for governor in the previous general election.[7] Such a change would increase significantly the signature threshold and inhibit the use of the participatory device by grassroots citizen groups but not by well-financed special interest groups. Similarly, a geographical signature requirement is undesirable, unless it is very low, as it might keep an important policy question off the referendum ballot because of the lack of support in certain areas of the state or local government despite widespread support in other areas where voters are faced with a major problem and an unresponsive legislative body.

To reduce the opportunity for initiative sponsors to enshrine statutory-like propositions in the state constitution or local government charter, the signature threshold for a constitutional amendment should be higher than the threshold for a statutory provision and might well be in the range of 12 percent to 15 percent of the total votes cast for the governor in the preceding general election.

An additional safeguard against such propositions and to ensure that the constitution contains only fundamental law is a stipulation that a proposed constitutional amendment is ratified only if there is an affirmative majority vote that includes a specified minimum percentage, such as thirty, of the registered voters.[8] In addition, the constitutional authorizing provision could stipulate that the courts must interpret the single subject rule narrowly when reviewing a constitutional initiative proposition.

To overcome the objection that the direct initiative does not permit compromises and restricts the electorate to casting an affirmative or negative ballot, the state constitution or local government charter could be amended to require the concerned legislative body to place a minimum of three alternative provisions on the ballot and authorize use of preferential voting to determine the proposition approved, if any.

THE APPLICATION PROCESS

The state or local government should be required to provide assistance, particularly with respect to drafting the wording of a proposition, to citizens desiring to file an initiative petition, and the response time for providing such assistance must be short.

The sponsors of an initiative petition should be required to form a sponsoring committee that might have as few as three to five sponsors. A committee of the National Municipal League (now National Civic League) in 1979 recommended that an individual or group desiring to sponsor an initiative petition must form a ten- to twenty-five–member committee whose officers sign the original filing papers and will be responsible for all subsequent petition decisions.[9]

The league's committee recommended only the indirect initiative, activated by the filing of petitions containing voter signatures equal to 5 percent of those who cast ballots for governor in the last general election, and suggested the sponsoring committee should be authorized to decide whether any legislative amendment(s) of the petition are satisfactory and to terminate the initiative process if satisfied with the amendment(s).[10] Under the committee's proposal, should the state legislature fail to enact the initiative petition within a stipulated time period or adds unsatisfactory amendments, the sponsoring committee can demand that the proposition be placed on the next general election ballot provided the committee collects additional voter signatures equal to 1 percent of those who participated in the last gubernatorial election and also can withdraw the petition before the ballot printing deadline.[11]

The authorizing provisions should direct sponsors of a proposition to file a notice of intention to launch an initiative campaign and a copy of the proposed petition with a specified election officer and the attorney general or local government attorney, and include a list of the names and addresses of members of the sponsoring committee. To protect the integrity of the process, the enabling provisions must require the sponsoring committee to include in its filing a statement whether it intends to use paid signature collectors and to notify the appropriate state or local government election officer in the event the committee subsequently changes its decision on using such collectors. A small filing fee, $100 to $200, could be imposed subject to a refund if the proposition qualifies for the ballot.

The effectiveness of the initiative process would be enhanced by a constitutional or statutory initiative provision mandating that the sponsors confer with the attorney general or local government attorney who would explain drafting problems, if any, and suggest alternative wording to overcome the problems and achieve the sponsors' goals. The concerned attorney also could be directed to issue an opinion with respect to any conflicts of the proposition with the U.S. Constitution, statutes, administrative rules and regulations, and state and U.S. court decisions. If the proposition is a statutory one, the attorney must issue an opinion whether the proposal conflicts with the state constitution. The attorney, however, should not be authorized to rule that a proposition is unconstitutional or outside of the authorized scope of the initiative and prohibit the placement of the proposition on the referendum ballot. Nevertheless, the attorney should be allowed to reject any initiative petition containing a nonsensical proposition subject to an appeal of the decision by the sponsor to a court.

The mandated conference of sponsors with a designated state officer can address the coordination of a statutory proposition with related statutes to prevent unintended consequences and the need for court clarification of conflicting provisions. In addition, sponsors could be urged by the attorney to consider incorporating an amendment or repeal section in the proposition empowering the legislative body to address unanticipated problems. Printing initiative petitions is also a responsibility of the sponsoring committee. Upon approval of the petition form by the concerned election officer, three camera-ready copies of the petition should be provided to the sponsoring committee.

Control of the initiative proposition remains in the hands of the sponsoring committee that will make decisions by a majority vote of its members. The committee should be allowed to make technical amendments to its proposition during the signature collection campaign provided the attorney general or a municipal attorney certifies that the amendments are technical ones.[12]

SIGNATURE COLLECTION AND VERIFICATION

The enabling constitutional or statutory provisions must make it a crime for a solicitor to threaten or offer a registered voter money or anything of value as an inducement to sign an initiative petition. Only one circulator can collect voter signatures on any single petition sheet. To facilitate compliance with the requirement, the circulator must sign an affidavit attesting that all signatures on the petition were signed in the presence of the circulator who is legally responsible for controlling the petition forms. An intentional violation of circulating, signature attesting, and filing procedures automatically invalidates a petition sheet.

A warning must appear on each petition sheet that signing the name of another registered voter (impersonation) is a misdemeanor, except in the case of signing a petition sheet in the presence of an individual unable to sign his or her name because of a physical infirmity. Additionally, the warning must emphasize that signing more than one petition in support of the identical proposition or signing a petition while knowingly not a qualified voter is a misdemeanor.

A person willing to sign a petition sheet must be instructed to sign and print his or her name on the sheet legibly and to include his or her full residential address, including street or box number, city, state, and postal code. An adequate description of the address should be included on the petition sheet in the event there is no street or box number.

Each circulator of an initiative petition must take an oath or affirm before an officer competent to administer oaths or affirmations that each signature on a petition sheet is the genuine signature of the person whose name it purports to be. Each circulator must sign each sheet, include his or her address and dates between which the signatures were collected, and certify the circulator witnessed each appended signature written by a registered voter of the electoral jurisdiction and each signature is that of the person whose name it purports to be.

A member of the initiative sponsoring committee must be forbidden to notarize a circulator's affidavit. Should a sponsor do so, the concerned signatures automatically are disqualified.

Any registered voter who signed an initiative petition sheet should be permitted to withdraw his or her signature until 5:00 p.m. on the last date for filing petitions with the concerned election officer for verification by filing an intention to withdraw signature affidavit in person or by mail with the petition receiving officer. After a petition sheet has been submitted for verification of signatures, no voter who signed a petition sheet should be permitted to remove his or her signature from the sheet. Any individual who gives money or receives anything of value for signing a withdrawal statement commits a misdemeanor.

To assist grassroots sponsors, petition signatures should be valid for one year after collection provided they are filed with the certification officer by the filing deadline that should be ninety days prior to the referendum. Any individual has the right to challenge in writing the validity of signatures and whether the signers are registered voters of the concerned jurisdiction.

The certification officer plays a key role in protecting the integrity of the initiative process against fraudulent and forged signatures. This officer should be authorized to conduct representative, random, statistical samplings of petition sheet signatures by means of postal cards, telephone calls, or other accepted information-gathering techniques to determine whether the signatures were signed by the registered voters whose names appear on the sheets. The officer must report violations of the petition-signing law to the appropriate public office for investigation and possible prosecution.

The certification officer also must make a determination within thirty days of the filing of petition sheets of their sufficiency and notify the sponsors *in personam* or by certified mail, within three days of the determination, whether the petition signatures were filed during the eligible time period and contained the required number of certified signatures.

A signature on a petition sheet should not be invalidated because a post office box address in the same jurisdiction is listed on the sheet and the voter's registration form contains a rural route number or street address. Similarly, a signature should not be invalidated for the absence of a middle initial or use of a nickname, such as Bob, in lieu of Robert or use of an incorrect election district number provided the individual concerned is a registered voter residing at the address listed on the petition. No technical violation should result in the invalidation of a signature if a registered voter signed it in good faith.

Nullification of a signature on a single petition sheet does not invalidate automatically other signatures on the sheet. In the event the certifying officer discovers invalid signatures, only members of the sponsoring committee should be allowed to examine the petitions in question to determine the reason(s) the signatures were rejected.

If the petition lacks the minimum number of verified signatures of voters, the petition can be amended within ten days of the certification officer's determination. The officer has ten days to review an amended petition that, if inadequate, is returned to the sponsors without prejudice to the filing of a new initiative petition. The failure of the certifying officer to comply with any required procedure automatically allows an elector within ten days of the refusal to comply to apply to the appropriate court of equity for issuance of a writ of mandamus to compel compliance.

Citizens generally are unaware of the identity of contributors who finance initiative campaigns or spend funds in opposition to an initiative proposition. To help inform voters, each sponsoring committee must file periodic financial reports identifying contributors, amounts contributed, and purposes for which expenditures were made in a format prescribed in the state's corrupt practices act, including a report at the time of the filing of petition signatures and a final report. Although paid signature gatherers cannot be prohibited, as explained in Chapter 3, it is desirable to forbid sponsors to pay such gatherers on the basis of the number of signatures collected. A political action committee with civic or good government names, such as concerned citizens for good government, must disclose in the reports the name and nature of the special interest. These reports should be publicized widely. Consideration could be given to requiring each print, radio, and television advertisement to identify the largest financial contributor.[13]

With respect to the indirect initiative, the state or local legislative body must be given a reasonable amount of time to act upon a petition and failure to act within the specified time period results in the proposition appearing on the referendum ballot. Similarly, a legislative amendment(s) of the petition unsatisfactory to the sponsoring committee triggers automatic placement of the proposition on the ballot.

BALLOT QUESTION TITLE AND SUMMARY

It is preferable for a constitutional, statutory, or charter initiative provision to assign responsibility to the attorney general or local government attorney for preparing a ballot question title and nonargumentative summary, and transmitting the information to the concerned election officer.

It is essential that the attorney general or local government attorney ensure that two or more propositions with the same number do not appear on the ballot in order to avoid voter confusion and to facilitate groups desiring to urge voters to cast a yes or no vote on a proposition. As noted in Chapter 3, the November 4, 1972, ballot in Yonkers, New York, contained a state proposition one and a city proposition one, resulting in considerable voter confusion.[14]

A commendable Washington statute requires the attorney general to use wording in the ballot title "in such a way that an affirmative answer to such question and an affirmative vote on the measure would result in a change in then current law, and a negative answer to the question and a negative vote on the measure would result in no change to then current law."[15]

Similarly, there should be a constitutional, statutory, or charter directive that the short ballot summary of the proposition must be nonargumentative and clearly indicate the change in policy that would occur if the proposition were approved. Additionally, the attorney general or local government attorney should identify hidden effects, if any, if the proposition is approved by the voters.

The falloff in the number of votes cast on propositions if they appear at the end of the ballot or bottom of the voting machine in comparison with votes for candidates at the top of the ballot strongly suggests that initiated propositions be placed at the top of the ballot before the listing of the names of candidates for elective office. Special efforts also should be made to encourage the print, radio, and television media to provide extensive coverage of the views of the proponents and opponents of an initiative provision.

VOTER INFORMATION PAMPHLET

Unassembled voter law-making admittedly lacks the benefits of face-to-face debate on issues, but many of the benefits of such debate can be gained through informational campaigns, including debates between supporters and opponents of a proposition. Civic organizations can assist the information dispersal process by scheduling such debates and preparing and distributing analytical pamphlets.

Although implementation of the above suggestions will prove helpful to citizens, it is essential that each state or local government be required by a constitutional or statutory provision to distribute an official pamphlet to each registered voter describing the propositions that will appear on the forthcoming election ballot and names of candidates for elective office. If a proposition is short, it should be printed in full below its title and number. Long propositions should be summarized in an impartial manner.

If a proposition mandates expenditures, the pamphlet should indicate the impact of the approval of the proposition on a balanced budget, need for tax increases, or estimated savings. A qualified fiscal officer must be assigned responsibility for preparing the cost estimate that includes the proposition's initial year costs and multi-year costs over the next decade. If the fiscal note is complex and long, it should be summarized in the section of the pamphlet devoted to the proposition, and the entire note should be published in the appendix. Each initiative state has assigned the responsibility to a specific officer. The Missouri state auditor is responsible for assessing the fiscal impact of a proposition and for preparing a fifty-word note summary, and the Mississippi Constitution directs the chief legislative budget officer to prepare a fiscal note analysis.[16]

It is conventional to list the pro and con arguments for each proposal in the pamphlet. Each set of arguments should be limited to a maximum of 500 words to reduce voter fatigue. In the event a large number of propositions will appear on the referendum ballot, the voter information pamphlet should include a summary of each proposition and fiscal note with a brief listing of the arguments of proponents and opponents followed by an appendix containing the full text of each proposition, a more extensive listing of pro and con arguments, and the full fiscal notes.

If the state legislature or local governing body has placed an alternative or counter proposition on the ballot, the assigned officer should group the legislative alternative with the voter-sponsored proposition to facilitate a comparison of their respective provisions. Similarly, if several propositions relate to the same general topic, they should be grouped together. Voters, or course, must steer a careful course between the Scylla and Charybdis of competing proposals.

Proponents and opponents of a proposition could be allowed to list a limited number of endorsements of their respective positions, such as six, by prominent individuals and organizations in the pamphlet to provide additional guidance to the electorate. Consideration also can be given to publishing paid advertisements pertaining to propositions in the appendix of the pamphlet to defray its printing and distribution costs. Grassroots proponents of a proposition, lacking major financial resources, would benefit greatly if the Federal Communications Commission would extend its fairness doctrine to initiative campaigns as well as election campaigns.

THE REFERENDUM

Approval of a statutory proposition should require the affirmative vote of a majority of those casting a vote on the proposition at a general election because voter turnout at primary elections often is low. In view of the declining percentage of registered voters participating in elections and referenda, serious consideration should be given to requiring an affirmative majority vote to approve a proposition to include a specified minimum percentage, such as thirty, of the registered voters casting ballots in the election. An approved proposition becomes effective thirty days after certification unless the proposition is challenged or provides a different effective date.

The electorate will be aided in reaching a decision on propositions if the state legislature or local governing body is directed to identify on the ballot alternative or conflicting statutory propositions.[17] In the event that each of two or more alternative or conflicting propositions that comprehensively change an existing policy are approved, only the proposition receiving the most votes should become effective. This policy is followed by Arkansas, Michigan, Missouri, Nevada, North Dakota, Ohio, Washington, and Utah.

Similarly, a provision should be included in the state constitution or local government charter providing for the harmonization of conflicting provisions in two or more approved measures. This approach is utilized for state initiative propositions by Arizona, Colorado, Idaho, Massachusetts, and Nebraska. Only sections of the proposition(s) receiving the fewest votes conflicting with the provisions of the proposition(s) receiving the most votes are invalidated.

If a proposition is rejected by the voters, the identical or similar proposition should be ineligible for placement on the referendum ballot by use of the initiative for a period of two years. Alternatively, a defeated proposition could be placed on the ballot during the two-year period if sponsors collect double the number of certified signatures required to qualify an ordinary initiative petition for placement on the ballot.

The Nebraska Constitution allows an identical or substantially identical proposition to appear on the ballot only once during a three-year period, and the Wyoming Constitution allows a resubmittal of a rejected proposition after five years.[18] A three-year restriction appears to be too long and a five-year restriction clearly is excessive, particularly if a proposition was rejected by a narrow margin.

In the event two or more competing propositions divide the votes cast and are defeated, consideration could be given to placing the proposition receiving the highest number of votes above a specified percentage, such as thirty-five, on the next general election ballot. The Maine Constitution and the Oklahoma statutes allow the highest defeated competing proposition to appear on the next referendum ballot provided the proposition received one-third of the total votes cast on the competing measures.[19]

AMENDMENT OR REPEAL

The state legislature or local governing body should be empowered to enact needed implementing legislation if the constitutional or charter initiative provision is a brief one. A constitutional or charter provision forbidding the legislative body to amend or repeal a statute or ordinance proposition approved by the voters in effect enshrines it in the constitution or charter and gives a semi-constitutional or semi-charter character to the proposition.

A more reasonable provision is one providing that an initiated measure is not subject to amendment or repeal by the concerned legislative body during a two-year period following the measure's approval by the voters, unless the proposition allows the legislative body to amend or repeal the statute or ordinance. The reason for this restrictive recommendation is the possibility that a hostile legislative body otherwise might frustrate the public will by amending or repealing the proposition. An approved proposition, however, can empower the legislative body to amend or repeal the measure if evidence reveals such action is desirable.

Alternatively, amendment or repeal could be permitted by a two-thirds vote of the legislative body or by a majority vote on receipt of an emergency message from the governor or local chief executive officer outlining the need for amendment(s) to correct technical deficiencies or alleviate unexpected major adverse consequences flowing from an initiated law. A strong case can be made for allowing unrestricted legislative amendment or repeal of such an approved measure if the constitution or local government charter authorizes use of the protest referendum described in a subsequent section.

OPEN AND ETHICAL GOVERNMENT

Responsible representative government is open and ethical government.[20] The exposure of in camera decision-making and unethical behavior by certain legislators with respect to bills to be enacted, amended, or rejected generate public pressure for employment of the initiative and two allied correctives — the protest referendum and the recall. In consequence, provisions for open and ethical governance are included in the model. Open governance assists citizens to obtain vital information essential for determining whether governmental actions are ethical ones. It also enables citizens to make sound decisions with respect to employing the initiative and, if employed, to make considered decisions on propositions. Ethical governance helps to reassure voters that the act of legislating is conducted in a manner that promotes the public weal and reduces the need for employment of the popular correctives.

Open Government

The power of information in the hands of the citizenry should not be underestimated. This fact is recognized by a number of elected officers who understand the danger to their positions if official records and meetings of public bodies are completely open to the public and consequently have a vested interest in preventing the widespread availability of information.

Freedom of Information

Governments have a legitimate need to deny access to certain information in order to protect the privacy of individuals and the citizenry at large. The deliberate withholding of information or delay in responding to citizen requests can raise ethical concerns with respect to the action or non-action of the concerned government officer. The latter, however, might be faced with a conflict between two statutes — a freedom of information law and a privacy law.[21]

The lack of a clear dividing line between public and confidential information in all cases presents a clear need for an appeals mechanism if a government officer(s) refuses to disclose information requested by a citizen or denies the citizen access to official records. New York State has provided an effective appeals mechanism since 1977 in the form of the Committee on Public Access to Records, which is responsible for developing guidelines for state and local government officers on the release of official information and for issuance of advisory opinions requested by persons denied access to records.[22] The advisory opinions and associated publicity often result in the government officers reconsidering their denial of access to requested information and a partial or total reversal of the initial decisions to deny access.

Open Meetings

Citizen participation in the governance process is hindered by in camera decision-making. To allow citizens to monitor governmental activities with less difficulty and promote ethical decision-making, many state and local governing bodies have enacted open meeting statutes or ordinances mandating that decisions be made only at a previously announced public meeting with a few specified exceptions where an open decision would be injurious to the public interest.

The Council of State Governments recommends the exercise of care in drafting an open meeting statute and that the term meeting be defined as the convening of a governing body for which a quorum is required in order to make a decision or to deliberate toward a decision on any matter."[23] Adequate advance notice, of course, must be given regarding the place, date, and time of a meeting, and whether any subjects to be considered are exempt from the open meeting requirement. Accurate and complete records of meetings must be made and permanently maintained for future consultations by those who attended as well as others who did not attend the meetings.

Ethical Government

Ethical government and citizen participation in policymaking and implementation are promoted by freedom of information and open meeting statutes and ordinances, yet they need to be supplemented by conflict of interest statutes, codes of ethics, mandatory information disclosure, and whistle blower protection.

Conflict of Interest Statutes

Individual legislators have entangled the public business with their own business on occasions despite the fact they have sworn or affirmed they faithfully and impartially will discharge and perform the duties of their respective office. The violations of oaths or affirmations can be subtle ones, and it is essential that statutes be enacted and supplemented by rules and guidelines to assist in the ethical education of legislators and their avoidance of conflicts of interest, and the detection of such conflicts.

Conflict of interest statutes, whether constitutional or statutory, should be broad in scope and include definition of interest, dual office holding, contracts, disclosure of confidential information, gifts, outside employment, representing private parties before governmental bodies, and post-employment restrictions. The definition of interest must be a wide one and include family members but exclude remote interests that would cause no harm to the public, such as entitling a legislator to receive a benefit offered by the government on the same terms offered to other persons. Alternatively, a legislator could be allowed to retain a remote interest provided it is disclosed publicly.

Codes of Ethics

Conflict of interest statutes deal with black and white issues with respect to actions a public officer is forbidden to take and actions the officer can take; that is, actions that are unethical and others that are clearly ethical. These statutes need to be supplemented by a legislatively enacted code of ethics addressing behavior that falls between what is permissible without question and what is proscribed clearly.

In common with conflict of interest statutes, codes of ethics cannot address adequately every conceivable ethical question that might arise. In consequence, the statute containing the code of ethics typically provides for a board with power to conduct investigations of allegations of unethical behavior and to render advisory opinions in response to questions filed by public officers. The board's published advisory opinions with names deleted over time become a type of common law of ethics providing guidance to all public officers. It is not uncommon for boards of ethics to conduct continuing education programs and to offer suggested amendments to the enabling statutes.

Mandatory Information Disclosure

Statutes requiring candidates for elective office, campaign committees, lobbyists, and public officers and employees to file periodic financial reports assist in the detection and reduction of unethical behavior in government, thereby strengthening citizen confidence in the legitimacy of a government and its decisions. The early corrupt practices acts forbid betting on elections, treating (offering something of value in exchange for a vote), and payment of a voter's poll tax by another person. These acts were supplemented in the late nineteenth century by statutes designed to reduce political patronage and assessment of officeholders to raise campaign funds for a political party. The more recent corrupt practice laws restrict the amount of funds that can be contributed to election campaigns and require periodic reports of contributions and campaign expenditures.

Financial disclosure statutes have become common in the second half of the twentieth century. To reduce unethical behavior and to provide voters with information to enable them to monitor the behavior of the elected representatives, thirty-two states require lobbyists to register, identify their employers, and reveal their compensation and the purposes for which expenditures were made. In common with corrupt practices acts, the lobbyist registration and reporting acts are subject to lax enforcement.

Legislators and other public officers are required to make an annual disclosure of their financial interests to assist citizens in determining whether there is an entanglement of personal interests with the public interest. These laws are of relatively little effect unless they are audited periodically to ensure their accuracy. The nature of the audit will vary according to the specific types of disclosures made in each financial statement.

Whistle Blower Protection

A knowledgeable person, called a whistle blower, often has disclosed unethical behavior on the part of a legislator. In the absence of legal protection for whistle blowers against various forms of retaliation, there is a natural reluctance on the part of knowledgeable government officers and employees to blow the whistle on a legislator who is engaging in unethical behavior.

Protest Referendum and Recall

An initiative proposition can repeal a statute or ordinance enacted by a legislative body, but it is preferable to have constitutional provisions allowing the electorate to use the protest referendum for this purpose because collection of the requisite number of certified signatures on petitions immediately suspends the statute or ordinance.[24]

Similarly, the recall should be made available, by a constitutional provision, as a remedy to be exercised by the voters in the event the legislative body ignores the wishes of a majority of the voters.[25] In common with the initiative and the protest referendum, the recall process is activated by filing petitions containing the required number of signatures of voters with a designated election officer. Certification of the adequacy of signatures filed results in a special election to determine whether the targeted officer should be recalled. Not all legislators would have to be recalled to enable the electorate to ensure their will is respected fully in the process of enacting bills into statutes or ordinances because removal of a small number of legislators might persuade the other recalcitrant legislators to change their positions on bills.

Concluding Comments

This review and analysis of initiated law-making by voters reveal that the process has not always lived up to the highest democratic ideals, yet a need remains for this political corrective in the state and local governments where it is authorized. Furthermore, the many important political reforms instituted through the initiative process support the recommendation that the device should be available to the electorate in all state and local governments.

In conclusion, the direct and indirect initiatives are supplements to representative law-making, allow voters to convert themselves into a temporary unassembled legislative body, have not undermined representative legislative bodies, and act as pressure valves releasing the constructive energies of concerned citizens. The indirect initiative is preferable to the direct initiative and should be employed by voters only if the representative law-making body proves to be unresponsive to the views of a significant portion of the electorate on important policy issues. This type of initiative can obviate the need for a referendum and its associated costs, and result in the enactment of a statute or ordinance superior to the original initiative proposition.

The model provisions are designed to eliminate certain abuses and reduce others while encouraging the legislative body to address major grassroots concerns. Any democratic process, however, is subject to abuse. The most egregious problem associated with the initiative today is the abuse by monied interests whose thirty- and sixty-second television advertisements can result in the defeat of a sound grassroots proposition and enactment of one not in the best interest of the citizenry at large. There is a hopeful but limited sign that states might be allowed to impose referendum campaign spending limits, although they might be very modest ones. The U.S. Supreme Court on January 25, 1999, issued a writ of certiorari to review a decision of the U.S. Court of Appeals for the Eighth Circuit that invalidated a Missouri corrupt practices law, which imposed an individual contribution limit of $1,075 in election campaigns.[26] If the Supreme Court modifies its 1976 *Buckley v. Valeo* decision, there is a possibility the court, in a subsequent review of a lower court decision, might modify its 1978 *First National Bank of Boston v. Bellotti* decision striking down a Massachusetts corrupt practices act that restricted corporate spending in referenda campaigns.

Democracy requires informed, active, and vigilant voters to ensure that the public weal is promoted by the initiative, other participatory devices, and representative law-making bodies. The United States accurately can be termed a reluctant democracy as measured by the secular decline in the number of eligible individuals casting ballots in elections for candidates and referenda propositions.

The non-participation by a large percentage of voters in an initiative-sponsored referendum can be interpreted as evidence that the non-voters have confidence that those who do cast ballots will represent, in a responsible manner, the interests of the non-voters. Nevertheless, the failure of many members of certain groups to vote raises the question whether those who cast ballots are representative of the citizenry at large.

To make the initiative a more democratic process, special efforts need to be made by governments and civic groups to encourage younger, lower income, and less formally educated citizens to register and vote in elections and particularly to express their preferences on ballot issues. Today, ballot issue decisions unfortunately often are made by an elite group — a minority of the voters.

The quintessential task for the electorate in a representative democracy is to obtain full information to permit rational decisions with respect to employing the initiative and acting upon ballot issues. It is the responsibility of the concerned government to ensure that voters have all the information they need through issuance of voter information pamphlets and public service announcements.

In sum, the leitmotif of the initiative is voter rule on issues inadequately addressed or ignored by elected assemblies that appear to be beholden to special interests. In an ideal world, open and ethical enactment of statutes and ordinances by legislators free of the corrupting influence of large campaign financial contributions by special interests will obviate the need for the electorate to take the process of law-making into their own hands on a regular basis.

NOTES

1. *Buckley v. Valeo*, 424 U.S. 1 at 143 (1976). See also *Federal Election Campaign Act Amendments of 1974*, 88 Stat. 1263, 2 U.S.C. §§ 431-37.

2. *First National Bank of Boston v. Bellotti*, 435 U.S. 765 (1978).

3. For a thoughtful analysis of constitutional and statutory initiative provisions, consult Richard B. Collins and Dale Oesterle, "Structuring the Ballot Initiative: Procedures That Do and Don't Work," *University of Colorado Law Review*, vol. 66, 1995, pp. 47–127.

4. See Robert Kurfirst, "Direct Democracy in the Sunshine State: Recent Challenges to Florida's Citizen Initiative," *Comparative State Politics*, August 1996, pp. 1–15.

5. *Constitution of Arkansas*, amendment no. 7.

6. *South Dakota Codified Laws*, § 2-1-11.

7. Philip L. Dubois and Floyd Feeney, "Improving the California Initiative Process: Options for Change," *CPS Brief*, November 1991, p. 2.

8. The *Mississippi Constitution* stipulates an initiated constitutional amendment is ratified if the affirmative majority vote is "not less than forty percent (40) of the total vote cast at the election." See art. 15, § 273(7).

9. "Recommendation of the Initiative Committee of the National Municipal League" (New York: National Municipal League, March 12, 1979), p. 1.

10. *Ibid.*, p. 2.

11. *Ibid.*

12. Philip L. Dubois and Floyd Feeney, *Lawmaking by Initiative* (New York: Agathon Press, 1998), p. 228.

13. See John S. Shockley, "Direct Democracy, Campaign Finance and the Courts: Can Corruption, Undue Influence, and Declining Voter Confidence Be Found? *University of Miami Law Review*, May 1985, pp. 417–18.

14. Linda Greenhouse, "Voters Can Be For and Against a Proposition One in Yonkers," *The New York Times*, November 4, 1972, p. 19.

15. *Washington Revised Code Annotated*, § 20.79.015. A 1997 Maine statute contains a similar requirement. See *Maine Revised Statutes Annotated*, tit. 21-A, § 906(6)(C).

16. *Missouri Code Annotated*, § 116.175(1) and *Mississippi Constitution*, art. 15, § 273(6).

17. See the *Massachusetts Constitution*, art. 48, the Initiative, part 6.

18. *Nebraska Constitution*, art. 3, § 2 and *Wyoming Constitution*, art. 52(d).

19. *Maine Constitution*, art. IV, part 3, § 18 and *Oklahoma Statutes Annotated*, tit. 34, § 24.

20. Joseph F. Zimmerman, *Curbing Unethical Behavior in Government* (Westport, CT: Greenwood Press, 1994).

21. *Ibid.*, pp. 101–19.

22. *New York Laws of 1977*, chap. 933; *New York Public Officers Law*, §§ 84-90.

23. *Guidelines for State Legislation on Government Ethics and Campaign Financing* (Lexington, KY: The Council of State Governments, 1974), p. 4.

24. Joseph F. Zimmerman, *Participatory Democracy: Populism Revived* (New York: Praeger Publishers, 1986).

25. Joseph F. Zimmerman, *The Recall: Tribunal of the People* (Westport, CT: Praeger Publishers, 1997).

26. *Nixon v. Shrink Missouri Government* PAC, 119 S.Ct. (1999).

Bibliography

BOOKS AND MONOGRAPHS

Allswang, John M. *California Initiatives and Referendums: A Survey and Guide to Research*. Los Angeles: The Edmund G. Brown Institute of Public Affairs, California State University, 1991.

Bacon, Edwin M. and Morrill Wyman. *Direct Elections and Law-Making by Popular Vote*. Boston, MA: Houghton Mifflin Company, 1912.

Bain, Henry M., Jr. and Donald S. Hecock. *Ballot Position and Voter's Choice*. Detroit, MI: Wayne State University Press, 1957.

Barber, Benjamin R. *Strong Democracy: Participatory Democracy for a New Age*. Berkeley: University of California Press, 1984.

Barnett, James D. *The Operation of the Initiative, Referendum, and Recall in Oregon*. New York: The Macmillan Company, 1915.

Beard, Charles A. *American Government and Politics*, 7th ed. New York: The Macmillan Company, 1935.

Beard, Charles A. and Birl E. Shultz. *Documents on the State-Wide Initiative, Referendum, and Recall*. New York: The Macmillan Company, 1912.

Bolt, Ernest C., Jr. *Ballots Before Bullets: The War Referendum Approach to Peace in America 1914–1941*. Charlottesville: University Press of Virginia, 1977.

Bone, Hugh A. *The Initiative and the Referendum*, 2nd ed. New York: National Municipal League, 1975.

The Book of the States. Lexington, KY: The Council of State Governments. Published biennially.

Bowler, Shaun and Todd Donovan. *Demanding Choices: Opinion, Voting, and Direct Democracy*. Ann Arbor: University of Michigan Press, 1998.

Bowler, Shaun, Todd Donovan, and Caroline Tolbert, eds. *Citizens as Legislators: Direct Democracy in the United States*. Columbus: Ohio State University Press, 1998.

Boyle, James. *The Initiative and Referendum: Its Folly, Fallacies, and Failure*, 3rd ed. Columbus, OH: A.H. Smythe, 1912.

Bryce, James. *The American Commonwealth*, new ed. New York: The Macmillan Company, 1922.

Butler, David and Austin Ranney. *Referendums Around the World: The Growing Use of Direct Democracy*. Washington, DC: American Enterprise Institute for Public Policy Research, 1994.

Butler, David and Austin Ranney, eds. *Referendums: A Comparative Study of Practice and Theory*. Washington, DC: American Enterprise Institute for Public Policy Research, 1978.

California Commission on Campaign Financing. *Democracy by Initiative: Shaping California's Fourth Branch of Government*. Los Angeles: Center for Responsive Government, 1992.

Cherny, Robert W. *Populism, Progressivism, and the Transformation of Nebraska Politics, 1885–1915*. Lincoln: University of Nebraska Press, 1981.

Childs, Richard S. *The First 50 Years of the Council-Manager Plan of Municipal Government*. New York: National Municipal League, 1965.

Childs, Richard S. *The Short Ballot: A Movement to Simplify Politics*. New York: The National Short Ballot Organization, 1916.

The Citizens' Conference on State Legislatures. *State Legislatures: An Evaluation of Their Effectiveness*. New York: Praeger Publishers, 1971.

Commager, Henry S., ed. *The Era of Reform: 1830–1860*. New York: Van Nostrand Reinhold, 1960.

Croly, Herbert. *Progressive Democracy*. New York: The Macmillan Company, 1914.

Cronin, Thomas. *Direct Democracy: The Politics of Initiative, Referendum, and Recall*. Cambridge, MA: Harvard University Press, 1989.

Crouch, Winston W. *The Initiative and Referendum in California*, rev. ed. Los Angeles: The Haynes Foundation, 1950.

Deploige, Simon. *The Referendum in Switzerland*. London: Longmans, Green, and Company, 1898.

Deverell, William and Tom Sitton, eds. *California Progressivism Revisited*. Berkeley: University of California Press, 1994.

De Witt, Benjamin P. *The Progressive Movement*. New York: The Macmillan Company, 1915.

Dubois, Philip L. and Floyd Feeney. *Lawmaking by Initiative*. New York: Agathon Press, 1998.

Durkee, Michael P. et al. *Land-Use Initiatives and Referenda in California*. Point Arena, CA: Solano Press Books, 1990.

Eaton, Allen H. *The Oregon System: The Story of Direct Legislation in Oregon.* Chicago, IL: A.C. McClurg & Company, 1912.

Ford, Paul L., ed. *The Writings of Thomas Jefferson.* vol. 4. New York: G.P. Putnam's Sons, 1894.

Galbrath, C.B., compiler. *Initiative and Referendum.* Columbus: Ohio State Library, 1911.

Godkin, Edwin L. *Unforeseen Tendencies of Democracy.* Boston, MA: Houghton Mifflin Company, 1898.

Goldman, Eric F. *Rendezvous with Destiny.* New York: Alfred A. Knopf, 1952.

To Govern Ourselves: Ballot Initiatives in the Los Angeles Area. Los Angeles: California Commission on Campaign Financing, 1992.

Hahn, Harlan and Sheldon Kamieniecki. *Referendum Voting: Social Status and Policy Preferences.* Westport, CT: Greenwood Press, 1987.

Hartz, Louis. *The Liberal Tradition in America.* New York: Harcourt, Brace and Company, 1955.

Hedges, Gilbert L. *Where the People Rule.* San Francisco, CA: Bender-Moss Company, 1914.

Hicks, John D. *The Populist Revolt: A History of the Farmers' Alliance and the People's Party.* Lincoln: University of Nebraska Press, 1961.

Hofstadter, Richard. *The Age of Reform.* New York: Alfred A. Knopf, 1955.

Hyslop, James H. *Democracy: A Study of Government.* New York: Charles Scribner's Sons, 1899.

Initiative and Referendum in California: A Legacy Lost? Sacramento: League of Women Voters of California, 1984.

Initiative and Referendum... "NO" for Minnesota. Minneapolis: Citizens League, 1979.

Issacharoff, Samuel, Pamela S. Karlan, and Richard H. Pildes. *The Law of Democracy: Legal Structure of the Political Process.* Westbury, NY: The Foundation Press, Incorporated, 1998.

Jowett, Benjamin, trans. *Aristotle's Politics.* New York: Carlton House, n.d.

Kales, Albert M. *Unpopular Government in the United States.* Chicago, IL: The University of Chicago Press, 1914.

Kaufman, George G. and Kenneth T. Rosen, eds. *The Property Tax Revolt: The Case of Proposition 13.* Cambridge, MA: Ballinger Publishing Company, 1981.

Key, V.O., Jr. and Winston W. Crouch. *The Initiative and the Referendum in California.* Los Angeles: University of California at Los Angeles, 1939.

Kobach, Kris W. *The Referendum: Direct Democracy in Switzerland.* Aldershot, England: Dartmouth Publishing Company, 1993.

LaPalombara, Joseph G. *The Initiative and Referendum in Oregon: 1938–48.* Corvallis: Oregon State College Press, 1950.

Lazarsfeld, Paul F., Bernard Berelson, and Hazel Gaudet. *The People's Choice.* New York: Duell, Sloan, and Pearce, 1944.

Lecky, William E. *Democracy and Liberty*. London: Longsman, Green, and Company, 1912.

Lieb, Hermann. *The Initiative and Referendum*. Chicago: H. Lieb, Jr. & Company, 1902.

Lloyd, Henry D. *A Sovereign People: A Study of Swiss Democracy*. New York: Doubleday, Page & Company, 1907.

Lobinger, Charles S. *The People's Law or Popular Participation in Law-Making*. New York: The Macmillan Company, 1909.

Lowell, A. Lawrence. *Governments and Parties in Continental Europe*. Boston, MA: Houghton Mifflin Company, 1896, vol. II.

Lubenow, Gerald C. and Bruce E. Cain, eds. *Governing California*. Berkeley: Institute of Governmental Studies Press, 1997.

Lydenberg, Steven D. *Bankrolling Ballots Update 1980*. New York: Council on Economic Priorities, 1981.

Magleby, David. *Direct Legislation: Voting on Ballot Propositions in the United States*. Baltimore, MD: Johns Hopkins University Press, 1984.

Margolis, Michael and Gary A. Mauser. *Manipulating Public Opinion*. Pacific Grove, CA: Brooks/Cole Publishing Company, 1989.

McGuigan, Patrick B. *The Politics of Direct Democracy in the 1980s: Case Studies in Popular Decision Making*. Washington, DC: Free Congress Research and Education Foundation, 1985.

McKenna, George, ed. *American Populism*. New York: G.P. Putnam's Sons, 1974.

Merriam, Charles E. *American Political Ideas*. New York: The Macmillan Company, 1920.

Meyer, Hermann H., compiler. *Select List of References on the Initiative, Referendum, and Recall*. Washington, DC: Government Printing Office, 1912.

Model City Charter, 7th ed. Denver: National Civic League, 1989.

Morton, Edwin M. and Morrill Wyman. *Direct Elections and Law-Making by Popular Vote*. Boston, MA: Houghton Mifflin Company, 1912.

Mowry, George E. *The California Progressives*. Berkeley: University of California Press, 1951.

Munro, William B. *The Government of the United States*, 4th ed. New York: The Macmillan Company, 1937.

Munro, William B., ed. *The Initiative, Referendum, and Recall*. New York: D. Appleton and Company, 1912.

Nelson, Bruce. *Land of the Dacotahs*. Minneapolis: University of Minnesota Press, 1946.

Oberholtzer, Ellis P. *The Referendum in America Together with Some Chapters on the Initiative and the Recall*. New York: Charles Scribner's Sons, 1900.

Phelps, Edith M., compiler. *Selected Articles on the Initiative and Referendum*. Minneapolis: The H.W. Wilson Company, 1909.

Pollack, Norman. *The Populist Response to Industrial America: Midwestern Political Thought*. Cambridge, MA: Harvard University Press, 1962.

Pollock, James K. *The Initiative and Referendum in Michigan.* Ann Arbor: University of Michigan Press, 1940.

Proceedings of the Rochester Conference on Good City Government and Seventh Annual Meeting of the National Municipal League. Philadelphia, PA: National Municipal League, 1901.

Ranney, Austin, ed. *The Referendum Device.* Washington, DC: American Enterprise Institute for Public Policy Research, 1981.

Rittinghausen, Martin. *Direct Legislation by the People.* New York: The Humboldt Library, 1897.

Samish, Arthur H. and Bob Thomas. *The Secret Boss of California.* New York: Crown Publishers, Incorporated, 1971.

Schmidt, David D. *Citizen Lawmakers: The Ballot Initiative Revolution.* Philadelphia, PA: Temple University Press, 1989.

Schmidt, David D. *Initiative Procedures: A Fifty-State Survey.* Washington, DC: Initiative News Service, 1983.

Schrag, Peter. *Paradise Lost: California's Experience, America's Future.* New York: The New Press, 1998.

Sears, David O. and Jack Citrin. *Tax Revolt: Something for Nothing in California.* Cambridge, MA: Harvard University Press, 1982.

Shockley, John S. *The Initiative Process in Colorado Politics: An Assessment.* Boulder: Bureau of Governmental Research and Service, University of Colorado, 1980.

Shultz, Jim. *The Initiative Cookbook.* San Francisco, CA: The Democracy Center, 1996.

Sturm, Albert L. *Thirty Years of State Constitution-Making: 1938–1968.* New York: National Municipal League, 1970.

Taft, William H. *Popular Government.* New Haven, CT: Yale University Press, 1913.

Talbot, C.H. *The Initiative and Referendum: State Legislation.* Madison: Wisconsin Library Commission, 1910.

Tallian, Laura. *Direct Democracy.* Los Angeles, CA: People's Lobby Press, 1977.

Torelle, Ellen, compiler. *The Political Philosophy of Robert M. LaFollette.* Madison, WI: The Robert M. LaFollette Company, 1920.

Weyl, Walter E. *The New Democracy: An Essay on Certain Political and Economic Tendencies in the United States.* New York: The Macmillan Company, 1912.

White, William Allen. *The Autobiography of William Allen White.* New York: The Macmillan Company, 1946.

Wilcox, Delos F. *Government by All the People or the Initiative, the Referendum, and the Recall as Instruments of Democracy.* New York: The Macmillan Company, 1912.

Wilson, Woodrow. *The State: Elements of Historical and Practical Politics.* Boston, MA: D.C. Heath and Company, 1907.

Zimmerman, Joseph F. *The Federated City: Community Control in Large Cities.* New York: St. Martin's Press, 1972.

Zimmerman, Joseph F. *Federal Preemption: The Silent Revolution.* Ames: Iowa State University Press, 1991.

Zimmerman, Joseph F. *Participatory Democracy: Populism Revived.* New York: Praeger Publishers, 1986.

Zimmerman, Joseph F. *The Recall: Tribunal of the People.* Westport, CT: Praeger Publishers, 1997.

Zimmerman, Joseph F. *State-Local Relations: A Partnership Approach,* 2nd ed. Westport, CT: Praeger Publishers, 1995.

Zimmerman, Joseph F. *State and Local Government,* 3rd ed. New York: Barnes & Noble Books, 1978.

Zisk, Betty. *Money, Media, and the Grass Roots: State Ballot Issues and the Electoral Process.* Beverly Hills, CA: Sage Publications, 1987.

GOVERNMENT REPORTS AND DOCUMENTS

The Acts and Resolves of the Province of the Massachusetts Bay. Boston, MA: Wright and Potter, 1874.

Charter of the City and County of San Francisco (1898).

Constitution of Georgia (1777).

Constitution of South Dakota (1898).

Durbin, Thomas M. and M. Ann Wolfe. *Initiative, Referendum, and Recall by Citizen Petition.* Washington, DC: Congressional Research Service, 1993.

Federal Attempts to Influence the Outcome of the June 1976 California Nuclear Referendum. Washington, DC: U.S. General Accounting Office, 1978.

Frankenthl, Leo J. *The Practical Working of the "Popular Initiative" in Switzerland.* Washington, DC: Government Printing Office, 1909. (Senate Document 126).

Haynes, John R. *Direct Government in California.* Washington, DC: Government Printing Office, 1917.

Jones, Bill. *California Initiative Process.* Sacramento: Secretary of State, 1997.

Oakley, Lisa and Neale, Thomas H. *Citizen Initiative Proposals Appearing on State Ballots, 1976–1992.* Washington, DC: Congressional Research Service, 1995.

Referendum Handbook, 6th ed. Harrisburg: Pennsylvania Department of Community Affairs, 1994.

Report Relative to Revising Statewide Initiative and Referendum Provisions of the Massachusetts Constitution. Boston, MA: Legislative Research Council, 1975.

Report of the Joint Subcommittee Studying the Initiative and Referendum to the Governor and General Assembly of Virginia. Richmond: The Senate, 1981.

Report of the Special Commission Created to Make an Investigation with a View to Improving the Procedure Under the Initiative and Referendum Provisions of the Constitution for the Purpose of Rendering Questions Submitted Thereunder More Understandable to the Voters and of Eliminating Certain Inconsistencies in Said Provisions. Boston, MA: Wright & Potter Printing Company, 1932.

Report of the Subcommittee on Initiative and Referendum to the Majority Leader of the New York State Senate. Albany: 1980.

Zimmerman, Joseph F. *Measuring Local Discretionary Authority.* Washington, DC: U.S. Advisory Commission on Intergovernmental Relations, 1981.

ARTICLES AND CHAPTERS IN BOOKS

Adams, Greg D. "Legislative Effects of Single-Member Vs. Multi-Member Districts." *American Journal of Political Science.* 40 (February 1996): 129–44.

Albury, Cherie B. "Amendment Nine and the Initiative Process: A Costly Trip to Nowhere." *Stetson Law Review.* 14 (1985): 350–73.

Allen, Scott. "Question 3 Backers to Push Case on Hill." *The Boston Globe.* (November 5, 1992): 43.

Amar, Akhil R. "The Central Meaning of Republican Government: Popular Sovereignty, Majority Rule, and the Denominator Problem." *University of Colorado Law Review.* 65 (1994): 749–86.

Arington, Michele. "English-Only Laws and Direct Legislation: The Battle in the States over Language Minority Rights." *Journal of Law & Politics.* 7 (1991): 325–52.

Arrow, Dennis W. "Representative Government and Popular Distrust: The Obstruction/Facilitation Conundrum Regarding State Constitutional Amendment by Initiative Petition." *Oklahoma City University Law Review.* 17 (Spring 1992): 5–88.

Ayres, B. Drummond, Jr. "Court Blocks California on Alien Rules." *The New York Times.* (November 17, 1994): A16.

Ayres, B. Drummond, Jr. "Gun-Control Measure is Decisively Rejected." *The New York Times.* (November 6, 1997): A28.

Baker, Lynn A. "Constitutional Change and Direct Democracy." *University of Colorado Law Review.* 66 (1995): 143–58.

Ballot Measures in Some States Face Hurdles Despite Vote Totals." *The Union Leader* (Manchester, N.H.). (November 5, 1998): A4.

"Ban on Same-Sex Marriage on Ballot." *The Sacramento Bee.* (November 18, 1998): A5.

Bell, Charles. "California's Continuing Budget Conflict." *Comparative State Politics Newsletter.* 4 (October 1983): 9.

Bell, Derrick A. "The Referendum: Democracy's Barrier to Racial Equality." *Washington Law Review.* 54 (No. 1, 1978): 3–29.

Benedict, Robert et al. "The Voters and Attitudes Toward Nuclear Power: A

Comparative Study of 'Nuclear Moratorium' Initiatives." *Western Political Quarterly.* 33 (March 1980): 7–23.

Bernstein, Dan. "Lottery Initiative Was One Consultant's Roll of the Dice." *The Sacramento Bee.* (August 5, 1996): 1 and A6.

Biddle, Frederic M. "Filling the Gap Created by Proposition $2^1/_2$." *The Boston Globe.* (February 24, 1989): 1 and 8.

"Bigger and Worse Fictions?: An Analysis of the 'Definition' of the Signature Machinery in the 48th (the I. & R.) Amendment, Recently Quoted in an Advisory Opinion of the Justices, 1945 Advance Sheets." *Massachusetts Law Quarterly.* 30 (October 1945): 49–54.

Bishop, Katherine. "Rural Counties are Still Gasping from California's Tax Revolt." *The New York Times.* (August 18, 1988): A16.

Black, J. William. "Maine's Experience with the Initiative and Referendum." *Annals of the American Academy of Political and Social Science.* 43 (September 1912): 159–78.

Bone, Hugh A. "The Initiative in Washington: 1914–1917." *Washington Public Policy Notes.* 2 (October 1974): 2.

Booth, William. "The Ballot Battle." *The Washington Post.* (November 5, 1998): A33.

Boskin, Michael J. "Some Neglected Economic Factors Behind Recent Tax and Spending Limitation Movements." *National Tax Journal.* 32 (June 1979): 37–42.

Bowler, Shaun and Todd Donovan. "Two Cheers for Direct Democracy or Who's Afraid of the Initiative Process?" *Representation.* 35 (Winter 1998): 247–54.

Bradbury, Katharine L., Karl E. Case, and Christopher J. Meyer. "School Quality and Massachusetts Enrollment Shifts in the Context of Tax Limitations." *New England Economic Review.* (July/August 1998): 3–20.

Bradbury, Katharine L. and Helen F. Ladd. "Proposition $2^1/_2$: Initiative Impacts." *New England Economic Review.* (March–April 1982): 48–62.

Break, George F. "Interpreting Proposition 13: A Comment." *National Tax Journal.* 32 (June 1970): 43–46.

Brooke, James. "5 States Vote Medical Use of Marijuana." *The New York Times.* (November 5, 1998): B10.

Brown, R. Steven and John M. Johnson. "Four State Environmental Protection Initiatives for the 1990s." *The Book of the States: 1990–91.* Lexington, KY: The Council of State Governments, 1990. 501–07.

Burke, Bari R. "Constitutional Initiative 30: What Constitutional Rights Did Montanans Surrender in Hopes of Securing Liability Insurance?" *Montana Law Review.* 48 (Winter 1987): 53–83.

Calhoun, Emily. "Initiative Petition Reforms and the First Amendment." *University of Colorado Law Review.* 66 (1994): 129–41.

"California Court Upsets Legislative Initiative." *Public Administration Times.* 8 (January 1, 1985): 6.

"California's Tobacco Initiative." *The New York Times.* (October 8, 1998): A34.

Callies, David L., Nancy C. Neuffer, and Carlito P. Caliboso. "Ballot Box Zoning: Initiative, Referendum, and the Law." *Journal of Urban and Contemporary Law.* 49 (1991): 53–98.

Castello, James E. "The Limits of Popular Sovereignty: Using the Initiative Power to Control Legislative Procedure." *California Law Review.* 74 (January 1986): 491–563.

Clayton, Joseph C. "Some Aspects of the Constitution." Washington, DC: Government Printing Office, 1911.

Colantuono, Michael G. "The Revision of American State Constitutions: Legislative Power, Popular Sovereignty, Constitutional Change." *California Law Review.* 75 (1987): 1473–512.

Collins, Richard B. and Dale Oesterle, "Structuring the Ballot Initiative: Procedures that Do and Don't Work." *University of Colorado Law Review.* 66 (1995): 47–127.

Cottrell, Edwin A. "Twenty-Five Years of Direct Legislation in California." *Public Opinion Quarterly.* 3 (January 1939): 30–45.

"Courts Intervene in Initiative Process." *Public Administration Times.* 8 (March 1, 1985): 3.

Cummings, Judith. "Ruling on Transit Stirs Coast Hopes." *The New York Times.* (May 8, 1982): 8.

Cummings, Judith. "San Francisco's Absentees Decide Smoking and Building Measures." *The New York Times.* (November 10, 1983): D26.

Curatolo, Tina and Jason Teel. "Want to Pass an Initiative?" *Public Affairs Report.* 39 (July 1998): 15–16.

Curtin, Daniel J., Jr. and M. Thomas Jacobson. "Growth Control by the Ballot Box: California's Experience." *Loyola of Los Angeles Law Review.* 24 (June 1991): 1073–107.

D'Souza, Dinesh. "The Education of Ward Connerly." *Forbes.* 159 (May 5, 1997): 90.

"Dangers of the Initiative and Referendum." *Civic Federation of Chicago Bulletin.* (No. 3, 1911): 1–36.

deCourcy Hinds, Michael. "Frustrated Governors Bypass Legislators with Voter Initiatives." *The New York Times.* (October 16, 1992): A10.

DeVivier, K.K. "By Going Wrong All Things Come Right: Using Alternative Initiatives to Improve Citizen Lawmaking. *University of Cincinnati Law Review.* 63 (1995): 1185–221.

"District Judge Rules Houston City Council Made Illegal Change in Initiative Language." *Election Administration Reports.* 28 (July 20, 1998): 3.

Dodd, W.F. "Some Considerations Upon the State-Wide Initiative and Referendum." *The Annals of the American Academy of Political and Social Science.* 43 (September 1912): 203–15.

Drage, Jennifer. "Direct Democracy Delivers." *State Legislatures.* 24 (December 1998): 18–19.

Dubois, Philip L. and Floyd Feeney. "Improving the California Initiative Process: Options for Change." *CPS Brief* (California Policy Seminar). 3 (November 1991): 1–5.

"Effect of Pending Initiative Petition on Legislature's Power to Enact Inconsistent Law." *Columbia Law Review.* 49 (May 1949): 705–08.

Egan, Timothy. "Assisted Suicide Comes Full Circle, to Oregon." *The New York Times.* (October 26, 1997): 1 and 25.

Egan, Timothy. "Blacks Recruited by 'Rights' Drive to End Preferences." *The New York Times.* (December 17, 1997): A18.

Egan, Timothy. "How an Idea Grew from the Fairground Up." *The New York Times.* (December 7, 1997): 1 and 36.

Egan, Timothy. "The New Politics of Urban Sprawl." *The New York Times.* (November 15, 1998): 1 and 3.

Egan, Timothy. "In Oregon, Opening a New Front in the World of Medicine." *The New York Times.* (November 6, 1997): A26.

Egan, Timothy. "Struggle over Gun Control Laws Shifts to States and Tests N.R.A." *The New York Times.* (October 13, 1997): B1 and B6.

Egan, Timothy. "Voters in Oregon Back Local Anti-Gay Rules." *The New York Times.* (July 1, 1993): A10.

Ertukel, A.D. "Debating Initiative Reform: A Summary of the Second Annual Symposium on Elections at the Center for the Study of Law & Politics." *Journal of Law & Politics.* 2 (1985): 313–34.

Eule, Julian N. "Checking California's Plebiscite." *Hastings Constitutional Law Quarterly.* 17 (Fall 1989): 151–58.

Everson, David H. "The Effects of Initiatives on Voter Turnout: A Comparative State Analysis." *Western Political Quarterly.* 34 (1981): 415–25.

Fairlee, John A. The Referendum and Initiative in Michigan." *Annals of the American Academy of Political and Social Science.* 43 (September 1912): 146–58.

Farmer, Rod. "Direct Democracy in Arkansas, 1910–1918." *Arkansas Historical Society.* 40 (Summer 1981): 99–118.

Ford, Henry J. "Direct Legislation and the Recall." *The Annals of the American Academy of Political and Social Science.* 43 (September 1912): 65–77.

Fountaine, Cynthia L. "Lousy Lawmaking: Questioning the Desirability and Constitutionality of Legislating by Initiative." *Southern California Law Review.* 61 (March 1988): 735–76.

Frey, Bruno S. "The Role of Democracy in Securing Just and Prosperous Societies." *American Economic Review.* 84 (May 1994): 338–42.

Gable, Richard W. "The Sebastiani Initiative." *National Civic Review.* 73 (January 1984): 16–23.

Gafke, Robert and David Leuthold. "The Effect on Voters of Misleading, Confusing, and Difficult Ballot Titles." *Public Opinion Quarterly.* 43 (Fall 1979): 394–401.

Gamble, Barbara S. "Putting Civil Rights to a Popular Vote." *American Journal of Political Science*. 141 (January 1997): 245–69.

Garcia, Phil. "Prop. 3's Defeat a Primary Issue for State Parties." *Sacramento Bee*. (November 5, 1998): A15.

Garrow, David J. "The Oregon Trail." *The New York Times*. (November 6, 1997): A31.

"Generals of the California Taxpayers' Revolt." *The New York Times*. (June 8, 1978): 25.

Gerber, Elisabeth R. "Legislative Response to the Threat of Popular Initiatives." *America Journal of Political Science*. 40 (February 1996): 99–128.

Gerber, Elisabeth R. "Reforming the California Initiative Process: A Proposal to Increase Flexibility and Legislative Accountability" in Bruce E. Cain and Roger G. Neil, eds. *Constitutional Reform in California: Making State Government More Effective and Responsive*. Berkeley: Institute of Governmental Studies, University of California, 1996. 291–311.

Gerber, Elisabeth R. and John E. Jackson. "Endogenous Preferences and the Study of Institutions." *The American Political Science Review*. 87 (September 1993): 639–56.

Getty, Tara and John Culver. "Initiative Policymaking in California." *Comparative State Politics*. 19 (October 1998): 13–19.

Gillette, Clayton P. "Plebiscites, Participation, and Collective Action in Local Government Law." *Michigan Law Review*. 86 (April 1988): 930–88.

Glickfeld, Madelyn, LeRoy Graymer, and Kerry Morrison. "Trends in Local Growth Control Ballot Measures in California." *Journal of Environmental Law*. 6 (1987): 111–58.

Goldberg, Carey. "Logging Debate in Maine Turns into Babbling." *The New York Times*. (October 31, 1997): A14.

Goldberg, Carey. "2 States Consider Boldly Revamping Campaign Finance." *The New York Times*. (October 19, 1998): A12.

Gordon, James D., III and David B. Magleby. "Pre-Election Judicial Review of Initiatives and Referendums." *Notre Dame Law Review*. 64 (1989): 298–320.

Grant, Paul. "Citizen Initiatives Under Attack in Colorado." *Independence Issue Paper*. (February 23, 1996): 1–10.

Gray, Alexander G., Jr. and Thomas R. Kiley. "The Initiative and Referendum in Massachusetts." *New England Law Review*. 26 (Fall 1991): 27–109.

Greenhouse, Linda. "High Court Hears Case on States' Power in Referendum Process." *The New York Times*. (October 15, 1998): A20.

Greenhouse, Linda. "Voters Can be For and Against a Proposition One in Yonkers." *The New York Times*. (November 4, 1972): 19.

Gregory, John M. "The Referendum and Initiative in Switzerland." *Public Opinion*. (January 1895–June 1895): 439–40.

Grinnell, F.W. "Does the Initiative and Referendum Amendment Authorize an 'Initiative' Petition for Another Constitutional Convention?" *Massachusetts*

Law Quarterly. 9 (July 1924): 35–51.

Guerin, Stan P. "Pre-Election Judicial Review: The Right Choice." *Oklahoma City University Law Review.* 17 (1992): 222–40.

Gunn, Priscilla F. "Initiatives and Referendums: Direct Democracy and Minority Interests." *Urban Law Annual.* 22 (1981): 135–59.

Hadwiger, David. "Money, Turnout, and Ballot Measure Success in California Cities." *Western Political Quarterly.* 45 (June 1992): 539–47.

Hager, Philip. "Remapping Vote Voided by High Court." *Los Angeles Times.* (September 15, 1983): 1 and 20.

Hahn, Gilbert, III and Stephen C. Morton. "Initiative and Referendum — Do They Encourage or Impair Better State Government?" *Florida State University Law Review.* 5 (1977): 925–50.

Hall, Adam P. "Regulating Corporate 'Speech' in Public Elections." *Case Western Reserve Law Review.* 39 (1988–89): 1313–342.

Hatfield, Mark O. "Voter Initiative Amendment." *Congressional Record.* 125 (February 5, 1979): S. 1062.

"Hawaii Court Says Work on Resort Must End." *The New York Times.* (October 25, 1982): B12.

Haynes, John R. "The Actual Workings of the Initiative, Referendum, and Recall." *National Municipal Review.* 1 (October 1912): 586–602.

Helm, Mark. "Drug Adviser Attacks Pot Votes." *Times Union* (Albany, NY). (October 28, 1998): A12.

Henks, Joseph T. and Miles A. Woodlief. "The Effect of Proposition 13 Court Decisions on California Local Government Revenue Sources." *University of San Francisco Law Review.* 22 (Winter/Spring 1988): 251–92.

Herbers, John. "13 States Curb Taxes on Spending: A Variety of Other Initiatives Fail." *The New York Times.* (November 9, 1978): A20.

"Hindsale Won't Vote on Liquor Sales." *Chicago Tribune.* (September 2, 1983): sec. 2, p. 2.

Hirsch, Eric and Julie Lays. "Bilingual Education: Sí o No?" *State Legislatures.* 24 (December 1998): 24–27.

Hoff, Ross H. "Mayor, Council, and Electoral Characteristics in Cities under 25,000 Population." *Urban Data Service Report.* 13 (December 1981): 1–25.

Hollingsworth, Charles M. "The So-Called Progressive Movement: Its Real Nature, Causes, and Significance." *Annals of the American Academy of Political and Social Science.* 43 (September 1912): 32–48.

Holman, Frederick V. "Results in Oregon." *Dangers of the Initiative and Referendum.* Chicago: Civic Federation of Chicago, 1911. 10–22.

Holmes, Steven A. "Senator Seeks a Deal on Affirmative Action Policy." *The New York Times.* (November 1, 1997): A13.

Hurley, Sheila M. "The Constitutionality of the Massachusetts County Distribution Requirement for Initiative Petition Signatures." *Suffolk University Law Review.* 13 (1979): 113–23.

"The Indirect Initiative." *National Civic Review*. 68 (May 1979): 232–33.

"The Initiative and Referendum, The Australian Ballot, and the New England Town Meeting." *Massachusetts Law Quarterly*. (1917): 281–83.

"INR Campaign Spending Study: Negativism Effective." *The Initiative News Report*. 4 (December 2, 1983); 1.

"Islanders Back Zoning for Resort in Hawaii." *The New York Times*. (February 6, 1984): A14.

Jacobs, John. "How Special Interests Captured the Initiative Process." *The Sacramento Bee*. (October 12, 1997): Forum, p. 5.

Jacobs, John. "Poll: Voters Like Initiative Process, But Want It Fixed." *The Sacramento Bee*. (December 9, 1997): B7.

Jameson, P.K. and Marsha Hoback. "Citizen Initiatives in Florida: An Analysis of Florida's Constitutional Initiative Process, Issues, and Alternatives." *Florida State University Law Review*. 23 (1995): 417–61.

"Jersey High Court Upholds Ballot Bias Ruling." *The New York Times*. (October 7, 1981): B5.

Johnson, Claudius O. "The Adoption of the Initiative and Referendum in Washington." *Pacific Northwest Quarterly*. 35 (October 1944): 291–303.

Johnson, Claudius O. "The Initiative and Referendum in Washington." *Pacific Northwest Quarterly*. 36 (January 1945): 29–61.

Johnson, Lewis J. "Direct Legislation as an Ally of Representative Government" in William B. Munro, ed. *The Initiative, Referendum, and Recall*. New York: D. Appleton and Company, 1912: 139–63.

Johnson, Richard R. "The Continuing Evolution of the Direct Initiative in Oklahoma." *Comparative State Politics*. 17 (June 1996): 6–7.

Keller, David and Robert M. "Initiatives in the 1980s and 1990s." *The Book of the States: 1994–95*. Lexington, KY: The Council of State Governments, 1994. 279–93.

Keller, David, Amy L. Yonowitz, and Christy Almanzor. "Initiatives and Voter Turnout." *Initiative & Referendum Analysis*. (July 1992): 1–4.

Kennedy, Timothy J. "Initiated Constitutional Amendments in Arkansas: Strolling Through the Mine Field." *University of Arkansas at Little Rock Law Journal*. 9 (1986–87): 1–62.

Ladd, Helen F. and Julie B. Wilson. "Why Voters Support Tax Limitations: Evidence from Massachusetts' Proposition $2^1/_2$." *National Tax Journal*. 35 (1982): 121–48.

Lagasse, David R. "Undue Influence: Corporate Political Speech, Power, and the Initiative Process." *Brooklyn Law Review*. 61 (Winter 1995): 1347–397.

LaPalombara, Joseph G. and Charles B. Hagan. "Direct Legislation: An Appraisal and a Suggestion." *The American Political Science Review*. 45 (June 1951): 400–21.

Lasken, Douglas. "It's Time to Abandon Bilingual Education." *The New York Times*. (January 13, 1998): 21.

Lawrence, David M. "Initiative, Referendum, and Recall in North Carolina." *Popular Government*. 63 (Fall 1997): 8–18.

Leary, Patricia. "Power to the People? A Critique of the Florida Supreme Court's Interpretation of the Referendum Power" in *Florida Land Company v. City of Winter Springs*, 427 S.2d 170 (Fla. 1983)." *Florida State University Law Review*. 15 (Winter 1987): 673–86.

Lee, Eugene C. "The American Experience, 1778–1978" in Austin Ranney, ed. *The Referendum Device*. Washington, DC: American Enterprise Institute for Public Policy Research, 1981. 46–59.

Lee, Eugene C. "California" in David Butler and Austin Ranney, eds. *Referendums: A Comparative Study of Practice and Theory*. Washington, DC: American Enterprise Institute for Public Policy Research, 1978.

Lee, Eugene C. "The Initiative Boom: An Excess of Democracy" in Gerald C. Lubenow and Bruce E. Cain, eds. *Governing California*. Berkeley: Institute of Governmental Studies Press, 1997.

Lee, Eugene C. "750 Propositions: The Initiative in Perspective." *California Data Brief*. 2 (April 1978): 1–4.

Levenson, Rosaline. "California Supreme Court Upholds Crime Initiative." *National Civic Review*. 72 (February 1983): 105.

Levenson, Rosaline. "Zoning Initiative Overturned in Cal." *National Civic Review*. 72 (September 1983): 442.

Linde, Hans A. "When Is Initiative Lawmaking Not 'Republican Government?'" *Hastings Constitutional Law Quarterly*. 17 (Fall 1989): 159–73.

Linde, Hans A. "When Initiative Lawmaking is Not 'Republican Government': The Campaign Against Homosexuality." *Hastings Constitutional Law Quarterly*. 72 (1993): 1945.

Little, Joseph W. "Does Direct Democracy Threaten Constitutional Governance in Florida?" *Stetson Law Review*. 24 (1995): 393–415.

Lowe, Robert J., Jr., "Solving the Dispute Over Direct Democracy in Florida: Are Ballot Summaries Half-Empty or Half-Full?" *Stetson Law Review*. 21 (Spring 1992): 565–607.

Lowell, A. Lawrence. "The Referendum and Initiative: Their Relation to the Interests of Labor in Switzerland and in America." *International Journal of Ethics*. 6 (1895): 51–63.

Lowenstein, Daniel H. "Ballot Propositions." *Election Law: Cases and Materials*. Durham, NC: Carolina Academic Press, 1995. 259–95.

Lowenstein, Daniel H. "California Initiatives and the Single-Subject Rule." *UCLA Law Review*. 30 (1983): 936–75.

Lowenstein, Daniel H. "Money and Ballot Propositions." *Election Law: Cases and Materials*. Durham, NC: Carolina Academic Press, 1995. 545–80.

Lowenstein, Daniel H. and Robert M. Stern. "The First Amendment and Paid Initiative Petition Circulators: A Dissenting View and a Proposal." *Hastings Constitutional Law Quarterly*. 17 (Fall 1989): 175–224.

Lowery, David and Lee Sigelman. "Understanding the Tax Revolt: Eight Explanations." *The American Political Science Review*. 75 (1981): 963–74.

Lupia, Arthur. "Shortcuts Versus Encyclopedias: Information and Voting Behavior in California Insurance Reform Elections." *The American Political Science Review*. 88 (March 1994): 63–76.

Magleby, David H. "Ballot Initiatives and Intergovernmental Relations in the United States." *Publius*. 28 (Winter 1998): 147–63.

"Making Democracy More Interesting." *The New York Times*. (November 27, 1978): A18.

Mariotti, Steve. "An Economic Analysis of the Voting on Michigan's Tax and Expenditure Limitation Amendment." *Public Choice*. 33 (Winter 1978): 15–26.

Mastro, Randy M., Deborah C. Costlow, and Heidi P. Sanchez. "Taking the Initiative: Corporate Control of the Referendum Process Through Media Spending and What to Do About It." *Federal Communications Bar Journal*. 32 (1980): 315–59.

Mathewson, William C. "Michigan, Five Other States Reject Rollback Proposals." *Michigan Municipal Review*. (March 1985): 35.

McCuan, David, Shaun Bowler, Todd Donovan, and Ken Fernandez. "California's Political Warriors: Campaign Professionals and the Initiative Process" in Shaun Bowler, Todd Donovan, and Caroline J. Tolbert, eds. *Citizens as Legislators: Direct Democracy in the United States*. Columbus: Ohio State University Press, 1998. 55–79.

Medina, J. Michael. "The Emergency Clause and the Referendum in Oklahoma: Current Status and Needed Reform." *Oklahoma Law Review*. 43 (Fall 1990): 401–28.

Melcher, James P. "Abatements Unabated: Cleveland's Historic Vote and the Dilemma of Tax Abatements." *Comparative State Politics*. 18 (December 1997): 19–25.

Mikesell, John L. "The Path of the Tax Revolt: Statewide Expenditure and Tax Control Referenda Since Proposition 13." *State and Local Government Review*. 18 (Winter 1986): 5–12.

Nichols, Stephen M. "State Referendum Voting, Ballot Roll-Off, and the Effect of New Electoral Technology." *State and Local Government Review*. 30 (Spring 1998): 106–17.

Noam, Eli M. "The Efficiency of Direct Democracy." *Journal of Political Economy*. 88 (August 1980): 803–10.

Nossiter, Adam. "Ballot Losses Signal End of Gambling's Lucky Run." *The New York Times*. (November 19, 1996): A22.

"Ohio Rejects Tax Repeal." *The New York Times*. (November 10, 1983): D26.

"Oregon, California Ballot Pamphlets May Deliver Information Overload." *Election Administration Reports*. 28 (November 23, 1998): 5.

Owens, John R. and Larry L. Wade. "Campaign Spending on California Ballot Propositions, 1924–1984: Trends and Voting Effects." *Western Political*

Quarterly. 39 (December 1983): 675–89.

Polhill, Dennis. "Are Coloradans Fit to Make Their Own Laws?" *Independence Issue Paper.* (October 15, 1996): 1–33.

Pomeroy, Eltweed. "Direct Legislation in 1904" in Josiah Strong, ed. *Social Progress.* New York: The Baker and Taylor Company, Publishers, 1905. 153–56.

Price, Charles M. "Direct Democracy Works." *State Government News.* 49 (June/July 1997): 14–15 and 35.

"Private Financing of Public Election Issue in Kausi, Hawaii Initiative Vote." *Election Administration Reports.* 14 (February 20, 1984): 3–4.

"Prop. 227 is Constitutional." *The National Law Journal.* 20 (July 27, 1998): A8.

"Property Taxes Decline 9.3% with Massachusetts Measure." *The New York Times.* (December 20, 1982): B16.

Pully, Brett. "Casinos Widen Rivers to Increase Business." *The New York Times.* (October 30, 1998): A16.

Pully, Brett. "Gambling Proponents Bet $85 Million on Election." *The New York Times.* (October 31, 1998): A11.

Purdum, Todd S. "California G.O.P. Faces a Crisis as Hispanic Voters Turn Away." *The New York Times.* (December 9, 1997): 1 and A20.

Purdum, Todd S. "Court Declines to Hear Appeal of Ban on Affirmative Action." *The New York Times.* (November 4, 1997): A19.

Purdum, Todd S. "Judge Nullifies Most of California Immigrant Law." *The New York Times.* (March 19, 1998): A12.

Rahm, David M. "Citizens Versus Legislators — The Continuing Fight to Ensure the Rights of Initiative and Referendum in Nebraska: *State Ex Rel. Stenberg v. Beerman.*" *Creighton Law Review.* 26 (1992): 195–220.

Rappard, William E. "The Initiative, Referendum, and Recall in Switzerland" in Clyde L. King, ed. *The Annals of the American Academy of Political and Social Science.* 43 (September 1912): 110–45.

Rheinold, Robert. "10 Years Later, Voters in California Are Asked to Make Up for Lost Taxes." *The New York Times.* (June 5, 1988): 242.

Rimer, Sara. "In Clear-Cutting Vote, Maine will Define Itself." *The New York Times.* (September 25, 1996): 1.

Rishel, George F. "Illinois' Experience with Cumulative Voting." *Journal of Election Administration.* 18 (1997): 14–17.

Ritter, John. "English Only, Ready or Not." *USA Today.* (August 3, 1998): 2A.

Roosevelt, Theodore. "Nationalism and Popular Rule." *The Outlook.* (January 21, 1911): 96–101.

Rosenthal, Alan. "Sloppy Democracy." *State Government News.* 38 (January 1995): 19–21.

Salvato, Greg M. "New Limits on the California Initiative: An Analysis and Critique." *Loyola of Los Angeles Law Review.* 19 (May 1986): 1045–96.

Schacter, Jane S. "The Pursuit of 'Popular Intent': Interpretive Dilemmas in Direct Democracy." *The Yale Law Journal.* 105 (October 1995): 108–76.

Schrag, Peter. "California Elected Anarchy: A Government Destroyed by Popular Referendum." *Harper's Magazine*. 289 (November 1994): 50–58.

Shapiro, Perry, David Puryear, and John Ross. "Tax and Expenditure Limitation in Retrospect and in Prospect." *National Tax Journal*. 32 (June 1979): 1–10.

Sirico, Louis J., Jr. "The Constitutionality of the Initiative and Referendum." *Iowa Law Review*. 65 (1980): 637–77.

"Six in a Bond Drive Indicted for Forged Missouri Petitions." *The New York Times*. (September 17, 1972): 46.

Smith, Alfred F. "Can We Afford the Initiative?" *National Municipal Review*. 37 (October 1949): 437–42.

Smith, Daniel A. "Unmasking the Tax Crusaders." *State Government News*. 41 (March 1998): 18–21.

Smith, Larry J. and Mary M. Ross. "The Zoning Process: Exclusionary Zoning, Initiatives, and Referenda, Design Review, and Other Recent Developments in the Law." *The Urban Lawyer*. 27 (Fall 1995): 811–25.

Sponholtz, Lloyd. "The Initiative and Referendum: Direct Democracy in Perspective 1898–1920." *American Studies*. 12 (Fall 1973): 43–64.

Stabrowski, Donald J. "Oregon's Increasing Use of the Initiative and its Effect on Budgeting." *Comparative State Politics*. 20 (February 1999): 31–45.

Stolz, Preble. "Initiatives Sap Courts and Threaten Reform." *Public Affairs Report*. 31 (July 1990): 1 and 10.

Sturm, Albert L. "State Constitutional Developments During 1982." *National Civic Review*. 72 (January 1983): 38–39.

Sugarman, Stephen D. "California's Insurance Regulation Revolution: The First Two Years of Proposition 103." *San Diego Law Review*. 27 (September/October 1990): 683–714.

"Suicide Law Withstands a Challenge." *The New York Times*. (February 28, 1997): A20.

"Tax Revolt Measures Defeated by Ohio Voters." *State Legislatures*. 10 (January 1984): 5–6.

Teague, William L., Jr. "Pre-Election Constitutional Review of Initiative Petitions: A Pox on *Vox Populi?*" *Oklahoma City University Law Review*. 17 (Spring 1992): 201–20.

Terry, Don. "Cigarette Tax Supported by Unlikely Coalition." *The New York Times*. (October 18, 1998): 20.

Terry, Don. "Strong Blow is Delivered to State Law on Aliens." *The New York Times*. (November 15, 1997): A8.

Thompson, Carl D. "The Vital Points in Charter Making From a Socialist Point of View." *National Municipal Review*. 2 (1913): 416–26.

"A Tool of Democracy?" *National Civic Review*. 67 (September 1978): 353.

Toy, Vivian S. "Foes of Ballot Proposal to Ease Council-Term Limits Law Begin TV Campaign." *The New York Times*. (October 16, 1996): B3.

"Tucson Initiative Fails to Make Ballot." *Public Administration Times.* 6 (December 15, 1983): 1.

Turner, Wallace. "Developer Pays Expenses for Voting on Zoning on Little Hawaiian Island." *The New York Times.* (January 12, 1984): A22.

Turner, Wallace. "Effects of Proposition 13 to Strike California Cities." *The New York Times.* (January 24, 1983): A15.

Tweedy, John, Jr. "Coalition Building and the Defeat of California's Proposition 128." *Stanford Environmental Law Journal.* 11 (1992): 114–48.

"U.S. Balanced Budget Measure Taken Off Ballot." *The New York Times.* (August 28, 1984): B20.

Vellinga, Mary L. "Initiative Races' Tab: $200 Million." *Sacramento Bee.* (November 5, 1998): A15.

Verhovek, Sam. H. "From Same-Sex Marriages to Gambling, Voters Speak." *The New York Times.* (November 5, 1998): B1 and B10.

Verhovek, Sam. H. "Houston to Vote on Repeal of Affirmative Action." *The New York Times.* (November 2, 1997): A28.

Verhovek, Sam. H. "Referendum in Houston Shows Complexity of Preferences Issue." *The New York Times.* (November 6, 1997): 1 and A26.

Weintraub, Daniel M. "California Closes Its Doors." *State Legislatures.* 20 (December 1994): 16–17.

Weintraub, Daniel M. and Mark Katches. "Citizen-Set Campaign Limits Too Low, Says Judge." *State Legislatures.* 24 (March 1998): 30–31.

Wells, Roger H. "The Initiative, Referendum, and Recall in German Cities." *National Municipal Review.* 18 (January 1929): 29–36.

Whitehill, Lisa. "Direct Legislation: A Survey of Recent Literature." *Legal Reference Services Quarterly.* 5 (Spring 1985): 3–45.

Wicker, Tom. "Tale of Two Initiatives." *The New York Times.* (October 19, 1982): A27.

Wilson, Woodrow. "The Issues of Reform." *Case and Comment.* 18 (November 1911): 306–07.

Zimmerman, Joseph F. "Electoral Systems and Direct Citizen Law-Making." *Diskussionsbeitrage* (Forschungs-Schwerpunkt Hisorische Mobilität und Normenwandel, Universitatät Gesamhochschule Siegen, Deutschland). (April 1988): entire issue.

Zimmerman, Joseph F. "The Federal Voting Rights Act and Alternative Election Systems." *William & Mary Law Review.* 19 (Summer 1978): 621–60.

Zimmerman, Joseph F. "Initiative, Referendum, and Recall: Government by Plebiscite?" *Intergovernmental Perspective.* 13 (Winter 1987): 32–35.

Zimmerman, Joseph F. "The Initiative and the Referendum: A Threat to Representative Government?" *Urban Law and Policy.* 8 (1987): 219–53.

Zimmerman, Joseph F. "Law-Making by Citizens in the United States in Ruediger Voight, ed. *Law in the Welfare State: An Interdisciplinary Perspective.* Siegen, Deutschland: Universität Gesamhochschule Siegen, 1985. 71–107.

Zimmerman, Joseph F. "Populism Revived" in Thad L. Beyle, ed., *State Government: CQ's Guide to Current Issues and Activities: 1986–87*. Washington, DC: Congressional Quarterly, Incorporated, 1986. 24–28.

UNPUBLISHED MATERIALS

Gallagher, James H. *Corporate Influence on Initiative Campaigns in Massachusetts and Oregon, 1986–1992*. Unpublished Doctoral Dissertation, Boston University, 1995.

King, Edward J. "Testimony Before the Joint Economic Committee." Boston, MA: Executive Department, February 24, 1982.

Lee, Eugene C. "The Initiative Process in California." A paper presented at the 84th National Conference on Government, Louisville, KY, November 12–15, 1978.

Magleby, David B. "Voter Pamphlets: Understanding Why Voters Don't Read Them." A paper presented at the 1981 annual meeting of The American Political Science Association, New York.

"Memorandum to All Finance Committee Chairmen & Secretaries." Boston, MA: Association of Finance Committees, April 1, 1983.

Minstrom, Michael and Sandra Vergari. "Why Policy Innovations Change as They Diffuse: Analyzing Recent Charter School Laws." A paper presented at the annual meeting of the Midwest Political Science Association, Chicago, April 10, 1997.

Mulligan, Kenneth. "The Effects of Campaign Spending on Voting in Ballot Initiative Elections." Unpublished Master of Arts thesis, George Washington University, 1997.

"Testimony of Marcia Molay, Massachusetts Director of Elections, before the New York State Senate Subcommittee on Initiative and Referendum," September 17, 1979 (mimeographed).

Wrote, Andy. "Race and Resentment in California? The Politicization of Illegal Immigration in the Early 1990s." A paper presented at the annual meeting of the American Politics Group, University of Manchester, January 3, 1998.

Zimmerman, Joseph F. "Citizen Law-Making: The Initiative." A paper presented at the annual conference of the American Politics Group, Cambridge University, January 8, 1999.

Zimmerman, Joseph F. "Enforcing Continuing Responsibility: The Recall." A paper presented at the annual conference of the American Politics Group, University of Manchester, January 3, 1998.

Index

ABOUT THE AUTHOR

Joseph F. Zimmerman is Professor of Political Science in the Graduate School of Public Affairs at State University of New York at Albany. He is the author of numerous articles and books, including *The New England Town Meeting: Democracy in Action* (Praeger, 1999), *The Recall: Tribunal of the People* (Praeger, 1997), and *Interstate Relations* (Praeger, 1996).

ISBN 0-275-96729-8

9 780275 967291

EAN

90000>

HARDCOVER BAR CODE